NEVADA
Our Home

Gary BeDunnah

Gibbs Smith, Publisher
Salt Lake City

This book is dedicated to those of the past—my parents, Pat and Neillie BeDunnah, who moved to Nevada in 1929; to those of the present—my children, Robin, Sherri, and Terri, who grew up in Nevada; and to those of the future—my grandchildren, Craig, Michael, Jordi, Ashlee, Crystal, Hannah, Brady, Bailey, Brice, and Jesse—for whom this book was written.

A special thanks is given for the help that my daughter Robin Swainston gave in writing this history. My colleagues George Wells and Larry Benham also contributed.

Finally, thanks to my wife, Patricia, for her suggestions and proofreading. Her encouragement made this possible.

—Gary BeDunnah

Copyright © 2006 by Gibbs Smith, Publisher
All rights reserved. No part of this book may be reproduced by any means whatsoever, either mechanical or electronic, without permission from the publisher.

Published by
Gibbs Smith, Publisher
P.O. Box 667
Layton, UT 84041
800-748-5439
www.gibbs-smith.com/textbooks

Managing Editor: Kris K. Brunson
Associate Editors: Carrie Gibson, Valerie Hatch,
Jennifer Petersen, Rachel Pike, Courtney Thomas
Photo Editor: Kris K. Brunson
Book Design: Jeremy C. Munns
Cover Design: Jeremy C. Munns

Cover photo: Pyramid Lake Indian Reservation, © Scott T. Smith
See last page for interior image credits.

Printed and bound in China
ISBN 1-58685-821-1

12 11 10 09 08 07 06   10 9 8 7 6 5 4 3

ABOUT THE AUTHOR

Gary P. BeDunnah taught history to Nevada students for almost 32 years. He was born in Las Vegas but spent many of his early years in Greensburg, Indiana. BeDunnah earned a B.A. in History from Colorado State University in 1962. Then he began teaching at the John C. Fremont Junior High in Las Vegas. In 1966, he received an M.A. in History from the University of Nevada. He taught at Fremont Junior High until he retired from teaching in 1994.

BeDunnah published his first Nevada state history textbook, *Discovering Nevada,* in 1994. This text is an updated, more comprehensive version of that earlier work. He has enjoyed sharing his love of history with other Nevada history teachers and the school children of Nevada.

CONTRIBUTORS AND REVIEWERS

Jerome Edwards is an emeritus professor of history at the University of Nevada, Reno, where he taught from 1965 to 2001. He has been teaching Nevada history since 1976 and was awarded "The Distinguished Faculty Award" in 2004. Edwards is also the author of several books and articles on Nevada history and although retired, continues to teach history as well as other courses at the University of Nevada, Reno.

Vickie Higgins is a native Nevadan, teaching at Mountain View Elementary in Elko, Nevada. She received a B.S. in Elementary Education from the University of Nevada, Reno. Higgins is married with 5 children and has been teaching for the past 12 years.

Dominique Jones has been teaching at Lahontan Elementary School in Fallon, Nevada for the past seven years. She was born and raised in Nevada and graduated from the University of Nevada, Reno in Elementary and Special Education. She also serves on several educational committees and, in her spare time, loves to travel and spend time outdoors.

Renee Muraco is originally from Rochester, New York where she received a degree in Sociology and a teaching certificate. Later, she earned two masters degrees—one from Grand Canyon University in Elementary Teaching and the second from UNLV in Educational Administration. She was also named the Southeast Region's Distinguished Educator for 2000 and 2005. Muraco has been teaching fourth grade in the Clark County School District for more than 10 years.

Guy L. Rocha has been engrossed in Nevada history for more than 20 years. After growing up in Las Vegas, he received a B.A. from Syracuse University in New York, an M.A. from San Diego State University, and a post-graduate degree in History at the University of Nevada, Reno. He taught in the Washoe County School District and at Western Nevada Community College. In 1989, Rocha became a Certified Archivist. Since then, he has served in many advisory capacities, written extensively on Nevada history, and directed a few of his own historical documentaries. Today, he continues to work as a private consultant of Nevada history and as the Assistant Administrator for Archives and Records at the State Library and Archives.

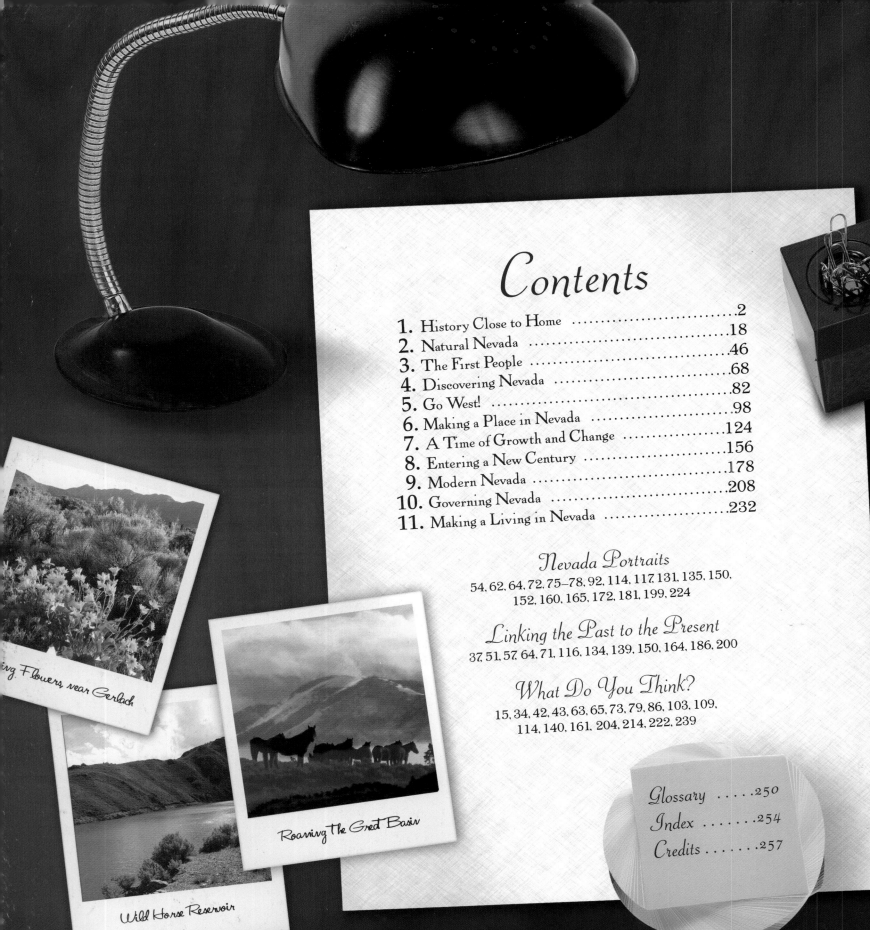

Contents

Nevada Portraits
54, 62, 64, 72, 75–78, 92, 114, 117, 131, 135, 150,
152, 160, 165, 172, 181, 199, 224

Linking the Past to the Present
37, 51, 57, 64, 71, 116, 134, 139, 150, 164, 186, 200

What Do You Think?
15, 34, 42, 43, 63, 65, 73, 79, 86, 103, 109,
114, 140, 161, 204, 214, 222, 239

Flowers near Gerlach

Wild Horse Reservoir

Roaming the Great Basin

Maps, Charts, and Graphs

Activities

Shoe Tree, Highway 50

Black Rock D

"*If there is magic on this earth it lies in water, and nowhere is water so beautiful as in the desert.*"

—Edward Abbey

History Close to Home

Boiling underground water leaking into a well, formed Nevada's Fly Geyser. It gets its bright colors from a special kind of plant that lives in hot water.

Discovering Your Tools

Welcome to *Nevada, Our Home*. Learning about our state will be like going on a great adventure. Have you ever been on an adventure? Maybe you've gone rafting on white water rapids. You may have been rock climbing or exploring in underground caves. Maybe you've even tried digging for buried treasure in your own backyard.

Did you take special tools on your adventure? You probably needed things like a flashlight, a life jacket, or a shovel. As we study Nevada history, we will use some important tools to help us along the way. Let's take a closer look at them.

Catch the Vision

Every great adventure begins with a vision. A vision is like a picture in your mind. It can show you where to go. On our adventure through Nevada history, we begin each **chapter** with a big picture. The picture might give you clues about what you will learn, see, and read. Someone once said, "A picture is worth a thousand words." What do you think that means? Can a picture tell a story?

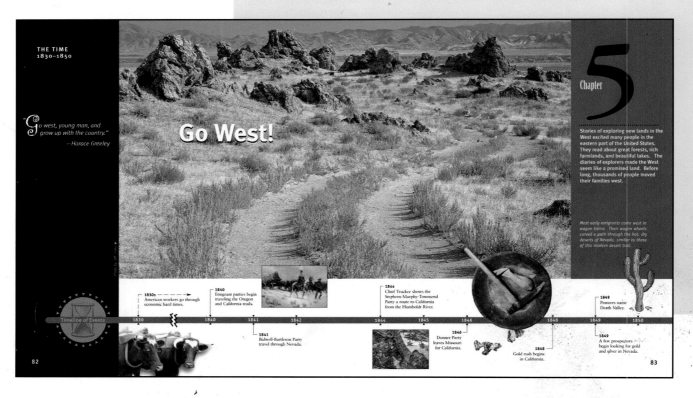

THE TIME
1830–1850

"*Go west, young man, and grow up with the country.*"
—Horace Greeley

Go West!

Chapter 5

Stories of exploring new lands in the West excited many people in the eastern part of the United States. They read about great forests, rich farmlands, and beautiful lakes. The diaries of explorers made the West seem like a promised land. Before long, thousands of people moved their families west.

Most early emigrants came west in wagon trains. Their wagon wheels carved a path through the hot, dry deserts of Nevada, similar to those of this modern desert trail.

Timeline of Events

1830s
American workers go through economic hard times.

1840
Emigrant parties begin traveling the Oregon and California trails.

1841
Bidwell-Bartleson Party travel through Nevada.

1844
Chief Truckee shows the Stephens-Murphy-Townsend Party a route to California from the Humboldt River.

1846
Donner Party leaves Missouri for California.

1848
Gold rush begins in California.

1849
Pioneers name Death Valley.

1849
A few prospectors begin looking for gold and silver in Nevada.

1830 1840 1841 1842 1844 1845 1846 1848 1849 1850

82

83

Keeping Track of Time

A **timeline** is another great tool that can teach us about history. Timelines help us see when important events happened. We can also see the order in which these things happened. Did you notice how the numbers on a timeline get bigger as you move from left to right? Timelines look a lot like rulers. What would a timeline of important events from your life look like?

Step by Step

Lessons are the next tool we'll use on our adventure. Each lesson has some important things to watch for:

PEOPLE TO KNOW
PLACES TO LOCATE
WORDS TO UNDERSTAND

Maybe you already know some of the words, people, or places on the lists. It's a good idea to look over each list before reading the chapter. Previewing each list is kind of like taking a peek at what's ahead.

Don't Be Afraid to Ask

Asking questions is one of the best tools you can use when you're on an adventure. Questions can help you learn new things. As you read, you will come across **What do you think?** questions. These questions ask what YOU think about certain things. There is no right or wrong answer. Look for What do you think? questions next to the big question marks.

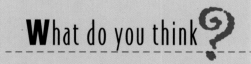

Connect the Dots

Have you ever wondered how the past affects your life today? Features called **Linking the Past to the Present** are a sure way to find out. Many things change over time. However, some things stay the same. As you read *Nevada, Our Home*, you will learn about both.

Linking the Past
to the Present

Meet the People

Nevada history is filled with stories of interesting people. Reading *portraits* is one way to learn about some of them. A **portrait** tells you a little about a person's life. Your teacher may have you write a report about an important person in Nevada history. Maybe you already know who you want to write about.

Activity

Just for Fun

Activities can be a fun way to learn about history. During our adventures, you will have a chance to enjoy many different kinds of activities. You might act out a moment from history. You might try foods from another country. You might write a story or make a map. What kinds of activities do you like best?

Activity

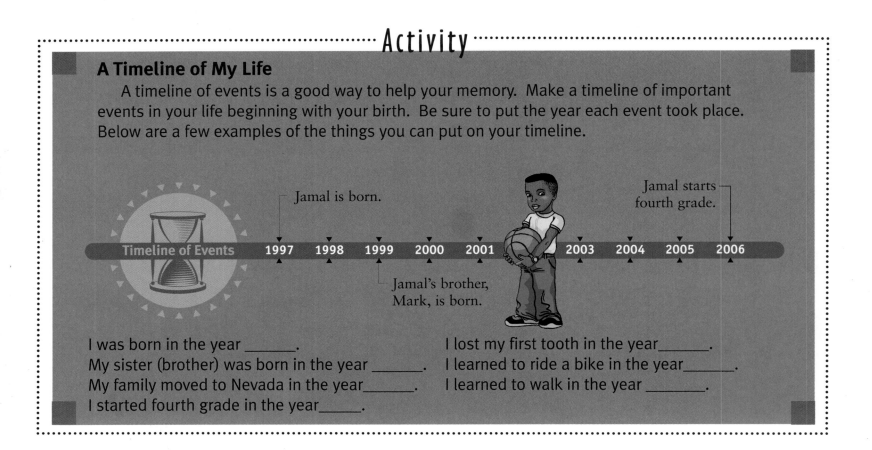

A Timeline of My Life

A timeline of events is a good way to help your memory. Make a timeline of important events in your life beginning with your birth. Be sure to put the year each event took place. Below are a few examples of the things you can put on your timeline.

Jamal is born.

Jamal starts fourth grade.

Timeline of Events 1997 1998 1999 2000 2001 2003 2004 2005 2006

Jamal's brother, Mark, is born.

I was born in the year _____.
My sister (brother) was born in the year _____.
My family moved to Nevada in the year _____.
I started fourth grade in the year _____.

I lost my first tooth in the year_____.
I learned to ride a bike in the year_____.
I learned to walk in the year _____.

Practice Remembering

Memory Masters are a good way to help you review what you have learned. Sometimes it's easy to forget the things you've read. If you do, just go back and read the lesson again.

Learning in Action

When you make it to the **chapter review**, you've reached the end of the chapter, but don't stop yet. One of the best parts of your adventure is still to come. It's the action part, where doing becomes part of learning. Here is a quick preview of what you will find there.

It's More Than Skin Deep

As you read *Nevada, Our Home*, you will learn about many different kinds of people. One of the chapter review exercises called **Consider Character** will ask you to think about the choices people make. Sometimes people do things that show good character, and sometimes they do not.

As you read this book, look for examples of how people show their character. Pay close attention to the kinds of examples you see.

Think Like an Explorer

Using maps and globes is a great way to explore the world. *Geography* is the study of the earth's land, plant, and animal life. With **Geography Tie-Ins**, we will learn about how Nevada's history relates to its geography.

Digging for Clues

Surfing the web may be something you already know how to do. **Technology Tie-Ins** will give you a chance to practice even more. *Technology* is a big word that means using tools and science together. Technology can help us do a job better. What kinds of technology do you like to use to learn something? Have you ever tried listening to books on tape or CDs?

WORDS TO UNDERSTAND

artifact
fact
historian
opinion
primary document
primary source
secondary source

History: A Study of the Past

Do you remember what you had for breakfast today? Of course you do. But do you remember what you ate two weeks ago? You probably don't. Our memories fade over time, so we forget. Sometimes we forget simple things, like what we ate for breakfast. Sometimes we forget important things, like doing homework.

To help us remember, we use pictures, diaries, and newspapers. The Internet, DVDs, CDs, and books can also help remind us of important people and events. Many people in our history have made Nevada the unique state that it is today. Studying our history will teach us how people and events shape our state.

Why Do We Study History?

The study of history tells us many things. It tells us how people of the past lived. We can learn what people liked to eat and drink. We can study the types of clothes they wore and what their schools were like. We can learn how people earned a living and spent their free time. A famous man once said, "To ignore the lessons of history is to repeat them." The lessons we learn from history can help us now and in the future.

Nevada history gives us a record of many different types of people. Native Americans, miners, farmers, and many others have helped develop our state.

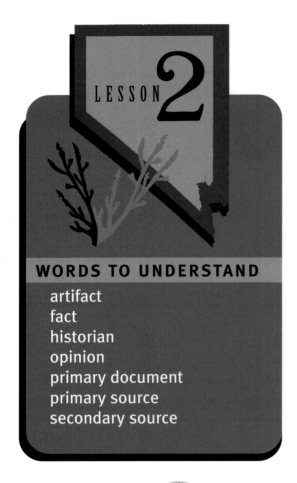

What can things that are old teach you about history?

How Do We Study History?

Historians are people who write and study other people's lives and important events. Historians study history for a living. Some study history just for fun. You and your classmates can be Nevada historians too. You can learn to use the same tools that real historians use.

Two important tools historians use are *primary sources* and *secondary sources.* Primary sources are things that were used or made at the time an event happened. Pictures, maps, and diaries are examples of primary sources. Sometimes historians call these *primary documents.* Toys, tools, clothing, and weapons are also primary sources. Historians call these things *artifacts.*

Now, can you guess what a secondary source is? It is something created by someone who heard or read about an event but who wasn't actually there. Secondary sources are made after an event. Books and movies are examples of secondary sources. They can help us understand what an event might have been like.

Is It Fact or Opinion?

Primary and secondary sources can teach us a lot about Nevada history. We will also learn many *facts* about Nevada's past. Facts are things you can prove. Facts can help you form *opinions.* Opinions are things you believe. Historians like to learn facts before they form opinions about people or events. With your teacher's help, you can discover how fun studying history can be.

Historians call things like this old lamp, artifacts.

Memory Master

LESSON 2

1. List some things that help us remember the past.
2. What are some examples of primary sources and secondary sources?
3. What is the difference between fact and opinion?

Activity

Primary or Secondary Source?

Tell whether the following are primary or secondary sources:

- birth certificate
- textbook
- photograph
- movie biography
- newspaper article
- diary

LESSON 3

Discovering Nevada

If you were asked to name an animal that stands for Nevada, what would you say? Could you name a flower that blooms all around the state? Do you know which tree has been an important part of our state's history? Nevada has many state *symbols.* Symbols are things that have a special meaning or that stand for something else. Our state has plants, animals, and minerals that stand for Nevada. They show how Nevada is different from other states in the United States.

Nevada's symbols are a source of pride for the people who live here. They are also keys to understanding Nevada's history.

Our State Seal

Nevada *adopted* the state seal as its first symbol. A seal is a stamp that is used on official state *documents,* or papers. Nevada's seal shows some of the ways Nevadans have made a living.

Try matching the symbols on the seal with the industry each stands for. Use your finger to draw an imaginary line to each correct choice:

- A miner and a mill
- A plow, a sheaf of grain, and a sickle
- The railroad and the telegraph line
- Transportation and communication
- Mining and milling
- Farming

Nevada made this seal its official choice in 1866.

You will also see 36 stars circling the seal. These symbols stand for the 36 states that were part of the United States when Nevada became a state. Do you see the words "ALL FOR OUR COUNTRY"? They were added to show Nevada's support for President Abraham Lincoln during the Civil War.

Our State Flag

Nevada has had four different state flag designs. The first flag had a blue background with 36 silver and gold stars. The stars stood for Nevada as the 36th state in the United States. The silver and gold stood for our mining wealth.

Our second flag had the state seal in the center. But a mistake was made when 37 stars were put on the flag instead of 36. The flag stayed that way for a long time.

On the third flag, the state seal was taken off. Two branches of sagebrush were added near the top left corner. The words "Battle Born" were also added. They remind us that Nevada became a state during the Civil War.

In 1991, the flag was changed for the last time. The letters spelling Nevada were changed to make them easier to read.

Next time you drive around your town or city, see how many times you can spot our state flag.

Our State Trees

Did you know Nevada has two state trees? The first tree our state adopted was the single-leaf piñon pine. It is one of Nevada's most common trees. It can grow even in dry, rocky places.

Pine nuts are the seeds of the piñon pine. Early Native Americans gathered pine nuts for food. Each year, Native Americans had a celebration to give thanks for the pine nut harvest.

Early miners also used the piñon pine. Trees were cut into timbers to support the walls and ceilings of the mines. The wood was also burned to make charcoal. Hot charcoal fires were used to **smelt,** or melt metals from rocks.

Not long ago, the bristlecone pine also became a state tree. It was the idea of students from Ely, Nevada. The bristlecone pine is one of the oldest living things on earth. These pines live in our state's highest mountains. Some bristlecone pines are more than 4,000 years old. Like the piñon pine, the bristlecone also thrives in Nevada's **harsh,** or rough, land.

The single-leaf piñon pine (above) was one of the main sources of food for Nevada's early native peoples.

Why do you think some bristlecone pines (below) are able to live so long?

Our State Flower

Sagebrush, our state flower, is really a bush with small yellow and white flowers. It blooms in the spring and can grow up to 12 feet high. Sagebrush also grows in dry soil, where most plants cannot. It was used in many ways by early Native Americans. They ground the leaves for medicine and stripped its bark to weave into mats.

Early settlers used sagebrush to help them learn about the soil. Where the sagebrush was tall, they knew the soil would also be good for growing crops. Sagebrush was important for animals too. Cattle, sheep, and wild animals ate it during the long winter months.

Our State Bird

The mountain bluebird is our state bird. The male is bright blue with a light blue belly. Like most birds, the female bluebird is not as colorful. Bluebirds live mainly in the higher, cooler regions of the state. They visit the desert floor in winter, looking for food.

Our State Song

Bertha E. Raffetto was living in Reno when she wrote and sang a song about our state. She wrote *Home Means Nevada* for a picnic celebration. The song is about the beauty of our deserts and mountains. Later, it became our state song.

Sagebrush has a strong, woodsy smell, especially after it rains.

The mountain bluebird stands about 6 to 8 inches tall.

Activity

Home Means Nevada

Way out in the land of the setting sun,
Where the wind blows wild and free,
There's a lovely spot, just the only one.
That means home sweet home to me.
If you follow the old Kit Carson trail,
Until desert meets the hills,
Oh you certainly will agree with me,
It's the place of a thousand thrills.

Chorus:
Home means Nevada,
Home means the hills,
Home means the sage and the pines.
Out of the truckee's silvery rills.
Out where the sun always shines.
There is a land that I love the best,
Fairer than all I can see.
Right in the heart of the golden west,
Home means Nevada to me.

Bertha Raffetto chose different words in her song to show Nevada's many parts. Find nouns that name the different landforms of Nevada. Can you find the adjectives she used? (Hint: adjectives are words that describe nouns.) Think of another adjective you would use to describe Nevada's beauty.

Our State Fossil, Grass, and Metal

The state *fossil* reminds us of a time when the land was very different. A fossil is a print of a plant or animal preserved in the earth or in rock. Over 160 million years ago, oceans covered parts of the western United States. Animals roamed the shores, and fish swam in the oceans.

One ancient creature was the ichthyosaur. It was a huge fish-like lizard, more than 50 feet long. It weighed thousands of pounds. Fossils of these huge lizards have been found in central Nevada. You can see them at the state park near the old mining town of Berlin.

Nevada is the only state with a full skeleton of the ichthyosaur It is almost 55 feet long.

Indian rice grass is Nevada's state grass. It grows throughout Nevada. Early Native Americans ate it, and desert animals grazed on it. Rice grass is a very hardy plant. It is still a favorite food of cattle and sheep.

Our state metal is silver. In fact, Nevada was settled by people who came looking for silver. Nevada has many minerals, but silver has been one of our most important. Silver mines in Nevada have helped our state grow.

Indian rice grass was a good source of food for early people because it is high in protein and fat.

Our State Animal

The desert bighorn sheep is Nevada's state animal. The male bighorn stands about 3 feet high and weighs about 170 pounds. Its large, curved horns can grow until they form almost a full circle. Female bighorns weigh around 125 pounds and usually have small, spiked horns.

Bighorns like to eat grasses and the fruits of small plants. Their official name is Nelson's Desert Bighorn. Native Americans called the bighorn sheep *Old Nagah*.

A long time ago, large numbers of sheep roamed all over Nevada. Then people began hunting them. The bighorn was forced to compete with other animals for space and food.

The bighorn were almost destroyed before people realized what was happening. Finally, a place was set aside where bighorns could be safe from hunters. Laws were passed to protect them. Today, the herds are growing, and the bighorn are able to live as they once did.

Bighorn sheep live from 9 to 15 years.

Our State Fish

The Lahontan cutthroat trout is our state fish. It lives in many of the lakes and streams of Nevada. The biggest cutthroat ever caught in Pyramid Lake was three feet long. It weighed over 41 pounds.

The cutthroat was important to the diet of Nevada's early Native Americans. Once, many of Nevada's lakes and rivers were filled with cutthroat trout, but today, there are very few. That is because people have taken too many cutthroats out of our lakes and rivers.

Years ago, people called this fish the "Tahoe trout" because there were so many of them in Lake Tahoe.

Our State Gemstones

The black fire opal is our state's **precious** gemstone. A precious gem is one that is rare and expensive. Virgin Valley, Nevada, is the only place in North America where the black fire opal is found.

Nevada turquoise is our state's **semi-precious** gem. It is not as rare or as valuable as the black fire opal. Nevada turquoise is known as the Jewel of the Desert. It is found in many parts of our state.

Turquoise was used by early Native American medicine men for healing.

Our State Rock

Out state rock is sandstone. It was formed by a process that took millions of years. Great pressure on layers of sand formed this soft rock. Sandstone can be seen in the Valley of Fire state park in southern Nevada. The mountains around Lake Mead are also made of sandstone.

Las Vegas school children came up with the idea to make sandstone our state rock. Our state government liked the idea. They made sandstone our official state rock at a ceremony at the Gene Ward Elementary School in Las Vegas.

Elephant rock is one of Nevada's most famous sandstone formations.

Our State Reptile

The desert tortoise is our state reptile. It can live on very little water, which makes it another good symbol of Nevada. The desert tortoise gets most of its water from eating plants.

Like the bighorn sheep, desert tortoises have been pushed out by people and buildings. Many people feared that tortoises would become *endangered*. Endangered animals are those that are almost all gone.

People worked to pass laws to protect tortoises. Workers now remove them from building sites and take them to protected areas. It's also against the law for people to take Nevada's tortoises out of the desert. Now, tortoises and people can live in harmony.

The desert tortoise spends most of its life in underground burrows.

Our State Artifact

Have you ever seen our state artifact, the tule duck decoy? You've probably seen a duck decoy before, but do you know what tule is? *Tule* is a tall plant that grows in a freshwater marsh. Early Native Americans twisted the stems of the plant into duck decoys. They used the decoys to attract ducks just like hunters do today. You will learn more about tule in a later chapter.

Can you see how tule reeds are twisted and wrapped to make this decoy?

Our State Colors and Nicknames

Silver and blue are Nevada's state colors. Silver stands for our most important mineral and blue for our beautiful skies. Our state nicknames are *The Silver State*, *Battle-Born State*, and *The Sagebrush State*. The word *Nevada* means "snow-capped" in Spanish.

Nevada symbols are very important to us. They remind us that Nevada is different from other states. Each symbol reflects strengths that are needed to survive in Nevada's harsh deserts. We can develop pride in Nevada by learning about our symbols and how they make our state unique.

What do you think?

1. What do all Nevada animal and plant symbols have in common?
2. What other symbols can you suggest for our state? How do they become official?

Memory Master

LESSON 3

1. List your favorite Nevada symbols and explain why you like them.
2. How many different state flags have we had in Nevada?
3. Which animal did Native Americans call "Old Nagah"?

Consider ★ Character

As you read the stories of our state's history, you will see how people faced many problems. You will learn how some people showed respect for others and some did not. You will read about times when people were honest and about times when they were not. You might even see that some wars started because people did not work together to solve problems. Here are six ways that people can show good character. Watch for them as you read.

Cooperation

Have you worked as part of a group at school? Maybe you and some friends made a project for a science fair. Maybe you had a role in a music program or play. Did you do your share of the work? Did you listen to other people's ideas? If you did, you were showing **cooperation**.

Courage

Have you ever done something just because you knew it was the right thing to do? If you saw people making fun of a student, and you asked them to stop, you showed **courage**. Showing courage means being brave—even when it is not easy.

Honesty

Have you ever made and kept a promise? Have you ever done something wrong and admitted it was your fault? Being **honest** means telling the truth and keeping your promises.

Perseverance

Have you ever worked really hard to make something happen? Did you have to wait to see the results? Maybe you wanted to get a good grade on your math test. When you keep trying even though things are hard, you are showing **perseverance.**

Respect

Differences between people help us learn from each other. Have you ever met someone who was different from you? Did you listen to what he had to say? Did you treat him with kindness? If you did, you were showing **respect.**

Responsibility

When you get your homework done on time, or when you do something your parents have asked you to do, you are showing **responsibility**. Responsibility means that you do what needs to be done.

Technology Tie-In

Do some research on the Internet to learn more about our state symbols. See if you can find out the year that each symbol became a state symbol. Record your findings on a separate sheet of paper. The first one is done for you.

• State Seal	1866		• Rice Grass	_____
• _____	1917		• _____	1981
• Home Means Nevada	_____		• _____	1983
• Piñon Pine	_____		• Sandstone	_____
• _____	1967		• Gemstones	_____
• _____	1973		• Bristlecone Pine	_____
• Ichthyosaur	_____		• _____	1989
• Silver	_____		• Tule Duck Decoy	_____

Geography Tie-In

Nevada history is not just stories about people. There are also many important places in our history. One such place is Pyramid Lake. Have you ever been there or read about it? Why is Pyramid Lake such an important part of Nevada's past? On a map of Nevada, find one place you have visited. Was it important to Nevada history? Use an encyclopedia, history book, or the Internet to find out. Remember, history is all around us. Then share what you learn with your class.

Activity

Design Time!

Design a new state seal for Nevada. What symbols can you draw to show jobs that your parents or relatives do today? Draw your idea for a state seal, and then color it.

Natural Nevada

Natural Nevada

"*All the wide world is beautiful, and it matters but little where we go, to highlands or lowlands, woods or plains...the spot where we chance to be always seems the best...*"

—*John Muir*

Nevada has more than 200 mountain ranges scattered across its desert lands.

Chapter 2

An airplane trip around Nevada would show you a strange and beautiful land. Parts of Nevada look like an alien planet. Rugged mountains and flat deserts appear to have no trees or plants. It seems as if nothing could survive here.

In other parts of our state, there are valleys covered with green farmland. Many Nevada mountains are covered in thick forests. Our grazing lands sometimes stretch for miles. Towns are few and often far apart. Nevada is, more than anything else, a land of contrasts.

LESSON 1

PLACES TO LOCATE

North America
North Pole
Northern Hemisphere
South Pole
United States of America

WORDS TO UNDERSTAND

astronomer
cardinal directions
continent
country
equator
exact location
hemisphere
intermediate directions
latitude
longitude
meridian
prime meridian
relative location

Our Place on Earth

The story of Nevada begins with our geography. How people change the land is also a part of geography.

On our adventure, you will learn about Nevada's land and waterways. You will learn about the plants and animals that live here. You will see how people live and how Nevada geography affects our lives.

Where in the World Is Nevada?

Of course you already know that we live on Earth. But just where on Earth is Nevada? Nevada is located in the Northern *Hemisphere.* A hemisphere is exactly one half of the Earth. Nevada is also part of the North American *continent.* Continents are the earth's largest bodies of land.

The United States is a *country* on the North American continent. Our state of Nevada is in the western United States. Five other western states touch the borders of Nevada. Can you name all of them?

Locating Home

By now you can probably find your way home from school or a friend's house. Can you also tell someone how to get to your home? What would you tell them about your home's location? You could give them its *relative location* or its *exact location.*

Relative location tells where a place is in relation to other things. For example, Nevada is west of Utah and east of California. It is between Oregon and Arizona. You could tell someone that you live near Reno or next to the school. You might say you live down the street from a friend.

Exact location tells someone exactly where to find a place. An address is an exact location. To give your exact location you would say, "I live at 309 Sidewinder Street in Ely, Nevada."

Finding Nevada

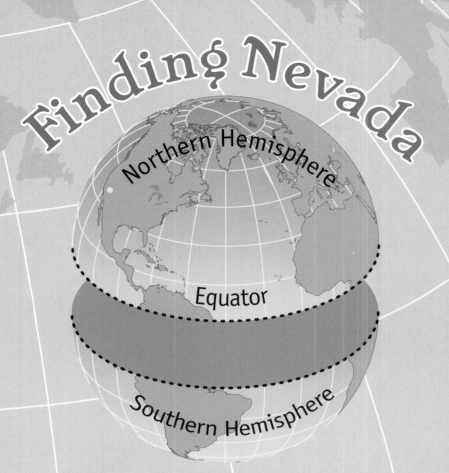

① *We live in the Northern **Hemisphere** of the Earth.*

② *Our **continent** is North America.*

③ *Our **country** is the United States of America.*

④ *Our **state** is Nevada.*

Natural Nevada

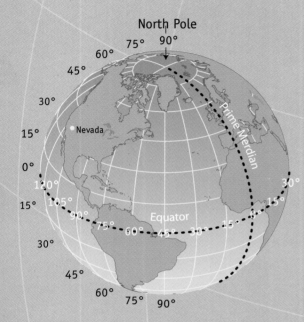

Lines Around the World

Every place in the world has an exact location using a set of imaginary lines on the Earth. These imaginary lines are called latitude and longitude lines. Latitude and longitude lines run up and down and side to side. They also cross each other at certain points. Each point marks a certain place, so if you know the longitude and latitude of a place, you can easily find it on a map.

A Greek astronomer named Ptolemy invented this system almost 2,000 years ago. His system helped travelers find their way.

Follow the Numbers

Latitude and longitude lines each have a number with a tiny circle next to it. We call these circles degrees. Degrees measure distance on a globe or map. They are numbered from 0 to 90.

The equator is at 0 degrees latitude. The North Pole and South Pole are at 90 degrees latitude.

Running From Side to Side

Latitude lines run across a map or globe from side to side or east and west. Because some latitude lines are above the equator and some are below it, latitude lines are labeled north (N) and south (S). Is 45 degrees N latitude above or below the equator? If you said above you, are correct because it is north of the equator.

Latitude lines also give us clues about how hot or cold a place gets. The farther away from the equator it is, the colder it gets. Did you know that there is snow year round at the North and South Poles? Can you locate the poles on a map or globe?

Going Up and Down

The second set of imaginary lines that help us locate places are called longitude lines. These lines run up and down, from the North Pole to the South Pole. Longitude lines are also called meridians.

A special longitude line is called the prime meridian. It goes from the North Pole to the South Pole at 0 degrees. Can you find the prime meridian on the globe pictured here? Because some longitude lines are to the right of the prime meridian and some are to the left, longitude lines are labeled east (E) and west (W). Is 15 degrees E longitude right or left of the prime meridian? If you said right, you are correct because it is east of the prime meridian.

Activity

Where Is Nevada?

On this map, find Nevada's latitude (side to side) and longitude (up and down) lines. On a globe, use your finger to trace these lines all the way around the world.

1. Which longitude line is near the western border of our state?

2. Locate the city of Ely on the map. What is its latitude and longitude?

3. Find the latitude and longitude of the city nearest your home.

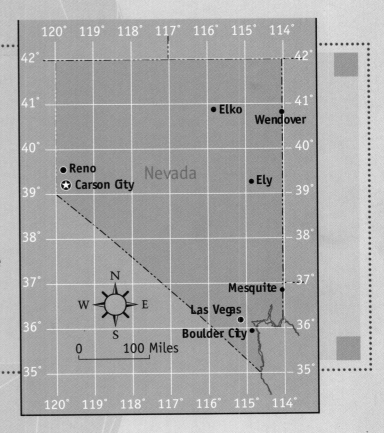

Which Half Is Which?

As you already know, the equator divides the earth into two equal halves. When the Northern Hemisphere is having winter, the Southern Hemisphere is enjoying summer.

Longitude lines also divide the earth into two parts. These are called the Western and Eastern Hemispheres. You can see them in the drawings below.

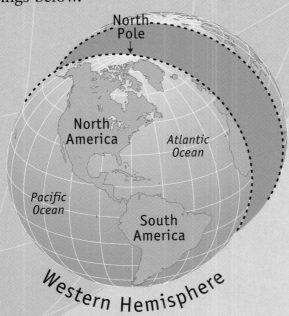

Western Hemisphere

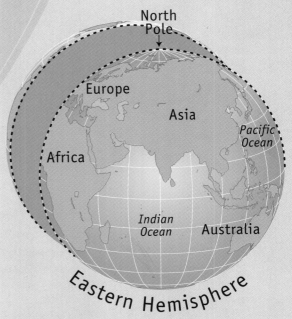

Eastern Hemisphere

Natural Nevada

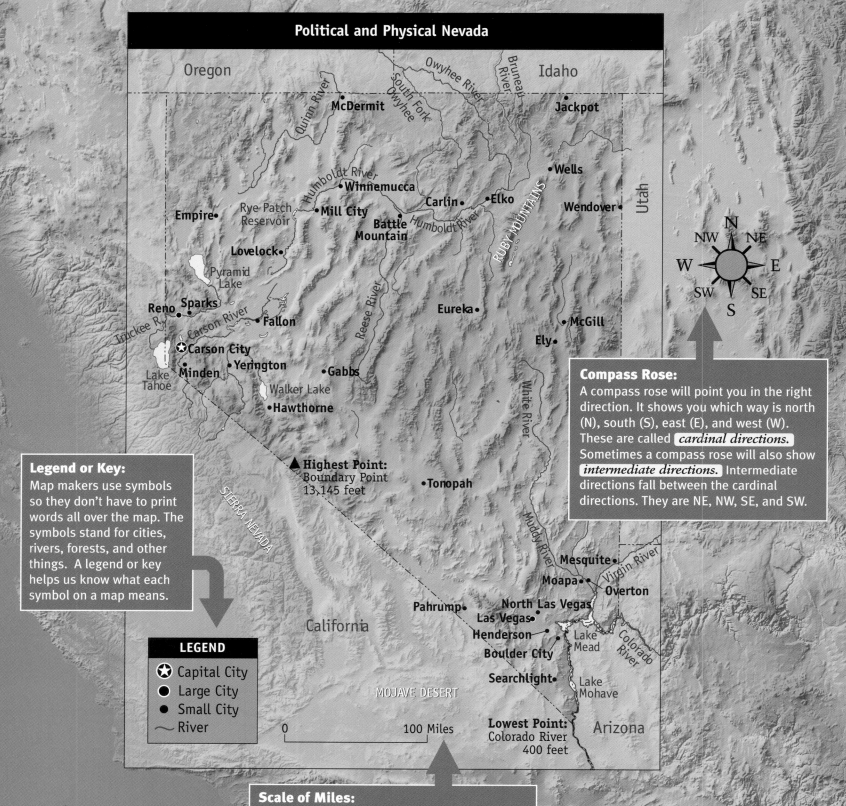

Political and Physical Nevada

Oregon
Idaho

Owyhee River
Bruneau River
South Fork Owyhee
Quinn River

McDermit
Jackpot

Humboldt River
Winnemucca
Wells

Carlin
Elko

Empire
Rye Patch Reservoir
Mill City
Wendover
Utah

Battle Mountain
Humboldt River

Lovelock
RUBY MOUNTAINS

Pyramid Lake
Reese River

Reno
Sparks
Carson River
Fallon
Eureka

Truckee R.
McGill

Carson City
Ely

Minden
Yerington
Gabbs

Lake Tahoe
Walker Lake
White River

Hawthorne

SIERRA NEVADA
▲ Highest Point:
Boundary Point
13,145 feet

Tonopah

Muddy River

Mesquite
Virgin River

Moapa
Overton

Pahrump
North Las Vegas

California
Las Vegas
Colorado River

Henderson
Lake Mead

Boulder City

Searchlight
Lake Mohave

MOJAVE DESERT

Lowest Point:
Colorado River
400 feet
Arizona

LEGEND

⊛ Capital City
● Large City
• Small City
∿ River

0 _____ 100 Miles

Legend or Key:
Map makers use symbols so they don't have to print words all over the map. The symbols stand for cities, rivers, forests, and other things. A legend or key helps us know what each symbol on a map means.

Compass Rose:
A compass rose will point you in the right direction. It shows you which way is north (N), south (S), east (E), and west (W). These are called *cardinal directions*. Sometimes a compass rose will also show *intermediate directions*. Intermediate directions fall between the cardinal directions. They are NE, NW, SE, and SW.

N
NW NE
W E
SW SE
S

Scale of Miles:
When you are planning a trip, it's nice to know how far you will travel. A scale of miles shows how far apart things are. It measures the distance between places.

Discovering Maps

Did you know that all modern maps begin as photographs? Photographs are taken from airplanes, satellites, or spacecraft. They help make maps more accurate by giving us more complete information. Older maps used to be drawn by hand using special tools. Sometimes mapmakers still use these tools when mapping small distances.

Maps come in all shapes and sizes. Can you think of some? Maybe you thought of a treasure map! Maybe you thought of the road maps your parents use on trips. Maps help us know where we are and where we want to go. Look at the map of Nevada on the previous page. The green boxes show us tools that help us read a map.

Have you ever compared a globe to a map? In what ways are they different? In what ways are they the same?

···· Activity ····

Nevada on a Map

Use the compass rose and legend on the map of Nevada to answer the following questions:

1. What direction do you travel to go from Reno to Las Vegas?
2. What direction do you travel to go from Lake Mead to Lake Tahoe?
3. In what part of the state is the Humboldt River?
4. In what part of the state is Carson City?
5. Name the two cities that are nearest to Nevada's northern border.

Memory Master

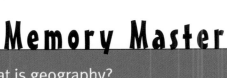

LESSON 1

1. What is geography?
2. Why do we use latitude and longitude lines?
3. How do modern maps begin?

Can you name one natural and one human feature found in this photograph?

LESSON 2

PLACES TO LOCATE

California
Humboldt-Toiyabe Forest
Lake Mead
Pacific Ocean
Sierra Nevada

WORDS TO UNDERSTAND

climate
ecosystem
elevation
fragile
graze
natural resource
precipitation
reservoir
shadow effect
species

What Kind of Place Is Nevada?

Nevada is a place with many beautiful features. Some of them are natural features, like soil, lakes, plants, and animals. Some of them are human features, such as cities, barns, homes, shopping malls, bridges, and roads. Many of these features make Nevada different from other states.

Our Natural Resources

Nevada is a state rich in ***natural resources.*** Natural resources are things found in nature that are useful to people. Today, our state mines more silver and gold than any other state. Turquoise and copper are other important metals found in our soil. Minerals such as gypsum, limestone, and salt, are Nevada resources too. Salt mined in our state is used to melt icy winter roads.

People in our state use the land as a resource to raise crops and animals. Many ranches in the northeast part of Nevada feed, or ***graze,*** their cattle and sheep on our state's rangelands. There are also farmers here who grow wheat, hay, potatoes, barley, and other important crops.

Water is another important natural resource in Nevada. We need water to drink, to cook, and to bathe. Our crops need water to grow, and our animals must have it to live. Water power is used to make electricity too. Nevada's lakes, rivers, and dams are our major sources of water since little rain falls here.

Natural resources are very important to our state. Using them wisely now will make life better for future Nevadans.

Nevada is a mineral-rich state. Do you know the names of any of these minerals?

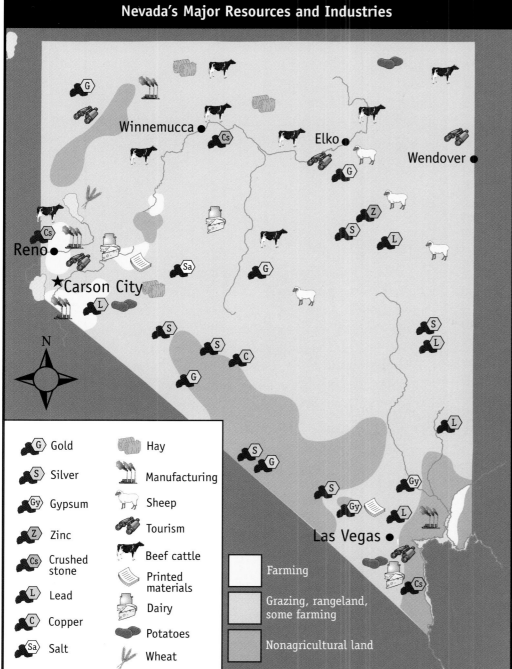

Nevada's Major Resources and Industries

Winnemucca •
Elko •
Wendover •
Reno •
★ Carson City
N
Las Vegas •

Legend:
- (G) Gold
- (S) Silver
- (Gy) Gypsum
- (Z) Zinc
- (Cs) Crushed stone
- (L) Lead
- (C) Copper
- (Sa) Salt
- Hay
- Manufacturing
- Sheep
- Tourism
- Beef cattle
- Printed materials
- Dairy
- Potatoes
- Wheat
- Farming
- Grazing, rangeland, some farming
- Nonagricultural land

Activity

Using the Land

This map shows some of our state's resources and industries. Each picture symbol shows the areas where a product is grown or produced. Study the map and answer these questions:

1. List four resources shown on this map.
2. Name two areas in Nevada where potatoes are grown.
3. If you lived in Las Vegas, would you grow wheat? Why or why not?
4. Pick one of our state's resources to learn more about. Try to find out why that resource is so important to Nevada.

Nevada's Natural Ecosystems

An *ecosystem* is a special community where certain plants and animals live. There are many natural ecosystems in Nevada. Here are just a few of them:

Desert

A desert is a hot, dry place with little rainfall and miles of sand and rock. Plants and animals that live in the desert know how to survive on little water. Some animals come out only at night when the ground cools off. Deserts are often cold at night. Do you know what kinds of animals live in such a place? Rabbits, coyotes, mice, insects, snakes, and lizards are just a few.

Rangeland

A rangeland is a place where grasses and shrubs grow and where animals are allowed to graze. In Nevada, we have thousands of acres of rangeland where cattle, sheep, horses, and wildlife graze. Much of this land is owned by the federal government. People also hunt, fish, and enjoy outdoor recreation on Nevada's rangelands. They are a very important ecosystem in Nevada.

Freshwater

Rivers, streams, and lakes all belong to the freshwater ecosystem. Many of our large rivers and lakes supply water for drinking, agriculture, and industries in Nevada. Lake Mead is a large *reservoir* in our state that catches water from snow and rain. A reservoir is a man-made lake used to store water. Are there any reservoirs near your home? Water is a very important resource for our state. We can each do our part to take care of Nevada's fresh waters.

Caves and Caverns

There are hundreds of natural limestone caves in Nevada. Some are large with odd rock formations, and some were used as shelter for Nevada's earliest people. The bones of many ancient people have been found in our caves. Caves and caverns are very *fragile,* or easily damaged, ecosystems. Even small changes made by people can place a cave or cavern at risk. All kinds of dark-loving creatures live in caves. Can you think of some? Bats, spiders, salamanders, and centipedes all live in dark places.

Forests

Forests are another important natural ecosystem in Nevada. Many kinds of trees and plants grow in our forests. Animals, like chipmunks, owls, mountain lions, and bears, live there too. The Humboldt-Toiyabe forest in our state is nearly 6.5 million acres. It is the largest national forest in the United States outside of Alaska. Nevada also has many state forests where people go to fish, hike, and enjoy nature.

Wetlands

Nevada's wetlands are a small but important part of our state. Many different types of plants and animals get food and freshwater there. More than 100 *species,* or types, of birds make their nests or stop to rest there every year. Fish, deer, elk, sage grouse, and owl are just some of the wildlife that depend on this ecosystem to survive. In Chapter 1, you read about a special plant called tule that was used by some of Nevada's earliest people. Tule is an example of a plant that grows in our wetlands.

Climate and Elevation

Are you wondering how climate is different from weather? Remember that climate is the way weather acts over time. Weather is what happens in a single day.

Climate is a very important part of a place. It tells us how weather acts over time. Climates in Nevada are different from place to place. That's because our mountains and our lowlands are at very different **elevations.**

Elevation tells us how high the land rises above sea level. For example, the Sierra Nevada Range rises more than 10,000 feet above sea level. Temperatures and *precipitation,* or rainfall, change at different elevations. Mountain areas are wetter and cooler than our desert lowlands. In Las Vegas, the summers are very hot. Las Vegas is part of our desert lowlands. The elevation there is less than 2,000 feet above sea level.

Weather Happenings

Nevada's climate is affected by other things besides elevation. Distance from large bodies of water affects our weather patterns too. Tall mountains on both sides of Nevada also play a part. Because our state sits like a bowl between tall mountains, we often experience a pattern called the **shadow effect.**

The shadow effect begins when winds from the Pacific Ocean blow clouds carrying moist air from west to east. As clouds filled with moisture cross California on their way to Nevada, they come up against the Sierra Nevada. Rising clouds are forced to move up the mountains to get over them. As they reach the top, the clouds cool down making it hard for them to hold their moisture. They begin dropping rain or snow as they travel over the mountains. By the time the clouds reach Nevada, very little moisture is left for Nevada's dry land.

The Shadow Effect

PACIFIC OCEAN

CALIFORNIA   SIERRA NEVADA   NEVADA

Nevada, Our Home

Activity

Reading Climate Maps

These maps give information about Nevada's climate. Use the maps to answer the following questions:

1. Which map shows how much rain falls in Nevada?
2. Which map shows how hot it gets in Nevada during the summer?
3. Name two counties in Nevada where 15 or less inches of precipitation fall each year.
4. What is the average temperature in Laughlin during the month of January?
5. What is the average temperature in Ely in the month of July?
6. What part of Nevada gets the most precipitation per year? North, South, East, or West?

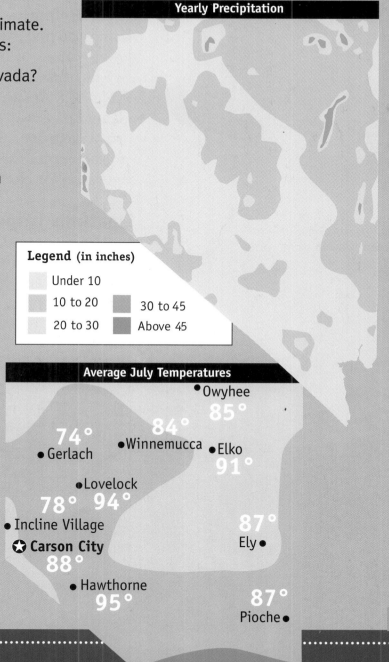

Yearly Precipitation

Legend (in inches)

- Under 10
- 10 to 20
- 20 to 30
- 30 to 45
- Above 45

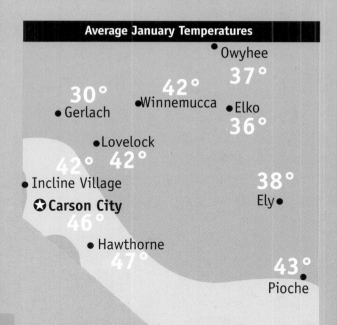

Average January Temperatures

- Owyhee 37°
- 30° Gerlach
- 42° Winnemucca
- Elko 36°
- Lovelock
- 42° 42°
- Incline Village
- ✪ Carson City
- 46°
- Hawthorne 47°
- Ely 38°
- Pioche 43°
- Las Vegas 57°
- Laughlin 64°

Average July Temperatures

- Owyhee 85°
- 74° Gerlach
- 84° Winnemucca
- Elko 91°
- Lovelock
- 78° 94°
- Incline Village
- ✪ Carson City
- 88°
- Hawthorne 95°
- Ely 87°
- Pioche 87°
- Las Vegas 105°
- Laughlin 108°

Our Plants and Animals

Nevada is home to many different kinds of plant and animal life. Some plants grow in dry areas while others need more water. Plants such as cactus, creosote bush, greasewood, and sagebrush live in the desert regions of Nevada.

Sagebrush, our state flower, grows in practically all parts of Nevada. It can live on very dry land. Its long root system takes advantage of water from deep within the soil. Sagebrush plants are also very strong. They produce yellow flowers in the spring and can sometimes reach over 12 feet tall. Early Native Americans used sagebrush for clothing, medicine, and shelter.

Creatures Large and Small

The animals of Nevada come in many shapes and sizes. Can you name some of our smaller desert animals? There are snakes, tortoises, spiders, lizards, mice, desert squirrels, rabbits, and birds. We also have many larger animals like mountain lions, bears, deer, coyotes, and bighorn sheep. Mountain lions, bears, and deer live mainly in our cooler mountain areas. Many animals were used for food by Nevada's early native people.

Lizards, like this one, love to sun themselves on warm rocks.

Nevada deserts can be beautiful following a wet winter or spring.

Memory Master

LESSON 2

1. Name three of Nevada's natural resources.
2. How is climate different from weather?
3. Name two ways early Native Americans used sagebrush.

Our Ancient Land

Nevada's land was formed over millions of years by volcanoes, earthquakes, glaciers, water, and wind. It's been called the land that was never finished. Rivers flow for miles and disappear into the earth. Mountains push up across the land. Rocks lie scattered as if sprinkled from the sky.

Today, Nevada is a desert and mountain region. But it has not always been that way. Millions of years ago, the area we call Nevada was part of a giant ocean. As time passed, the ocean dried up. Great periods of *drought* followed. Volcanoes erupted and earthquakes caused mountains to rise. Over time, mountains were *eroded,* or worn away, by wind and rain. Water covered Nevada once again.

Many animals and sea creatures lived here then. The ichthyosaur swam in warm waters. Horse-like animals, sloths, and mammoths also roamed the land.

As the earth became warmer the waters dried up, leaving only one large lake in the Nevada area. It was called Lake Lahontan. It covered much of the west-central part of Nevada.

Weather patterns continued to change in ancient Nevada. The climate that was once hot and wet, like in tropical areas, later became hot and dry, like the desert we see today. Many prehistoric animals living in the area disappeared when the plants they ate stopped growing. Eventually, Lake Lahontan turned into two smaller lakes. Today, we know these lakes as Pyramid and Walker Lakes.

LESSON 3

PLACES TO LOCATE

Colombia Plateau
Great Basin
Lake Lahontan
Mojave Desert
Pyramid Lake
Sierra Nevada
Walker Lake

WORDS TO UNDERSTAND

adapt
custom
drought
environment
erode
ethnic group
fault line
immigrant
landform
movement
plate tectonics
region
tourist
unique

Larry Jacox created this painting of giant ichthyosaurs swimming in the ancient waters of Nevada.

 ## Activity

Shaking Things Up

Let's see how erosion really works. Try this experiment. Record your findings in as much detail as possible.

Put a few small limestone rocks about the same size into three plastic bottles. Cover them with water and cap the bottles. Put a few rocks aside to look at later.

Shake one bottle for 3 minutes. Shake the second bottle for 5 minutes. Shake the third bottle for 10 minutes.

Compare the rocks in the three bottles with each other. What has happened to them? Compare the rocks from the bottles with the rocks you set aside.

What kinds of things have you learned from this experiment? Do you think water has had the same effect on the land in Nevada?

What do you think?

What types of landforms are near your home? If you had to rename your town using a landform, what would you would name it?

A Land of Change

Because much of Nevada is without plant life, it's easy to see how nature has affected the land. Our state has had many volcanoes and earthquakes. Some scientists study the movement of the earth's crust. They call this study *plate tectonics.*

The earth's crust is split into many sections called plates. Each plate is many miles thick and millions of miles wide. Two plates affect Nevada and the states nearby. The North American and Pacific plates come together in several places in our region. Scientists call the place they touch a *fault line.* As the plates rub against each other, it puts great pressure on the earth's crust. This underground pressure can lead to earthquakes and volcanic activity.

Huge forces of nature have shaped Nevada, leaving many strange and interesting *landforms.* A landform is a natural feature of the earth. Mountains, valleys, hills, and plateaus are examples of natural landforms. Lehman Caves, Cathedral Gorge, and the Valley of Fire are some of Nevada's most interesting landforms. Rivers and lakes are sometimes called landforms. They help shape the land too.

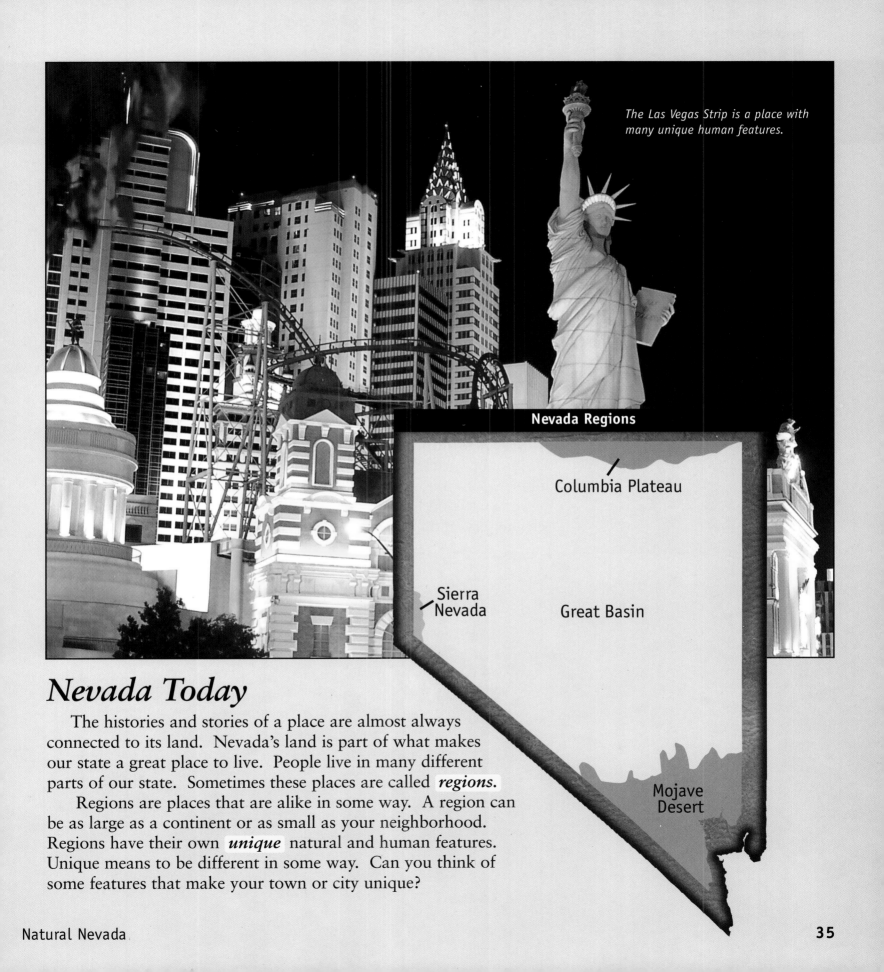

The Las Vegas Strip is a place with many unique human features.

Nevada Regions

Columbia Plateau

Sierra Nevada

Great Basin

Mojave Desert

Nevada Today

The histories and stories of a place are almost always connected to its land. Nevada's land is part of what makes our state a great place to live. People live in many different parts of our state. Sometimes these places are called *regions*.

Regions are places that are alike in some way. A region can be as large as a continent or as small as your neighborhood. Regions have their own *unique* natural and human features. Unique means to be different in some way. Can you think of some features that make your town or city unique?

The Great Basin

Nevada is part of a very large land region called the Great Basin, or the Basin and Range region. It covers more than half of our state and parts of Utah, Oregon, Idaho, Wyoming, and California. The region was given its name by explorer John C. Fremont. He named it that because of its very large bowl shape.

Sometimes the Great Basin is called a cold desert. It's the only one of its kind in the United States. In the winter, temperatures drop and the ground is often dusted with snow. Summers are mostly hot, dry, and dusty. Sheep and cattle graze across the sagebrush-covered land. Ghost towns, old mines, and mountain ranges also dot the region.

One of the world's oldest living trees grows in the Great Basin. It's also one of our state symbols. Can you guess which one? If you guessed the bristlecone pine, you guessed right!

Sagebrush, saltbush, and many types of grasses grow here too. Riverbeds of the Great Basin are often lined with cottonwood trees. During the spring, beautiful wildflowers, like Indian paintbrush, lupines, sego lilies, and sunflowers, cover the ground. Lake Tahoe, Nevada's second largest lake is part of this region. Many farmers, vacationers, and industries draw water from the lake.

Nevada's rangelands are home to the desert fox.

This photograph shows the Highland Range that lies northwest of Pioche.

© Airphoto-Jim Wark

Reno is sometimes called "the Biggest Little City in the World"

Animals of the Great Basin have had to adapt to a harsh climate. You might see pronghorn, bobcat, coyote, badger, and fox. Miles of open land are home to birds, ducks, and geese. Rabbits, squirrels, rats, mice, and the Great Basin rattlesnake are also at home here.

Reno and Carson City are just two of the larger cities in the Great Basin region. Ely, Elko, Fallon, Wells, Lovelock, and Virginia City are some of the smaller towns that spread across our state.

People from many different *ethnic groups* live in our towns and cities. Ethnic groups are people of the same race or heritage. Some of them are *immigrants.* An immigrant is a person who lives in a country other than where he or she was born.

To keep their traditions alive, immigrants celebrate their heritage in a number of ways. People of all cultures look forward to the Basque festivals held each year in our state.

People living in the Great Basin region work in factories or mines. Others work as ranchers or farmers. Many people work in state parks, hotels, restaurants, or other places visitors, or *tourists,* like to go. Providing services for tourists is big business all over our state.

Linking the Past to the Present

Think about a festival you celebrate or a custom you enjoy. How many years have you been doing it? Can you think of any customs you enjoy that people have celebrated for more than 5 years? 10 years? 50 years? 100 years?

These children are dressed in traditional clothing for the annual Basque Festival in Elko.

Photo by Travis Miller

The Mojave Desert

At the southern tip of our state is a region that is part of the Mojave Desert. Las Vegas, Henderson, and Boulder City are a few of the cities found here. This region also covers parts of California, Utah, and Arizona.

Wide valley floors and fewer mountains make this area hot, dry, and windy. Temperatures here often reach freezing during the winter months. But the area usually gets less than five inches of precipitation a year.

Because there is little rainfall, the plants in the area survive without much water. Creosote bush, shadscale, blackbush, and sagebrush are a few of the most common plants. The Joshua tree is also found here.

Animals living in the Mojave region have learned to live on very little water too. They stay in cool places while it's hot. Then they search for food and water when the sun goes down. Wild burros, coyotes, lizards, desert tortoises, roadrunners, jackrabbits, barn owls, and Desert Bighorn are a just a few of the animals that make their homes here.

More than half of Nevada's people live in the Mojave region. They work for hotels and the gaming and entertainment industries. They teach at local schools and universities. They work for the government and for the United States Air Force.

People from all over the world come to the Mojave region for fun. They gamble, shop, attend shows, take thrill rides, go boating, get married, and enjoy all-you-can-eat buffets. They also enjoy sporting events like rodeo, tennis, NASCAR, boxing, and off-road motorcycle racing.

Lake Mead, at the base of Hoover Dam, is the area's largest water resource. It is 115 miles long.

Callville Marina on Lake Mead has thousands of visitors each year.

The Columbia Plateau

Near the Nevada-Idaho border, a small corner of our state lies in a region called the Columbia Plateau. Some of the land in this corner of Nevada looks very different. Rivers and streams run through deep rock canyons. These layers of rock were left behind by ancient volcanoes.

Only a few small towns are found in this region. Most of the land is wide-open prairie. Like the Great Basin region, cattle and sheep graze the grasslands. Hunting, fishing, and other outdoor activities are an important part of life.

Here, rivers and streams receive more precipitation than in other parts of our state. The increased moisture makes it the perfect place for aspen and juniper trees to grow.

The South Fork of the Owyhee River winds through a deep, rocky gorge.

40

The Sierra Nevada

The Sierra Nevada region of western Nevada is our state's most tree-rich region. The smell of pines and deep green forests fills the air. During summer months, people like to hike, camp, fish, and ride horses in the area. Winter brings skiers, young and old, to the snow-covered slopes. Beautiful vacation homes are built among the trees, and area casinos are alive with tourists.

The people who live and work here find jobs in casinos, ski resorts, and in area shops. Some work in construction, real estate, or in banks. Jobs like these are part of Nevada's large service industry. Nevada workers serve the needs of visitors and people all over our state.

"Three months of camp life on Lake Tahoe would restore an Egyptian mummy to his pristine vigor, and give him an appetite like an alligator."

–Mark Twain

Living and Learning From the Land

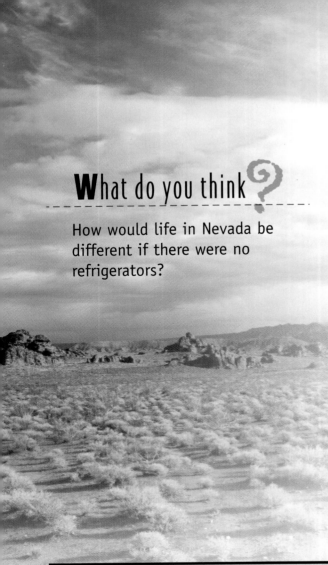

What do you think❓

How would life in Nevada be different if there were no refrigerators?

Sometimes people must learn to *adapt* to new ways of living. To adapt means to change. Sometimes people have to change the way they live when they move to the desert. They may have to eat different foods or wear different clothes.

Nevada's early native peoples had to adapt to living here. They had very little water and a limited food supply. Hot summers, cold winters, high winds, and blowing dust made life very hard. There were no buffalo and few deer to hunt.

Early native peoples lived on small animals, like rabbits. They learned to eat native plants. They wove mesquite bushes and tree limbs together to make their homes. Native peoples learned how to become part of the land. They didn't do much to try to change their surroundings, or *environment.*

Improving Nevada

Today, it is much easier to live in Nevada. Modern tools help make our environment more comfortable. Air conditioners and refrigerators help us stay cool. Highways, railroads, cars, and planes help us travel faster and protect us from bad weather. Wood for homes and other things now comes to our state from other places. Most of these changes are good, but some can harm our environment.

Caring for the Land

For many years, we didn't know we needed to take care of our environment. Now we know that resources will not last if we don't use them carefully. Nevada will still be a good place to live 20 years from now, if we take care of our land, air, and water today. Many people study how to protect these resources. Some groups have set aside special places for endangered animals. Some have created gardens where rare plants can grow. Other people study our rangelands and forests. Lawmakers pass laws to protect our lakes and rivers from pollution.

Everyone can help. You can put trash in a garbage can. You can recycle paper, plastic, and tin cans. You can save energy by turning off your lights or TV when you aren't using them. You can conserve water. Everyone can help take care of Nevada.

These students are learning how to test water quality and how to reduce erosion.

On the Move

People and goods have always moved from place to place or region to region. *Movement* is when ideas, goods, or people go from one place to another. Movement connects people and places to each other.

People first came to Nevada in search of gold and silver in our deserts and mountains. They brought with them their own *customs,* or ways of living, thinking, and acting.

People who moved out of Nevada took ideas and money with them. Cities like San Francisco, California were partly built with money made in Nevada mines. Mining methods used in Nevada are also used in mines around the world. People still come from other places to work in our mines or to learn from them.

Nevada's gold and silver are shipped to many places in the world. People, ideas, and resources are always moving in and out of our state.

© Airphoto-Jim Wark

Have you and your family ever moved from one place to another? What kinds of things did you take with you?

What do you think?

How are goods moved today? How are ideas moved today? What do you think is helpful or harmful about moving goods and ideas?

LESSON 3

Memory Master

1. Which lakes in Nevada are all that remains of Lake Lahontan?
2. What are scientists studying when they study plate tectonics?
3. Who named our state's largest region?

Natural Nevada

Consider ★ Character

On page 42 of this chapter, you've read about many ways to show respect for Nevada. Now let's look at how some of the students in our state are learning about the importance of caring for Nevada's water resources.

Each September, thousands of students across the United States participate in a national day of water education. It's called Make a Splash with Project WET. About 200 students were involved in Nevada's 2005 Make a Splash Festival. Students learned about different water environments through hands-on activities. They learned about conservation and water quality. They talked about underground water, or aquifers, and about protecting Nevada's wetlands. Take a look at a few of the activities students from West End Elementary School in Fallon participated in.

◄ Testing water samples helps these students learn about water quality.

These students ► are learning about where drinking water comes from.

Technology 🔬 Tie-In

How many different jobs can you think of where people study the characteristics of regions? Who works to gather information about weather, cities, small towns, land and population? What technology or tools do these people use to gather information? How is this information useful to our state?

Geography 🌐 Tie-In

As you read *Nevada, Our Home*, you will learn many new things about our state. You might be surprised, though, to find out how much you already know. You know that Nevada is part of a region called the West. In the West there are big cities, small towns, and many farms and ranches. We get rain, snow, wind, and lots of sunny days.

Some people live and work in the city. They live in houses and apartment buildings. Some people live on farms with open fields all around them. Make a list of other things you know about living in the West.

Now pick another region of the United States you might want to explore. Do you know the names of these regions? The map below will help you locate them. Once you choose which region you want to explore, make a list of at least three things in that region that are different from the West. Then make a poster or brochure that shows what types of land, plants, and animals are part of this region. Include other interesting things too, like what your region's weather is like or the kinds of food people eat. Think about working together with someone else from your class who is interested in learning about the same region. When you are finished, share what you learned with your class.

Regions of the United States

The First People

"It takes a thousand voices to tell a single story."

— Tribe Unknown

Timeline of Events

10000 B.C.
Desert Archaic culture develops.

5000 B.C.
Possible arrival of the Paiutes in the Great Basin.

A.D. 1150
- Anasazi abandon the Lost City.
- Paiutes live in Nevada.

8000 B.C.
Hunter-gatherers live in the Great Basin.

300 B.C.
Anasazi live in southern Nevada.

A.D. 1600s
Paiute, Shoshone, and Washoe spread out across the land.

2500 B.C.
People live in Lovelock Cave.

10000 B.C.   5000 B.C.   A.D. 1000   A.D. 1500

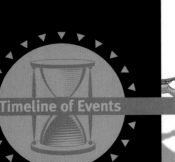

Nevada's earliest human remains are over 9,000 years old. These people had a difficult life trying to survive in our harsh desert lands. Artifacts left by these early people help us better understand their ways of life. They also remind us that from the very beginning, native peoples have been an important part of Nevada's heritage.

Thousands of years ago, Nevada's native people spent much of their time hunting for food.

A.D. 1820s
Explorers begin entering the region.

A.D. 1860–1890
The U.S. government establishes reservations in Nevada.

A.D. 1895
Dat-So-La-Lee's friends begin to document her baskets as works of art.

A.D. 1924
The U.S. government makes Native Americans U.S. citizens.

A.D. 1820   A.D. 1840   A.D. 1860   A.D. 1880   A.D. 1900   A.D. 1920   A.D. 1940

A.D. 1859
Thousands of white settlers begin coming to Nevada.

A.D. 1883
Sarah Winnemucca publishes her book, *Life Among the Piutes.*

A.D. 1925
Mark Harrington begins studying Pueblo Grande de Nevada.

A.D. 1940
Spirit Cave Man's remains are discovered in a cave near Fallon.

47

Some of Nevada's earliest people lived in caves like these.

PEOPLE TO KNOW

Desert Archaic people
Lovelock Cave people
Spirit Cave Man

PLACES TO LOCATE

Fallon
Lovelock Cave
Spirit Cave
Valley of Fire State Park

WORDS TO UNDERSTAND

archaeologist
atlatl
Clovis point
graffiti
hunter-gatherer
mummy
petroglyph
prehistoric
tule

Who Were the First People?

The earliest people to reach what is now Nevada came to this region more than 10,000 years ago. We call them Desert Archaic people. Sometimes, we also call them *prehistoric* people because they lived before written records were kept. These early people lived all over the southwestern United States in caves and small family groups.

Archaeologists have discovered many cave homes in our state. Archaeologists are people who study the clues left by people from long ago. Some of these caves are near the shores of Lake Lahontan. Archaeologists search caves for clues about people who might have lived there. By studying things left by ancient people, we can learn much about their way of life.

Discovery at Spirit Cave

More than 60 years ago, near the town of Fallon, the *mummy* of a man was found in a place called Spirit Cave. A mummy is a body that has been wrapped for burial. Some archaeologists think the man died over 9,000 years ago. His skeleton was found wrapped in matting and a rabbit-skin blanket.

This is a model of what scientists believe the Spirit Cave Man might have looked like.

The Lovelock Cave People

The Lovelock Cave is another important archaeological site in our state. Artifacts made of bone, stone, and wood have been found there. Scientists call the people who left these remains the Lovelock Cave People.

One special artifact found at this site and in other parts of Nevada is called a **Clovis point.** Clovis points are hand-made stone darts. They were often tied to sticks to make spears and used for hunting.

Over time, early people created new tools to make hunting easier. The **atlatl** was a tool that made it easier to throw a spear harder and faster.

The Lovelock Cave People also made duck decoys from tule reeds. They pulled the long, skinny reeds from the water and then wrapped them into the shape of a duck. Sometimes cave people painted and decorated their ducks with feathers to make them look real. Duck decoys were a good hunting tool for cave people, just as they are for hunters today. Once a decoy was complete, it was sent floating out into the water to attract live ducks. Decoys made it easier for cave people to kill live ducks for food.

The Lovelock Cave People were **hunter-gatherers.** This means they spent most of their time hunting and gathering food. They made nets and clothing from rabbit fur and other animal skins. They also fished and gathered wild plants and berries.

Sometimes cave people made baskets out of tule for storing food and for carrying things. Pieces of tule baskets were uncovered in the Lovelock Cave.

The **atlatl** was a small, narrow stick that early people attached to the end of a spear. It helped hunters throw their spears much farther and faster.

This 2000-year-old duck decoy was discovered in Nevada's Lovelock Cave.

Sometimes tule was dried and made into mats.

These rock carvings in Nevada's Valley of Fire State Park tell stories about some of Nevada' earliest people.

Photo by Tom Till

Nevada, Our Home

Writings on the Walls

Some of Nevada's earliest people left carvings called *petroglyphs* on rocks and cave walls. Archaeologists study these carvings to learn more about our state's first people. Some rock carvings are of animals. Some are of people and events. Many archaeologists believe early people carved pictures of deer on rocks or walls so their hunts would go well. Petroglyphs have been discovered all over Nevada. Nevada's most famous carvings are in the Valley of Fire State Park, north of Las Vegas. Many are thought to be more than 1,500 years old.

Activity

Petroglyphs

After looking at the picture of petroglyphs on page 50, design your own petroglyph on a piece of paper. Then find a few medium-sized rocks with at least one flat surface. Lightly draw your petroglyph on the rock with chalk. Carefully paint over your drawing with craft paint to make your petroglyph permanent. Create more than one design, or find a bigger rock and create a whole story. Tell your class why you picked your specific design.

Remember! Drawing or painting on small rocks you collect or have at home is alright. But writing or drawing on cave or rock walls is against the law. Writing or drawing things on canyon walls or someone else's property is called *graffiti.*

Linking the Past to the Present

Today it's against the law to take artifacts from caves in Nevada. It's also against the law to harm petroglyphs, or rock art. A few years ago, in a cave near the Utah-Nevada border, two teens broke through iron gates and used charcoal to draw over original rock art. They also dug a hole looking for artifacts. Have you ever seen graffiti on a wall or in a cave? Talk with your class about ways you can help stop graffiti.

Memory Master

LESSON 1

1. What do archaeologists do?
2. What did the Lovelock Cave people use to make duck decoys?
3. Where are some of our state's most famous petroglyphs found?

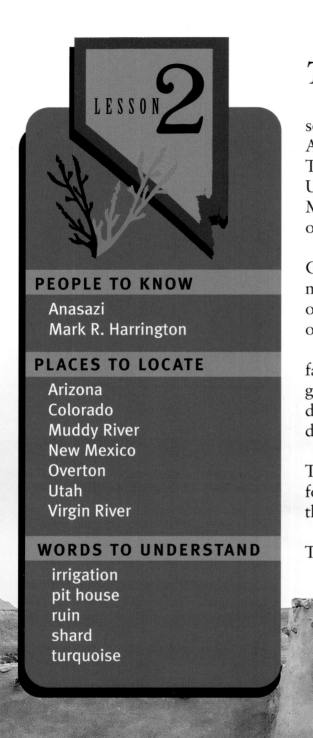

LESSON 2

PEOPLE TO KNOW

Anasazi
Mark R. Harrington

PLACES TO LOCATE

Arizona
Colorado
Muddy River
New Mexico
Overton
Utah
Virgin River

WORDS TO UNDERSTAND

irrigation
pit house
ruin
shard
turquoise

The Anasazi

About 2,000 years ago another group of people settled in the southern part of our state. We call them the Anasazi people. Anasazi is a Native American term that means *old* or *ancient ones*. The Anasazi built settlements in Nevada, Colorado, New Mexico, Utah, and Arizona. *Ruins* of Anasazi homes near the Virgin and Muddy Rivers tell us much about their lives. Ruins are what is left of a place after the people living there have gone.

The Anasazi built a large community known today as Pueblo Grande de Nevada, or the Lost City. This early community was made of *pit houses.* Some were built partly underground while others were built above the ground. Some pit houses had only one or two rooms while others had more than 100 rooms.

The Anasazi did more than hunt and gather. They were also farmers who grew corn, beans, and squash in their fields. They grew cotton and used it to make clothing. They dug *irrigation* ditches to bring water to their crops. Irrigation is a way of watering dry land through pipes, ditches, or canals.

Farming allowed the Anasazi to spend more time in one place. They did not have to move to follow animals or hunt for food. Staying in one place gave them time to improve their way of life and develop other skills.

The Anasazi also made beautiful baskets and pottery. They used most of them for storage. Some of their most

Archaeologist rebuilt parts of the Lost City so people today can see how the Anasazi lived thousands of years ago.

beautiful pieces were used for trade. Pieces of baskets and pots have been found in many Anasazi ruins.

The Anasazi were also our state's first miners. They dug salt and a bluish-green mineral called *turquoise* from the nearby hills. Salt was very important to the Anasazi. They used it to dry food to keep it from spoiling. The turquoise they found was often traded or used to make jewelry.

The Anasazi traded with people in Utah and Arizona. Trade was very important for their community. They gained new ideas, skills, and goods from other people.

The Three Sisters

Corn, beans, and squash were life-giving plants for early Nevada people. Sometimes they called these plants the Three Sisters because they helped each other grow. As cornstalks grow tall, they work like a pole to support the beans. The beans help feed the soil. The squash leaves spread out keeping the ground moist and weed-free. Ask your parents to help you plant a Three Sisters garden.

Pit houses were sometimes built partly underground. This helped keep people cooler during the hot summer months.

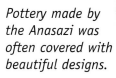

Pottery made by the Anasazi was often covered with beautiful designs.

Mystery of the Lost City

No one knows why the Anasazi left their homes in Pueblo Grande Nevada. Some people think they may have been forced out because of war with other tribes. Some believe disease or changes in the climate made it difficult for the Anasazi to stay in Nevada. Others believe these early people moved to find more food and water.

Many scientists think there was a long dry spell, or drought, about the same time the Anasazi left their homes here. They learned this by studying tree rings. Clues found in the rings of trees led scientists to believe that the drought may have lasted more than 20 years.

Thousands of years after the Anasazi left the Grand Pueblo Nevada, people began finding remains of the city. Scraps of pottery, called *shards,* and other small items were found along the banks of the Muddy River.

These ruins are part of the Lost City that was uncovered by archaeologists in 1926.

Can you imagine what it must have been like to live in homes like this?

LESSON 2

Memory Master

1. Which three plants did Nevada's early people use to create a three sisters garden?
2. What minerals did the Anasazi mine?
3. The ruins uncovered along the Muddy River have been called by two different names. Name one of them.

Activity

Write a Story About Anasazi Life

Now that you have read a little about the Anasazi, write a story about what life might have been like. Imagine yourself as a young Anasazi boy or girl. What was going on in your village? What kinds of things did you do each day? What did you do for fun? These are just a few of the things you could write about. You could even draw a picture to go with your story.

LESSON 3

PEOPLE TO KNOW

Dat-So-La-Lee
Mohave
Northern Paiutes
Shoshone
Southern Paiutes
Washoe·
Sarah Winnemucca

PLACES TO LOCATE

Carson Valley
Rocky Mountains
Sierra Nevada Range

WORDS TO UNDERSTAND

culture
historic groups
legend
nomadic
reservation
staple
tradition
tribe

Nevada's Historic People

Five native *tribes,* or groups, once made their homes in what is now Nevada. Historians call these people *historic groups* because written records were kept about their lives. Sometimes people kept records of their own lives. Sometimes people kept records about the lives of others.

When explorers and traders first came to the Great Basin, native groups had no written language. They passed their history on by talking to one another and by telling stories.

Our first written records of historic native people come from the records of early explorers and traders. Historians study these records to learn more about historic groups. They also learn about them by hearing the stories they have passed down.

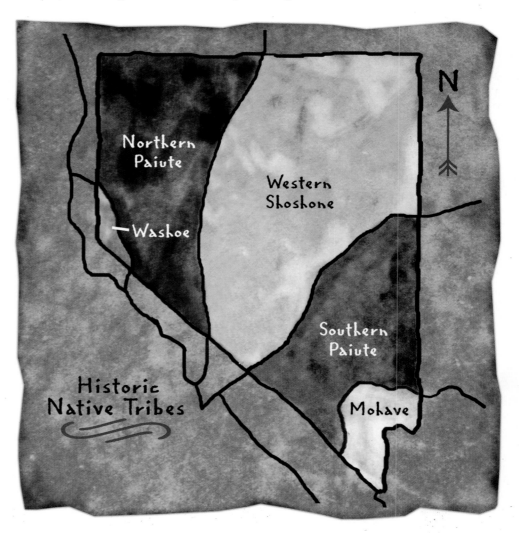

Historic Native Tribes

A Tribal Way of Life

Each of Nevada's five main tribes were different in some ways and alike in other ways. They spoke different languages and had different customs. They lived in different places and ate different foods.

One of Nevada's smallest historic groups was the Washoe. They lived near the Nevada-California border in the Lake Tahoe area. Before the white man came, the Washoe had rich hunting and fishing lands. Acorns were a major source of food for them. Washoe women were skilled basket-makers. Washoe men believed killing a bear was a sign of great bravery.

The Northern Paiutes settled in western Nevada and parts of California, and Oregon. They called themselves the pine nut eaters. More than 20 different bands, or groups, lived in the area when the first explorers came. Northern Paiutes were usually a peaceful group, often sharing what they had with other groups.

The Western Shoshone lived mostly in eastern Nevada and in parts of Utah and Idaho. Some believe these native groups were the first people explorers and trappers met when they reached the Great Basin. The Shoshone moved often, eating mostly roots, plants, and small animals.

The Southern Paiutes were at home in the southern regions of Nevada and in parts of California, Utah, and Arizona. These groups planted a few simple crops. Sometimes they traded goods with other groups. Many people think these were the first native people seen by Jedediah Smith as he crossed the southern tip of Nevada.

A group called the Mohave spent time along the Colorado River near the southern tip of Nevada. These people were Nevada's best gardeners. They planted corn, melons, beans, and pumpkin near the river. Spring floods would then water and fertilize their crops.

Nevada's main tribes were alike in some ways. All of them were *nomadic* at least part of the time. Nomadic people move from place to place. Nevada's nomadic people moved in search of food as they struggled to survive in the harsh desert land.

Linking the Past to the Present

Nevada's native people worked hard to get food. Did they eat foods that we eat today? What is different? What is the same?

Native women strapped their babies to their backs in cradleboards like this one from Overton's Lost Museum.

Hunting and Gathering

Nevada's historic groups were also hunter-gatherers. Tribes that lived near lakes and rivers ate fish and ducks. Some gathered natural plants like raspberries, wild carrots, and seeds.

Tribes in more wooded areas used the nuts from the Piñon pine to make many foods. The pine nut became a **staple,** or main food, for many tribes. To gather the nuts, tribes used long poles to hit the tree branches. After the pine cones fell, they were gathered, and the nuts were removed. Sometimes people made pine nut flour by grinding the nuts between two rocks.

Gathering nuts was so important for Nevada's historic tribes that at harvest time they gathered together for pine nut festivals. They celebrated with singing and dancing. Some people even taught their skills to members of other tribes.

Historic groups were able to make flour from pine nuts and grains by grinding them between two rocks.

Historic groups gathered nuts, seeds, roots, and berries for food.

Early mapmakers and explorers called some native groups digger Indians. Digger Indians dug up grubs and other insects to eat. They also used sticks to beat grasshoppers into a paste they could eat.

Other native groups had hunts called rabbit drives. A rabbit boss organized the hunt, and the main tool for the hunt was a large net. Tribe members walking in a line beat bushes with sticks and clubs. Frightened rabbits were then chased by hunters into a narrow canyon. A large net was stretched across the canyon opening to keep the rabbits from escaping. Hunts like this helped hungry tribes feed their families because they could catch so many rabbits at once.

Rabbit skins and meat were very important to early native groups. Most meat from their hunts was eaten quickly so it wouldn't spoil. Some of it was dried and stored for later. Rabbit skins were also used to make soft robes and warm blankets.

Baskets like this were used to store food and other important things. Most baskets were even woven tightly enough to hold water.

Rabbits were a source of food for Nevada's early native people.

Native Life and Customs

Life for native groups was not all work. Young girls often played a stick game called shinny. It was a mix between hockey and soccer. Players used sticks and a ball stuffed with deer hair. The object of the game was to get the ball into the other team's goal.

Gambling games were also very popular. In one game, called the hand game, players tried to guess who was holding the animal bones. Players often bet rabbit skins on who they thought might win.

Nevada's native people also believed in a Great Spirit or Creator. They taught their children that all creations have spirits. They believed some animals were messengers from the Creator or a sign of good luck. Native people also believed that people who die go to live in a better place.

Nevada's native people lived in simple shelters. In warmer months, their shelters were built from mesquite branches. Desert breezes could blow through these branches to cool them. When it turned cold, they covered pole frames with grass, reeds, or bark. Both shelters were easy to leave behind and build again when native groups moved to find food.

Paiute groups built wicki-ups like these to protect them from the weather.

Native groups believed that people, animals, plants, and even the wind and the stars would live forever with the Great Spirit after they died.

Nevada, Our Home

Have you ever had your picture taken in a photographic studio? Is this early photograph of Paiute children a lot different than photographs people have taken today?

Photographing Native Peoples

Not long after the camera was invented, a few early photographers came west to take pictures of native peoples. Sometimes they took pictures of native people in a studio and dressed them in fancy clothing or costumes. What do you think about the way these Paiutes are dressed? Do you think they wore clothes like these everyday?

Sarah Winnemucca
1844–1891

Sarah Winnemucca was a writer and speaker for the Paiute people. She grew up in northern Nevada and was called Thocmetony, (Tos-me-to-ne), which means Shell-Flower. White people who could not say her Indian name called her Sarah.

Sarah was the daughter of Old Chief Winnemucca and the granddaughter of Chief Truckee. Chief Truckee wanted her to be educated so she could survive in the white man's world. He sent Sarah and her sister to school in California.

The girls, however, were treated badly by other students and parents. After only a month, Sarah and her sister left the school and returned to Nevada, Sarah soon began speaking out about the poor treatment of her people. She spoke out about being forced to live on reservations.

Sarah gave more than 400 speeches about the rights of her people, all across the nation. She went to visit the *Great White Chief* in Washington, D.C. to see if he would help. Later, she started a school for Indian children in Nevada. She was also the first Native American woman to write a book. It was called *Life Among the Piutes*.

Learning From Legends

Historic native peoples taught their children about their world through stories and **legends.** Legends are stories that tell how something came to be. Some legends explain things, like why there are stars in the sky. Legends can also teach children important lessons. Native tribes used legends to teach their children respect for all living things.

Telling stories and legends was one of the ways native peoples taught their children.

Paiute Creation Legend

In the beginning, there was a great land between the Rocky Mountains and the Sierra Nevadas. The people who lived there were beautiful giants. They were always trying to protect themselves from outsiders.

One woman gave birth to a disfigured child who was treated badly by the other giants. The Great Spirit was angry because of this, so he brought fire and lightning down on the land. The land became hot and barren.

The Great Spirit also allowed the giants to be beaten by their enemies. Only two giants were left, a man and a woman. The man's name was Paiute, and the woman was his wife. They were burned dark brown and made to live in a land where only a few birds could be found for food. The land they lived in was called Nevada.

What do you think?

Nevada's historic people did not read or write, so they didn't keep written records. Do you think their stories and legends would be different today if they had written them down?

Nevada is a strange land where deserts and mountains live side-by-side.

Nevada Portrait

Dat-So-La-Lee
18??-1925

Dat-So-La-Lee was a famous Washoe basket maker who had many names. Her Indian name, Dabuda, means *Young Willow*. Louisa was her English name, and Dat-So-La-Lee was her nickname. She was born in the Carson Valley sometime between 1829 and 1850.

As a young girl, Dat-So-La-Lee learned how to cut different kinds of willows and reeds. She soaked them in mud to make them darker in color. After drying them, she cut them, shaped them, and wove them into baskets.

For many years Dat-So-La-Lee spent all her time cooking food and washing clothes for miners. The Cohn family heard about her basket-making skills. They helped her begin making baskets again. They also helped her sell them for a good price. They gave her food and a place to live so she could spend all her time making baskets. Her designs were very beautiful. Now her baskets are worth a lot of money. Some of them are in Nevada museums.

Dat-So-La-Lee never went to school. She didn't know how to read or write. She couldn't sign her name on important papers, so she signed with her hand print instead. Dat-So-La-Lee was one of the last Washoe basket weavers to practice this ancient art.

Reservation Life

Life became harder for native people as the problems of living with white settlers grew worse. Soon the U.S. government stepped in and began forcing native tribes to move to *reservations.* Reservations are pieces of land set aside by the government. However, native groups did not want to live on reservations. Life there was not as good as the government told them it would be.

Reservation life left native people very poor. Even though they were promised food and clothing, the clothes they got were often old and worn. Sometimes the food they were sent was not good quality. Farming and hunting on reservation land was not good either. But the government wouldn't let them hunt outside of the reservation. Native people were angry about how they were treated. They were angry about having to live on reservations.

Linking the Past to the Present

Native peoples and white settlers had a hard time getting along. Their ways of life were very different. How do people from different cultures treat each other today?

These Native American homes are on Nevada's Moapa reservation.

Many of Dat-So-La-Lee's baskets had beautiful patterns and designs.

Native Americans Today

Today's Native Americans no longer have to live on reservations. Many live in towns and do the same work as other Nevadans. Some live in rural areas, where they own ranches and farms.

Many of Nevada's Native Americans work together with other tribe members to improve their lives and the lives of other Nevadans. They own and operate hotels and casinos. They run their own stores and restaurants. Some sell handmade crafts or operate fisheries, campgrounds, or marinas.

Some Native Americans now choose to live on reservations. Living there is just like living in a small state. Reservations have their own governments that provide services, enforce laws, and collect taxes. People work hard to help improve reservation life. They help each other solve day-to-day problems. Today, the Paiute, Shoshone, Washoe, and Goshute tribes have reservations in Nevada.

Keeping *traditions* alive is another important part of Native American life in our state. A tradition is a way of life passed down from parent to child. Each year Nevada's Native Americans hold festivals and powwows. They dance and celebrate with traditional music, food, and costumes. These events help young Native Americans and others learn more about Native American *culture.* Culture is the way a group of people live.

Ranching near Elko is a way of life for this Shoshoni family.

What do you think?

What are some of your family's traditions? What are some of your community's traditions? What do these traditions tell people about your culture?

LESSON 3

Memory Master

1. Name the five main tribes that lived in Nevada before white settlers came.
2. Name two ways Nevada's native people used pine nuts.
3. Describe some of the problems native people had on reservations.

Consider ★ Character

Did you notice how early Nevada people had to cooperate to live together? They had to work together to get food, clothes, and shelter. Look back through the chapter and find one example of cooperation. Now imagine if someone in that example was not responsible and did not want to cooperate. Talk with your class about what happens when someone is not responsible.

Geography 🌍 Tie-In

Many Native Tribes

When early explorers came to North America, there were over 500 native groups living here. Each group had a different culture, a different language, and a different set of beliefs. Each group lived in ways that were unique. Take a few minutes to read about these groups. Then see if you can name the region where each group lived. If you need help, go back and review the land regions in chapter 2.

Native peoples living in the **Northwest** carved totem poles from tall tree trunks. They used animals and birds as symbols.

Native peoples of the **plains** often lived in tipis made from buffalo hides. Hides were also used to make clothing. Sometimes people decorated their tipis or clothing with special symbols or drawings.

Native peoples of the **Northeast** used trees to make canoes, boxes, baskets, and walls for their homes. They often ate wild cranberries.

Native American Nations

Western natives carried their water in tightly woven baskets. They lived in parts of what is now Nevada and California.

Native desert peoples of the **Southwest** built stone and adobe houses. They made pots from sandy red clay, which were often brightly painted.

Southeastern natives wove baskets of cypress and cane that grew in their lush green swamp lands. Brightly colored beads in zigzag patterns were sometimes added to baskets and clothing to make them more interesting.

Technology Tie-In

Can you imagine what it must have been like for early explorers and traders who first came to Nevada? What did they think about the native groups living in the area? What kinds of experiences did they have with them? How did they communicate with these groups? Many early traders and explorers wrote down what they saw and felt. Research online sources to find one of these early records. Remember, the records and journals of traders and explorers are primary sources. Records written by others about their experiences are secondary sources. (Hint: historical societies and museums have many early records.) After you have chosen and read one record, make a chart or diagram to show what you learned. The chart below is only one example of something you could make. Don't forget to make your own chart on a separate piece of paper.

Explorer	What He Found	What He Thought

Activity

Create Your Own Game

Native people used what was around them to make the things they needed. They didn't have stores where they could buy things. They didn't have computers or board games. Look around your room and in your desk. Invent a game using the things you find around you. Be creative! Make up the rules of the game. How do you know who wins? Try playing the game with your classmates.

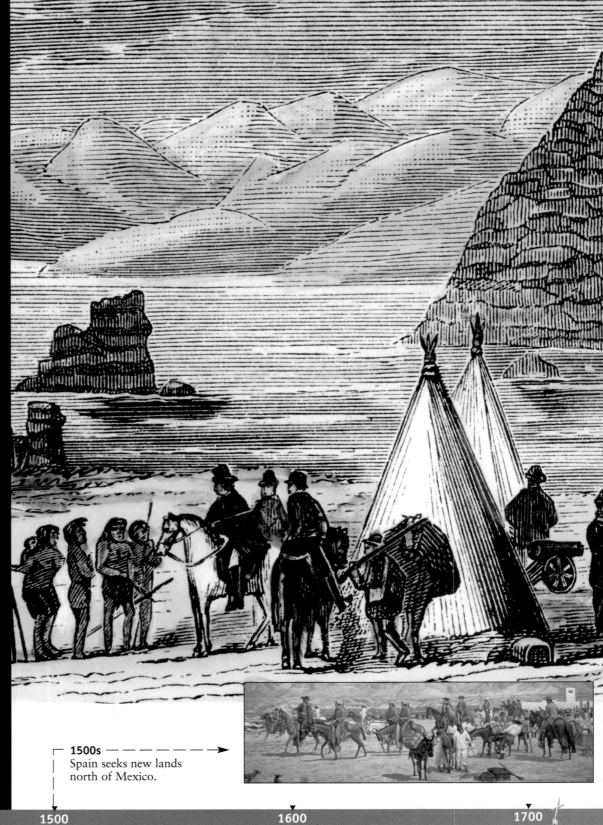

THE TIME
1492–1843

"*We encamped on the shore opposite a very remarkable rock in the lake,....[about] 600 feet above the water,... This striking feature suggested a name for the lake, and I called it Pyramid Lake...*"

—John C. Fremont

Timeline of Events

1500s
Spain seeks new lands north of Mexico.

1500

1600

1700

1492
Christopher Columbus finds the New World.

1610
Spain opens the first mission (Santa Fe) in the new territory.

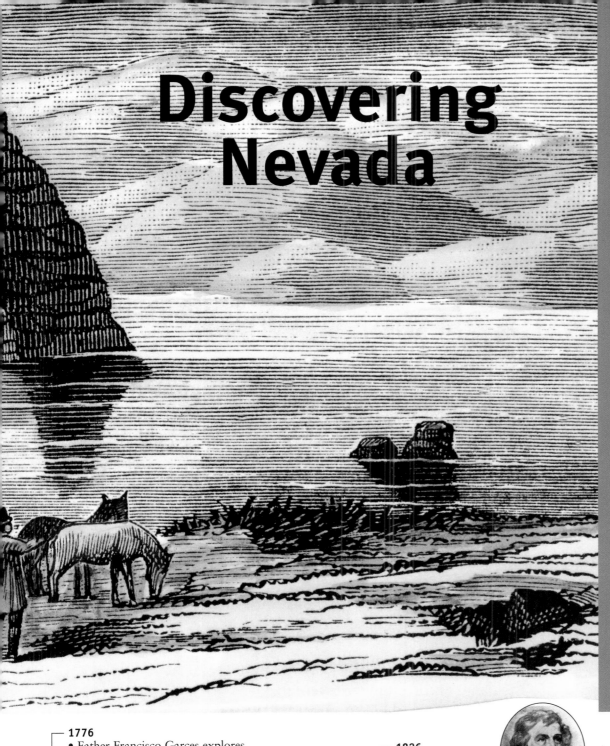

Discovering Nevada

Explorers are an important part of our nation's history. Some, like Christopher Columbus, came in search of new trade routes. Some traveled west looking for new lands to explore. In time, most of the land from the shores of the Atlantic to the Pacific had been explored. Each new adventure paved the way for others to follow.

John C. Fremont wrote many of his thoughts about seeing Pyramid Lake in his journal.

1776
- Father Francisco Garces explores near the southern tip of Nevada.
- Spanish priests Dominguez and Escalante explore western lands.

1826
Jedediah Smith enters the southern part of Nevada.

1843
John C. Fremont leads a mapmaking expedition into Nevada.

1820

1830

1840

1828
Peter Ogden explores northeastern Nevada.

1833
Joseph Walker fights in the first battle between white men and Indians in Nevada.

69

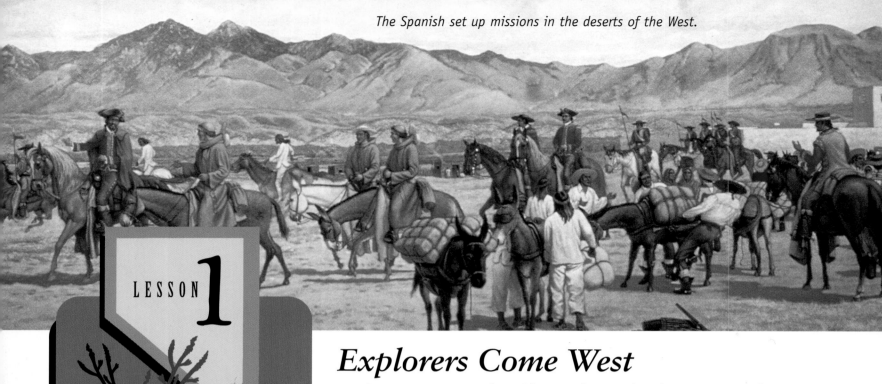
The Spanish set up missions in the deserts of the West.

LESSON 1

PEOPLE TO KNOW

Father Dominguez
Father Escalante
Father Francisco Garces

PLACES TO LOCATE

Colorado
Monterey, California
Santa Fe, New Mexico
Spain
Utah

WORDS TO UNDERSTAND

convert
expedition
mission
trader

Explorers Come West

Over 200 years after Christopher Columbus came to the New World, most of western North America was still unexplored. Spain had control over much of the land. It even sent soldiers to look for gold in the area. Spain had also hoped to get Native tribes to join, or *convert* to, the Catholic Church.

Soon Spanish *missions* were opened in small western outposts, where priests could begin teaching native tribes. One of the first missions was built in Santa Fe in what is now New Mexico. Monterey was another mission built near the Pacific Ocean. Today it is part of the state of California. At first, not much was known about the land between the two missions. Soon Spanish explorers were sent into the region to learn more.

Exploring Spanish Lands

Escalante and Dominguez were the two Spanish priests chosen to explore and find a new route from Santa Fe to Monterey. The priests were also asked to learn about the native people in the area.

With a party of 12, the two priests left Santa Fe in the heat of July. They took pack animals and horses through what later became New Mexico, Colorado, Utah, and Arizona. In Utah, they found many rivers and hoped one might flow as far west as the

Painting by Keith Eddington.

An Indian guide shows Father Escalante Utah Lake.

Pacific Ocean. They wanted a river route that would make travel between the missions easier. In the southern tip of Utah, Escalante and Dominguez came upon a large river they called the San Buenaventura. They believed it might drain toward the Pacific Ocean. Their mapmakers even added the river to the maps they were making. But the group never got a chance to fully explore the river. Bad weather and problems with their guide forced them to return to Santa Fe.

Years later, *traders* and other explorers got lost trying to find the river route shown on the Escalante and Dominguez map. They soon found that the San Buenaventura didn't really exist. Today, some people think the river seen by Escalante and Dominguez was what we now call the Colorado River.

Even though some of the information on their early maps turned out to be false, the travels of Escalante and Dominguez are still important to our history. Many people seeking adventure eventually found their way to Nevada because of their writings.

Linking the Past to the Present

Can you imagine using a map with wrong information today? What do you think would happen? What could happen if we sent explorers into space with incorrect maps? Have you ever thought about how we get maps of space?

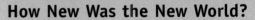

How New Was the New World?

Europeans called the land Columbus claimed the "New World". But it was not really new. Native people, like the Paiute, had been living there for thousands of years. The land was only new to the Europeans.

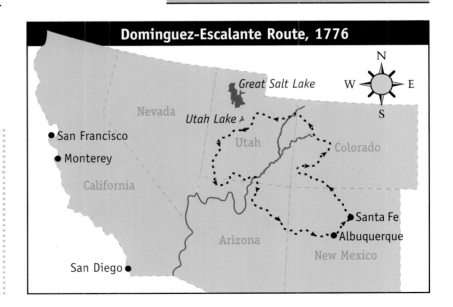

Dominguez-Escalante Route, 1776

NEVADA *Portrait*

Father Francisco Garces

Father Garces was one of many Spanish priests sent from Mexico to teach the native tribes. He lived at an outpost in the Arizona desert. Father Garces was also asked to help find the best route to California.

In 1776, Garces led an **expedition,** or journey, through present-day Nevada. He was most likely the first European to see our state. His writings were very helpful to others who later traveled through the area. Sadly, Garces and four others were killed by Indians at a mission in the Arizona desert.

This illustration shows Father Garces teaching native tribes.

Activity

Writing in a Journal

Many early explorers wrote in a journal, or diary, almost every day. This is just one of the ways we know so much about them. Explorers wrote about wild animals and finding food. They wrote about crossing new rivers or seeing new land. They wrote when they met new people.

Keep a journal for a week or more. Start with the date, and then write your thoughts or what you did that day. Talk about who you saw or what you learned. A few years from now, you'll love reading your journal.

LESSON 1 Memory Master

1. Name one reason Spain set up missions in the unexplored West.
2. Who had been living in the "New World" for thousands of years?

Mountain Men, Trappers, and Traders

Mountain men and fur trappers were some of the first explorers to enter the Nevada region. They came looking for animals to trap. Soon trading companies began to compete with one another. Each hoped to gather more furs than the others.

The Fur Trade

Beaver was one of the most popular furs of the time. Trappers went looking for beaver in ponds and streams. They placed baited traps in the water and checked them often. When a beaver went after the bait, the trap would snap shut, holding the beaver inside.

Trappers skinned beaver for their *pelts,* or furs, and took them to a trading post or settlement. Sometimes pelts were traded for food, money, or weapons. Trading posts often sent furs to Europe or large cities in the East. Companies then made them into clothing or fancy hats. In those days, nearly everyone wanted something made from beaver or fox fur.

What do you think?

Today, many people feel that killing animals for their furs is wrong. What do you think? Is it fair to judge the actions of people from the past by our standards today?

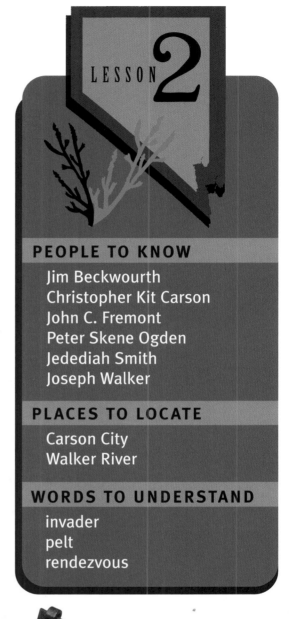

LESSON 2

PEOPLE TO KNOW

Jim Beckwourth
Christopher Kit Carson
John C. Fremont
Peter Skene Ogden
Jedediah Smith
Joseph Walker

PLACES TO LOCATE

Carson City
Walker River

WORDS TO UNDERSTAND

invader
pelt
rendezvous

How to Catch a Beaver

To catch a beaver, trappers used strong steel traps that had long chains. Traps were placed in shallow water. Then a twig covered in beaver oil was placed above the trap. When the smell brought the beaver to the twig, the trap snapped shut. Most beavers drowned while trying to break free. Trappers then skinned the beaver and dried the fur. A fur pelt weighed up to two pounds. Trappers pressed pelts into bundles and tied them together.

Mountain Men

This painting by Alfred Jacob Miller shows a mountain man riding ahead of his Native American wife.

Mountain men often tried to catch fish with sticks, spears, or their bare hands.

Mountain men were trappers who often spent long periods of time hunting in the mountains. They lived off the land, finding their food and shelter in the mountains and deserts of the West.

Mountain men often hunted where Indian tribes lived. Many of them became friendly with native people. Sometimes they traded food and supplies with each other. Some mountain men even joined native tribes and married Indian women. But many native people didn't like trappers. They saw them as *invaders* of the land. This caused many problems between the mountain men and Indian tribes. Some of these problems turned into battles that later became legends of the West.

74

Jedediah Smith

Jedediah Strong Smith was one of the first white men to travel through what is now Nevada. He came west after joining the Rocky Mountain Fur Company in Missouri. A few years later, Smith led 15 men on an expedition from Utah to California. They followed the Virgin and Colorado Rivers through Nevada in search of rich fur trapping areas. He also looked but never found the San Buenaventura river route mentioned by Escalante and Dominguez.

Like most mountain men, Smith had to deal with wild animal attacks. One attack by a grizzly bear left him without an ear. After finally killing the bear, Smith asked a friend to sew his ear back on. But the legend claims his friend sewed the ear on upside down. Many people believed that was why Smith wore his hair long on that side.

When Smith and a few of his men made another trip through Nevada, they could not find food in the desert. They had to kill some of their mules and eat them to survive. To rest and escape the heat, the men crawled into tunnels they dug in the ground.

Smith wrote in his diary about his travels through the area. His writings encouraged many people to come west.

Jedediah Smith was killed by Indians when he was only 32 years old.

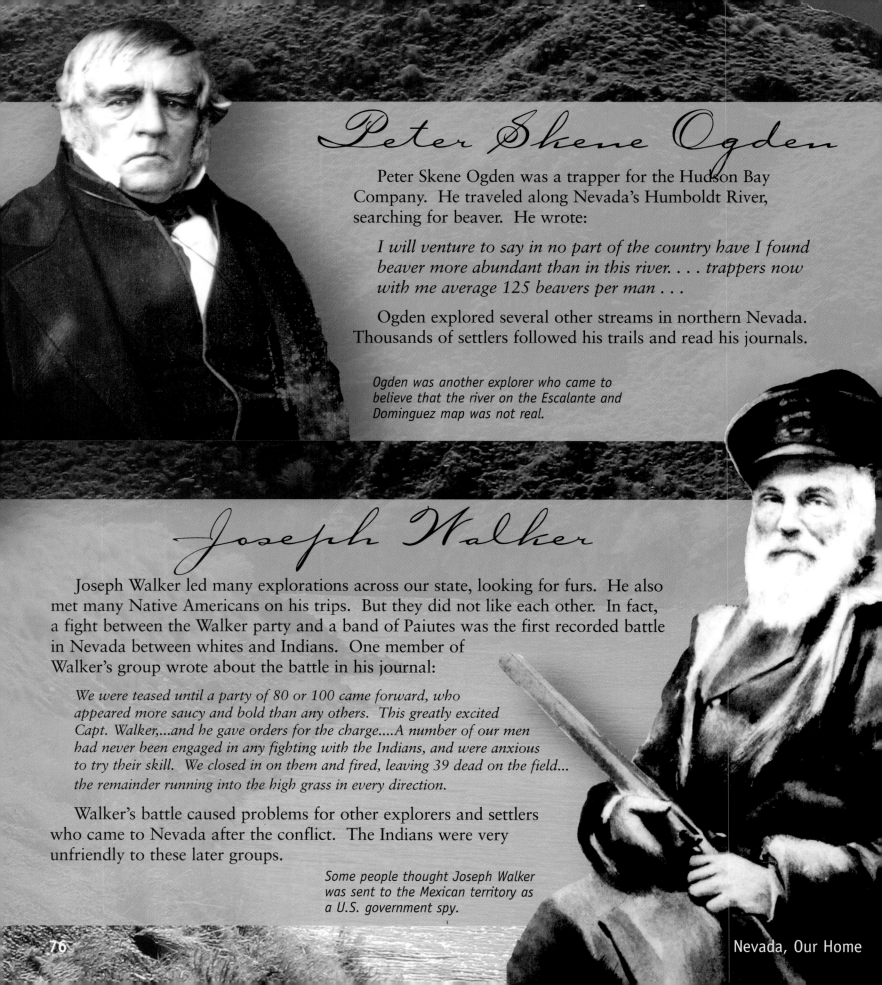

Peter Skene Ogden

Peter Skene Ogden was a trapper for the Hudson Bay Company. He traveled along Nevada's Humboldt River, searching for beaver. He wrote:

I will venture to say in no part of the country have I found beaver more abundant than in this river. . . . trappers now with me average 125 beavers per man . . .

Ogden explored several other streams in northern Nevada. Thousands of settlers followed his trails and read his journals.

Ogden was another explorer who came to believe that the river on the Escalante and Dominguez map was not real.

Joseph Walker

Joseph Walker led many explorations across our state, looking for furs. He also met many Native Americans on his trips. But they did not like each other. In fact, a fight between the Walker party and a band of Paiutes was the first recorded battle in Nevada between whites and Indians. One member of Walker's group wrote about the battle in his journal:

We were teased until a party of 80 or 100 came forward, who appeared more saucy and bold than any others. This greatly excited Capt. Walker,...and he gave orders for the charge....A number of our men had never been engaged in any fighting with the Indians, and were anxious to try their skill. We closed in on them and fired, leaving 39 dead on the field... the remainder running into the high grass in every direction.

Walker's battle caused problems for other explorers and settlers who came to Nevada after the conflict. The Indians were very unfriendly to these later groups.

Some people thought Joseph Walker was sent to the Mexican territory as a U.S. government spy.

Jim Beckwourth

Jim Beckwourth was one of the few African American mountain men in the West. He was a trapper and an army scout who ran trading posts. He married a Native American woman and later became a chief in her tribe. He also discovered a pass in the Sierra Nevada that was later given his name. The pass made it easier for pioneers to get through Nevada's high mountains on their way to California.

Beckwourth told his life story to a writer who put it in a book called *The Life and Adventures of James P. Beckwourth*. One man said of him, "That Beckwourth is surely one of the most [unusual] men I ever met." Others claimed his courage and strength helped change the West.

Beckwourth often dressed like the Crow Indians who adopted him into their tribe.

Kit Carson

Christopher "Kit" Carson was one of the West's most famous mountain men. He began traveling through the western territories when he was just 16. Carson worked as a trapper and guide even though he couldn't read or write. He tried to make up for it by learning all he could about western trails and lands. He also learned to speak Spanish, French, and many Indian languages.

Like other mountain men, his main job was to trap animals for their pelts. He also worked as a guide for John C. Fremont's expedition across Nevada. It was this trip that made him famous. Nevada's Carson River was named after this important trapper and guide.

Kit Carson was known as a tough mountain man who knew a lot about the trails of the West.

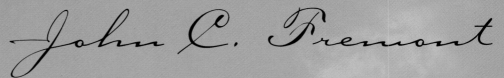

John C. Fremont

John C. Fremont was one of the most famous explorers of our state. Many people call him the great "Pathfinder". As an army officer, his job was to map the Southwest. He was the first to make correct maps of this region, which helped many settlers later find their way.

During his travels through Nevada, Fremont named several important lakes and rivers. He named the Humboldt River, Pyramid Lake, Walker River, and Walker Lake. You may remember that he named the Great Basin too. His maps made it clear that most of the rivers in Nevada run toward the center of the state. Fremont wrote about one Nevada river in his journal:

> *The most considerable river in the interior of the Great Basin is the one called on the map Humboldt River....It is a very peculiar stream...rising in mountains and losing itself in a lake of its own, after a long and solitary course. It lies on the line of travel to California and Oregon, and is the best route now known through the Great Basin, and one traveled by emigrants.*

On another of Fremont's trips through the area, he and his party tried crossing the Sierra Nevada during winter. There were 27 men, 67 horses and mules, and one cannon mounted on wheels. Two Washoe Indians tried to warn Fremont about crossing the mountains in the deep snow. Making signs with his hands and speaking loudly, one Indian said, "Rock upon rock . . . snow upon snow, even if you get over the snow, you will not be able to get down from the mountains."

When Fremont finally arrived in California, he was short on supplies and had only half of the 67 animals. Years later, Fremont published his writings. They proved to be a valuable resource to hundreds of emigrants who were traveling west.

Fremont's writings described the Great Basin as a huge land with waters running inward. His writings proved once and for all that the San Buenaventura River did not exist.

The Rendezvous

Each year mountain men, friendly Indians, and trappers came together for a ***rendezvous.*** Rendezvous is a French word that means "a place and time of meeting." A rendezvous was like a long, wild party. The men played games and competed in contests. They raced to see who could eat cooked buffalo intestine the fastest. They even shot cups of whiskey off of one another's heads to prove their bravery.

Gambling games were popular with both trappers and Indians. Trappers loved to bet on all kinds of things, from foot races to horse races. They especially liked playing the Indian hand game.

Sometimes a rendezvous lasted an entire week. After most of their money was spent, trappers went back to their work in the mountains for another year. The mountain men of the West and their yearly rendezvous soon became legends in American history.

What do you think ?

What do you think trappers wrote in their journals about the yearly rendezvous?

Memory Master

LESSON 2

1. Why were Spanish priests sent to explore our western lands?
2. Which explorer could neither read nor write?
3. What did Fremont name the largest region in Nevada?
4. What was the yearly mountain man meeting called?

William Henry Jackson painted this scene of an annual mountain man rendezvous.

Consider ⭐ Character

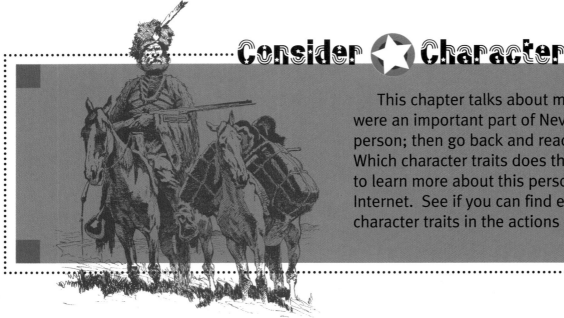

This chapter talks about many famous men who were an important part of Nevada history. Pick one person; then go back and read about him again. Which character traits does this person show? Try to learn more about this person from books or the Internet. See if you can find examples of other character traits in the actions of this person.

Geography 🌍 Tie-In

Pretend you are an early explorer to the area or neighborhood you live in. Suppose you want to keep a record of the regions you explore. Take a walk with a family member or with your entire class to a safe location nearby. Maybe you could go to a friend's house, a nearby store, office building, or a church. Make a map of the route you travel. Be sure to include important landmarks on your map, such as parking lots, walls, parks, or buildings you pass along the way. Do you think your map is correct and clear enough for others to follow? Compare your mapmaking experience to that of early explorers. How difficult is mapmaking?

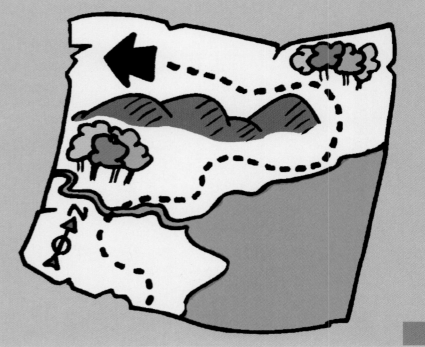

Technology  Tie-In

This chapter talks a lot about early explorers who came through Nevada. Do you think many women explorers came to Nevada then? What about Indian women living in Nevada when explorers came? What can you find out about these women? Do some research to find what life was like for the women who lived in Nevada at this time.

Activity

Mountain Man Slang

Like other groups of people, the trappers began using slang words among themselves. Slang words are words that are sometimes used instead of common words. Look at the words and meanings below. Can you match each word to its correct meaning?

Slang	Meanings
• buffler	• Rocky Mountains
• cache	• buffalo
• critter	• hiding places for furs
• fixins	• animal
• pill	• bullet
• give 'em a teach	• teach them a lesson
• make beaver	• an even trade
• para swap	• sack of things
• possible sack	• the way things happened
• Shining Mountains	• food
• the way the stick floats	• things needed in the trapping business
• vittles	• make money

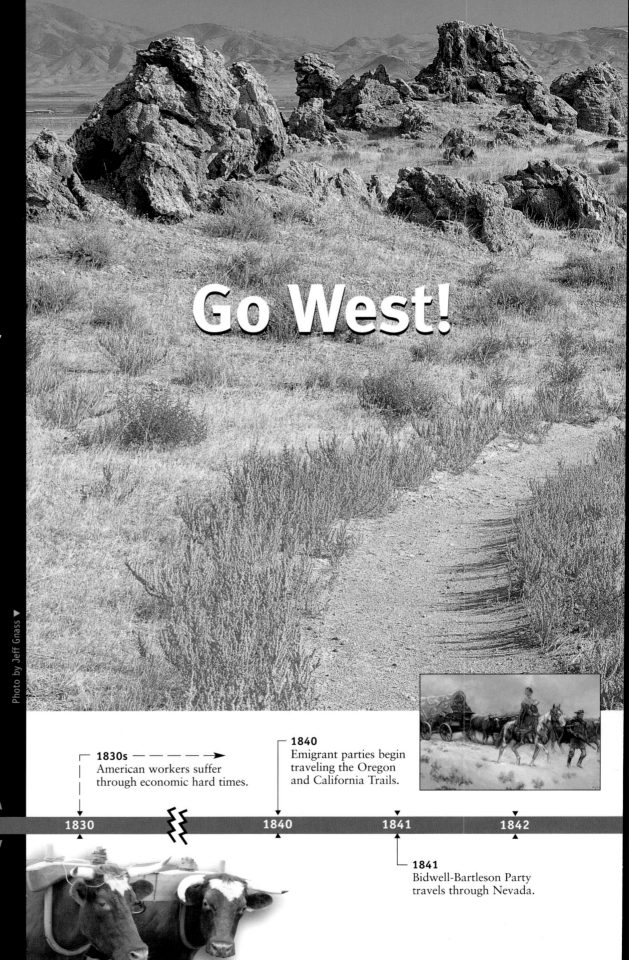

"Go west, young man, and grow up with the country."

—Horace Greeley

Go West!

Photo by Jeff Gnass ▶

Timeline of Events

1830s ----→
American workers suffer
through economic hard times.

1840
Emigrant parties begin
traveling the Oregon
and California Trails.

1830   1840   1841   1842

1841
Bidwell-Bartleson Party
travels through Nevada.

Chapter 5

Stories of exploring new lands in the West excited many people in the eastern part of the United States. They read about great forests, rich farmlands, and beautiful lakes. The diaries of explorers made the West seem like a promised land. Before long, thousands of people moved their families west.

Most early emigrants came west in wagon trains. Their wagon wheels carved paths through the hot, dry deserts of Nevada, similar to those of this modern desert trail.

1844
Chief Truckee shows the Stephens-Murphy-Townsend Party a route to California from the Humboldt River.

| 1844 | 1845 | 1846 | 1848 | 1849 | 1850 |

1846
Donner Party leaves Missouri for California.

1848
Gold rush begins in California.

1849
Pioneers name Death Valley.

1849
A few prospectors begin searching for gold in Nevada.

PLACES TO LOCATE

California
Forty-Mile Desert
Mississippi River
The West

WORDS TO UNDERSTAND

emigrant
pioneer
prairie schooner
wagon train

A Fresh Start

For a long time, most people in our country lived east of the Mississippi River. When it became difficult to earn a living because of economic hard times, people began to move west. Farmers hoped to find rich farmlands where they could grow many crops. Others hoped to find jobs out west. Some people just wanted to live where there was more space and fewer people. Others were looking for adventure.

Wagon Trains

The earliest travelers from the east did not come west to live in Nevada. The land here was very dry, and water was hard to come by. Most *emigrants* were only passing through on their way to California. Emigrants are people who leave one country to settle in another. Most emigrants came west in *wagon trains*.

Wagon trains were made up of many people traveling together. Sometimes emigrants moving west were also called *pioneers*. Many pioneers were single men. Others traveled as families. Pioneers packed only their most important belongings into their wagons. They took clothes, food, and a few pieces of furniture.

The pioneers went through many hardships to reach their new homes in the West. Today, people move to new places in comfort. Most travel in heated or air conditioned cars.

Traveling by wagon was very slow. On a good day, a wagon train could travel about 10 to 15 miles. At night, the wagons were moved into a circle to better protect the pioneers and their animals from danger or attack.

Covered Wagons

Pioneer wagons covered with white canvas tops were sometimes called *prairie schooners*. The round, stretched canvas looked like the sails of ships from far away. The canvas protected the pioneers and their belongings from the dust, sun, wind, and rain. Prairie schooners were also much lighter and easier for oxen or mules to pull than other wagons.

Imagine traveling by covered wagon during the winter months. How do you think the pioneers stayed warm?

Packing Up

Pioneers had to be well prepared for their long journey. They had to make sure they took enough food and supplies. Here are some of the things they packed for their trip:

flour	bacon	axe
cornmeal	medicine	hammer
sugar	salt	water bucket
fruit	rifle	soap
butter	pots and kettles	clothing
lard	rope	extra bedding
vegetables	shovel	wheel grease

If you had to leave your home and go on a long journey, what things would you take with you? Make a list of at least ten things you would need. Then compare your list to the pioneers' list. What things are the same? What things are different? How do you think the pioneers packed food items like butter and meat?

Pulling the Load

Emigrants used oxen or mules to pull their wagons. Oxen were the strongest, but the slowest of the two. They were cheaper to buy and could eat almost every type of grass along the trail. Mules were more stubborn than oxen. They ate mostly grains and some dry grasses. They were also better in the heat than oxen. But, like horses, they sometimes wandered off. Pioneers who could afford horses usually rode them instead of using them to pull their wagon. Horses were the hardest to care for and the most expensive to buy and feed.

Oxen wear a wooden frame called a yoke when pulling heavy loads. The yoke helps them bear the weight of the load together.

What do you think?

Which animals would you have chosen to pull your wagon? Why?

Nevada, Our Home

Some pioneer families struggled to stay on the trail when early storms made travel difficult.

Dangers on the Trail

Moving west was an exciting adventure, but it was also very hard. Every day there were problems and dangers to face. Week after week, pioneers walked in the dust and heat. When it rained, wagon wheels were often stuck in the mud. Many pioneers died along the trail because of freezing temperatures and deep snows.

Weather was just one of the many problems people faced during their travels west. Some got lost because the trails they followed were not marked. Others drifted off course while trying to follow maps made by early explorers or traders. Pioneers also had to protect themselves from bear, mountain lion, or other wild animal attacks.

Another problem people faced was unfriendly Indian tribes. Most tribes were friendly at first. They traded with the pioneers for goods, food, or other supplies. But as more wagon trains came west, some Indians began to attack the settlers. They wanted to stop the settlers from harming the land and the animals the tribes depended on for food.

Indian tribes and pioneers lived very different lives. Their ways of life did not always work well together. Indian tribes believed their way of life was in danger.

"Mosquitoes were as thick as flakes in a snow-storm, the poor horses whinnied all night, from their bites, and in the morning the blood was streaming down their sides."
—Margaret A. Frink, 1850

Go West!

Emigrant Diaries

Many pioneers wrote about their experiences in their diaries. They wrote about problems they faced and what their lives were like. Their words have given us much information about the trails they traveled and how they felt as they traveled them. One pioneer woman wrote about meeting Indians while traveling west: ⟶

After looking in vain for water, we were about to give up as it was near night, when my husband came across a company of friendly Cayuse Indians about to camp, who showed him where to find water. The men and boys have driven the cattle down to water and I am waiting for water to get supper. This forenoon we bought a few potatoes from an Indian, which will be a treat for our supper.

Amelia Knight

— Forty Mile Desert

Forty-Mile Desert

Crossing western deserts in the summer heat was one of the hardest things pioneers had to do. Nevada's Forty-Mile Desert was probably the worst. After leaving the western edge of the Humboldt River, wagon trains had to travel 40 miles before reaching water again.

Many pioneers knew the Forty-Mile Desert would be hard to cross. They knew their animals would not be able to pull heavy wagons that far without water. Many of them had to get rid of their belongings to make their wagons lighter. Sometimes they left things, like furniture, scattered along the desert trail.

LESSON 1

Memory Master

1. Name one reason people wanted to move west.
2. What is an emigrant?
3. Name two possible dangers pioneers faced on their journey west.

Blazing the Trail

Crossing the Sierra Nevada was never an easy task for early emigrants. Difficult weather conditions and narrow mountain passes made travel slow. Some people took their wagons apart so they could lower them down the steep granite cliffs.

One emigrant group, called the Donner Party, tried crossing the Sierra Nevada too late in the year. Snow drifts and freezing temperatures made it nearly impossible for them to reach California. Many of them lost their lives that cold, snowy winter.

LESSON 2

PEOPLE TO KNOW

Bidwell-Bartleson Party
Chief Truckee
Donner Party
Thomas "Broken Hand"
   Fitzpatrick

PLACES TO LOCATE

California Trail
Death Valley
Humboldt River
Missouri
Old Spanish Trail
Oregon Trail
Sierra Nevada

WORDS TO UNDERSTAND

cholera
disease
smallpox

Emigrant parties began crossing the Sierra Nevada as early as 1840. Their wagon wheels left rust and scrape marks along many rocky, narrow passes.

To protect themselves from the cold, some members of the Donner Party built small brush shelters. Then they covered the brush with the canvas from their wagons.

Nevada, Our Home

The Donner Party

It was late spring when the Donner Party left Missouri, headed for California. Near the end of September, the group of 87 reached Nevada's Humboldt River. By mid-October they followed the Truckee River into the Sierra Nevada.

The party had already faced problems of every kind. But their problems soon got worse. Wagons began to break down, people in the group began to argue, and many worried about the coming snow.

As the party climbed toward the summit, heavy snow began to fall. In less than 24 hours, the group could not go on because of the huge snow drifts. Slowly, they made their way back to the lake to try to find shelter.

One family in the group moved into an old shack at the edge of the lake. Others built log cabins or rough lean-tos. When the food ran out, they had to eat their animals to stay alive. They even ate the hides and hooves of their cattle.

Twelve-year-old Virginia Reed and her family were members of the party. Virginia wrote to her cousin about the horrible event after she was rescued.

We had nothing to eat but ox hides. O Mary I would cry and wish I had what you all wasted. . . we had to kill littel cash the dog and eat him....

A few members of the group got so hungry they ate the flesh of those who had died. Only 46 people survived that horrible winter. The hardships they faced caused many people to rethink their plans to go west.

Other problems, like finding good drinking water, caused problems for pioneers. Nevada's Humboldt River was the area's main source of water. Sometimes though, the water tasted bad, or was muddy, or nearly dried up.

Diseases, or illnesses, were another kind of problem. Things like cholera and smallpox spread very quickly. When one person got a disease, it didn't take long for others in the group to get it too. Without doctors or hospitals nearby, thousands of people died along westward trails. One woman wrote about it in her diary:

We passed a new made grave today... [of] a man from Ohio. We also met a man that was going back [as] he had buried his wife this morning. She died from the effects of measels...we passed another grave to day which was made this morning... [it] stated that he died of cholera. He was from Indiana.

—Lydia Rudd

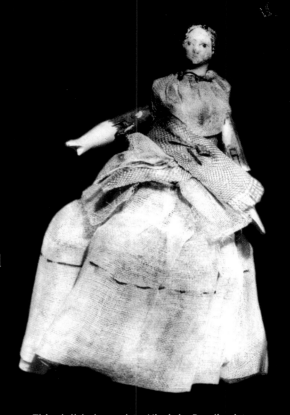

This doll belonged to Virginia Reed's sister Patty. She was eight years old when she and her family were rescued from the snowy pass. They were only one of two families to have every member survive.

Chief Truckee, sometimes called Captain Truckee, was a chief of the Paiute people. He was also the grandfather of Sarah Winnemucca. Chief Truckee became famous for guiding the Stevens-Murphy-Townsend Party. He led them from the western edge of the Humboldt Sink, up the Truckee River, and into California. Some people say the group named the Truckee River after him because he was such a good guide.

Chief Truckee also fought the Mexicans in California alongside John C. Fremont. After the war, he returned to Nevada, where he remained until he died. Many believe Chief Truckee was buried with a Bible given to him by Fremont.

The Bidwell-Bartleson Party

The Bidwell-Bartleson Party was one of the first groups to cross the Great Basin on the way to California. John Bartleson and John Bidwell were the leaders of the group. But neither knew how to lead a wagon train. They also didn't know much about the land they would cross.

With only a few details from a newspaper, the group headed west. They joined a famous explorer and trapper by the name of Thomas "Broken Hand" Fitzpatrick. Fitzpatrick guided them only as far as the Great Salt Lake. The party then traveled the rest of the way on their own.

Shortly after leaving the Great Salt Lake area, the party ran into trouble. Water was scarce, and the dry land was covered with salt and sand. The wagons had trouble moving through the sand, and many of them broke down. Travel became so slow that Bartleson and other men in the party left the group and went on ahead. Bidwell stayed behind.

He took the group down Mary's River, later called the Humboldt River, and across the Forty-Mile Desert to the Walker River. When they reached the Sierra Nevada, they decided to leave their wagons behind. They were too heavy to pull over the rugged mountains. Two weeks later the party reached California. It had been six months since they left Missouri.

This picture of pioneers camping along the Humboldt River was drawn by Daniel Jacks in 1859. Can you tell what kinds of activities are going on in camp?

More Emigrant Groups

Other wagon trains soon followed the trail across Nevada along the Humboldt River. Once they reached the river, groups took off in many different directions. Some traveled across the Black Rock Desert into northern California, Oregon, and Washington. Others followed the Carson River through the Sierra Nevada toward California. Some, like the Donner Party, took their wagons along the Truckee River route.

Not all groups that traveled the same route as the Donner Party had serious problems. The Stevens-Murphy-Townsend Party was one of the first groups to get their wagons safely to California. When they came to the Sierra Nevada, they took their wagons apart. They pulled and lifted the wagon parts over the mountains piece by piece.

Early Emigrant Trails

Many early emigrants followed the Old Spanish Trail, which cut across the southern tip of Nevada. One group of emigrants split off from this trail in search of a shortcut. They were led by a man named Lewis Manley. He led them into the hot, dry desert of Death Valley. They almost didn't make it out alive. After sending some of the party ahead to get supplies, the rest were finally able to get out of the area. It was this group that gave Death Valley its name.

Just as we were ready to leave and return to camp we took off our hats, and then overlooking the scene of so much trial, suffering and death [we said]…"Good bye Death Valley!"….

—William Lewis Manly

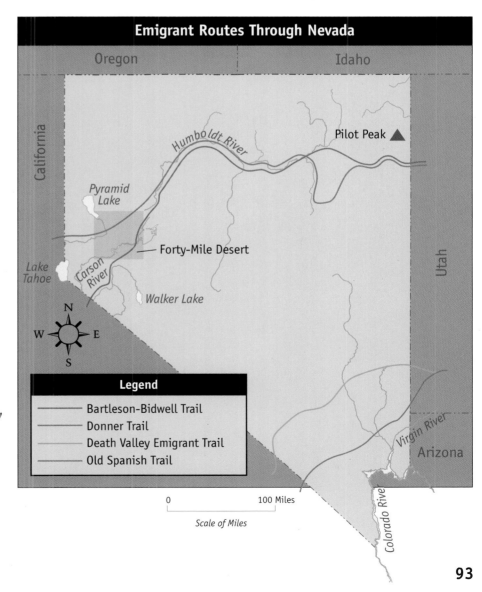

Emigrant Routes Through Nevada

Oregon

Idaho

California

Humboldt River

Pilot Peak ▲

Pyramid Lake

Forty-Mile Desert

Lake Tahoe

Carson River

Walker Lake

Utah

N
W — E
S

Legend
— Bartleson-Bidwell Trail
— Donner Trail
— Death Valley Emigrant Trail
— Old Spanish Trail

Virgin River

Arizona

0   100 Miles

Scale of Miles

Colorado River

More Trails

The Oregon Trail was the most popular wagon train route heading west. Winding from Missouri to Oregon, the trail was 2,100 miles long. More than 350,000 people made their way along the trail.

Splitting off from the Oregon Trail was the California Trail. It cut through Nevada into the Sacramento Valley of California. In ten years, more than 70,000 settlers traveled this route.

Both the Oregon and California trails were a series of trails, not just one trail. Many of our railroads and highways today follow these trails.

This photograph shows the point where emigrants bound for California left the Oregon Trail. They traveled southwest while emigrants going to Oregon or Washington traveled northwest.

This painting by William Henry Jackson shows his ideas about what the gold rush must have been like.

Gold Fever!

It didn't take long for the word to spread that gold nuggets had been found in California. Suddenly there was a new reason for people to come west. People came by the thousands to search for gold. Most fortune seekers were men who left their homes and families hoping to strike it rich.

Once they reached the Great Basin, they followed the main route to California along the Humboldt River and the Oregon and California Trails. Most didn't waste time looking for gold in Nevada. Only a few people stopped long enough to search our rivers and streams.

Gold seekers were excited to reach California. They had heard many stories claiming large nuggets of gold could be picked up off the ground. But few people ever found enough gold to get rich. Some people found they could make more money by selling food, tents, clothes, and other supplies to gold seekers.

Serious gold seekers didn't return to Nevada until gold fever in California began to die down.

Early prospectors used tools like this shallow tin pan and pick axe when they searched for gold.

Memory Master

LESSON 2

1. How did early emigrants get their wagons down steep cliffs?
2. What happened to the Donner Party?
3. How long did it take for the Bidwell-Bartleson Party to reach California?
4. Who was Chief Truckee?
5. What other major emigrant trail branched off from the Oregon Trail?

Consider ★ Character

Can you imagine what it would have been like to travel on trails for weeks at a time with no stores or shelter in sight? What character traits do you think these pioneers had? Review this chapter. Identify one character trait you see in the pioneers. Find examples of people in the text showing this trait. Then act out one these examples for your classmates. See if they can guess which character trait you are showing.

Geography  Tie-In

Today we have maps, roads, and sidewalks to help us get where we are going. Pioneers had rough trails, or made their own trails, through mountains and deserts. Look at the map on p. 91 and pick a trail. On a piece of paper, make two columns. On one side, list all the physical features along the trail that helped pioneers. On the other side, list all the physical features along the trail that made travel difficult for pioneers. Remember to think about the kinds of foods they ate and the types of weather they had!

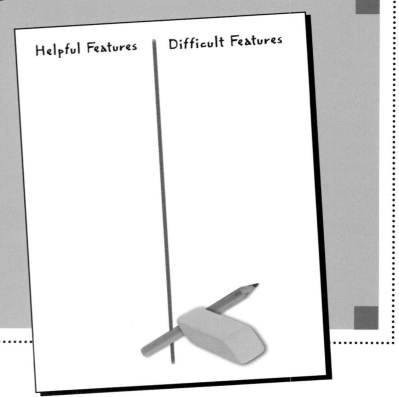

Helpful Features   Difficult Features

Technology Tie-In

Gold Fever!

Where was gold found in Nevada? Do you know how much gold has actually been found in Nevada? Are there any gold mines in Nevada today? Research these questions in an encyclopedia or on websites your teacher recommends. Then make a chart or graph to show where gold was found in Nevada. A pie chart would be an interesting way to show where gold was found. You would have the biggest slice of pie show the place where the most gold was found. Can you name other natural resources in Nevada? Look them up if you don't know!

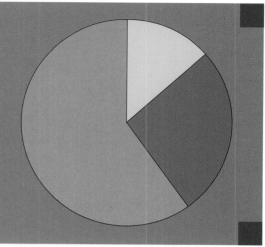

Activity

Pioneer Games

What if you were a pioneer child? What would you do for fun? Pretend you are on the trail and that you've been traveling for weeks. Make up a game you would play while you are walking along or when you have stopped to set up camp. Think about what physical objects might be nearby. What kinds of things would you use to create your game?

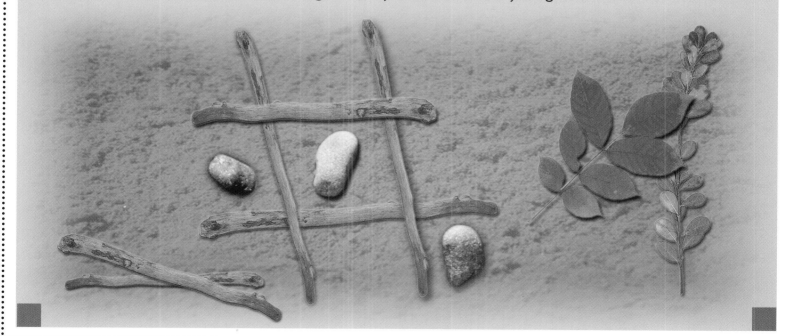

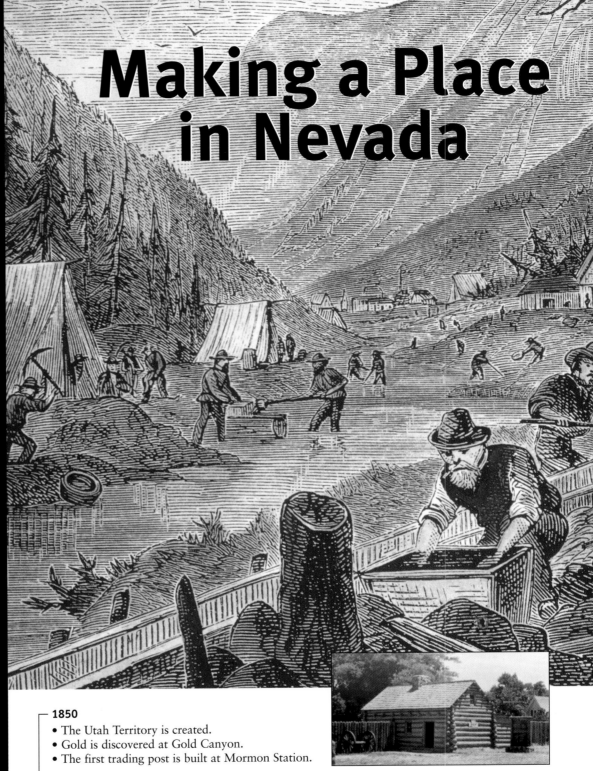

Making a Place in Nevada

"We built a small, rude cabin in the side of the crevice and roofed it with canvas, leaving a corner open to serve as a chimney, through which the cattle used to tumble occasionally at night and mash our furniture and interrupt our sleep."

—Mark Twain, *Roughing It*

Timeline of Events

1850
- The Utah Territory is created.
- Gold is discovered at Gold Canyon.
- The first trading post is built at Mormon Station.

1850   1851   1852   1853   1854

1851
- Mormon settlers form a community at Mormon Station.
- Settlers form the first government.

1853
First school opens in the Carson Valley.

98

Chapter 6

After gold was discovered in California, thousands of people began to come west. They came by wagon and on horseback. They walked through rain, snow, and blazing sun. Dreams of finding gold nuggets carried them across Nevada's driest deserts. Few people stopped to look for gold in Nevada until miners found a wide strip of precious metal buried deep in Nevada soil.

Early prospectors searched for gold along rivers and in canyons. They worked from dawn until dusk and often slept only a few feet away from where they worked.

1856
Chinese workers create Nevada's first Chinatown.

1859
• The Comstock Lode is discovered.
• Virginia City becomes a boom town of the West.

| 1855 | 1856 | 1857 | 1858 | 1859 | 1860 |

1855
• Mormon settlers open Fort Las Vegas.
• Lead is discovered at the Potosi Mine.

1860
Square-set timbering is invented. •
The Pony Express begins. •

LESSON 1

Discovery at Gold Canyon

Thousands of people traveled through Nevada on their way to find gold in California. One emigrant party stopped along the Carson River, where one man discovered a few gold specks. It wasn't enough gold, though, to convince the group to stay in Nevada. Soon, miners in other places heard about the find. By spring, nearly 100 men were searching for gold in a place called Gold Canyon.

Some miners reported that an old prospector was already living in Gold Canyon when they arrived. A trading post was opened at Hall's Station where miners held a New Year's Eve dance.

Later, Chinese workers from California were hired to dig a long ditch that would take water to Gold Canyon. They started Nevada's first Chinatown. Eventually, the town became known as Dayton.

When mining towns first began, there were not many places for people to gather. One-room trading posts or saloons were also used as meeting or dance halls.

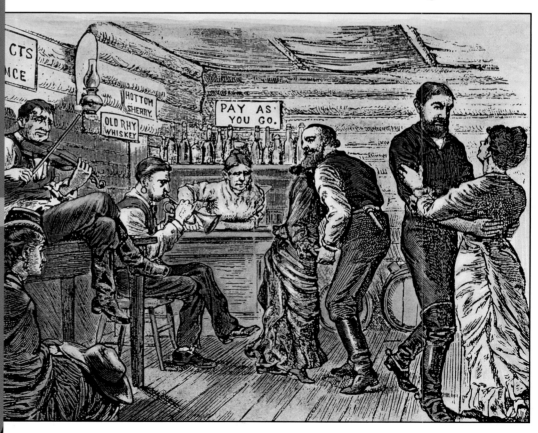

The Chinese were hard workers. They often worked for lower wages than white workers. They were also neat and clean, and they stayed out of trouble.

Laws Against the Chinese

Most miners didn't like the Chinese workers who moved to Nevada. They spoke a different language and had different customs. They also lived a different lifestyle and were willing to work for lower wages than white workers. Because of this, many miners were fearful that Chinese workers would take away their jobs.

They began treating the Chinese unfairly. They even passed laws to keep the Chinese from working in the mines or from owning mining land. The Chinese were only allowed to do things like wash laundry, chop wood, and cook meals for others. These were the lowest-paying jobs people could have.

Sometimes people's feelings about the Chinese turned violent. Angry white people burned homes and often beat the Chinese or the people who hired them.

Sadly, the poor treatment of the Chinese happened throughout much of the West. Even the U.S. Congress passed laws against the Chinese that made it impossible for new immigrants to come to the United States.

A Home in Carson Valley

Some of the first people to settle in the desert valleys of the Rocky Mountains were members of The Church of Jesus Christ of Latter-day Saints. Sometimes they were called Mormons. They were also one of the first groups to settle in Nevada's Carson Valley.

A few traders built a *trading post,* or small log store, near the base of the Sierra Nevada. They called it Mormon Station. It attracted many travelers and gold seekers on their way to California. The trading post carried basic supplies like flour, beans, and bacon. Travelers also traded with Mormon settlers in the area.

Carson Valley's first government came about because of these early settlers. They hoped to bring a little law and order to the area, which in those days was part of the Utah Territory. Brigham Young was the territory's first governor.

In time, other settlers started new trading posts in Eagle Valley and along the Humboldt and Carson Rivers. People along the eastern foothills of the Sierra Nevada began farming. They grew wheat, hay, barley, and vegetables. They planted fruit trees and raised milk cows and chickens. Some raised cattle and sheep, and others opened a sawmill nearby. Eliza and Israel Mott started the very first school in the Carson Valley in the kitchen of their home. The teacher of the school was a woman named Mrs. Allen.

Years later, as the area grew, its name was changed to Genoa.

A state park now stands where the original Mormon Station trading post once stood. The original building burned down in 1910. Many years later, the state built a historic copy of the old log cabin on the same site.

For settlers living in the West, trading posts were about the only places people could get supplies. What goods can you see for sale or trade?

· Activity ·

What Makes a Place a Settlement?

Today many people in Nevada disagree over where our state's first settlement started. Some say it was Mormon Station, now called Genoa. Others say our state's first settlement grew up in and around Gold Canyon, now called Dayton.

Now that you have read a little about both places, see if you can learn more. Search the Internet, or look for articles about each place. Then make a list that describes each settlement. Talk with your teacher and classmates about the kinds of things that you think make a place a settlement.

Nevada in 1851

CA

Truckee River

Truckee Meadows

Emigrant Trail

Dayton (Gold Canyon)

Lake Tahoe

Carson River

Genoa (Mormon Station)

N

MILES

0   15

What do you think?

Pretend you are opening a trading post in the early days out west. What supplies would you sell to your customers? Where could you get your supplies? How would you bring them to your trading post?

A Fort at Las Vegas

Brigham Young sent another group of settlers from Utah to open a trading post and mission just south of the Utah Territory. Spanish traders had already named the area Las Vegas, which means "the meadow." Fresh grasses grew wild there, and water bubbled up from underground springs. It was a good place to rest and water tired horses.

When the Utah settlers arrived in the area, they worked hard to make it feel like home. They planted gardens and built a small *adobe* fort that became the supply station and center for the rest stop. Thousands of people traveling the Old Spanish Trail stopped to rest and feed their animals there.

Mormon settlers were also interested in teaching area natives about their religion. Some tribes listened to their message, but others did not.

In another nearby area, one group of men opened a small mining camp where they mined lead. At first, they wanted to make metal tools and bullets, but the lead they mined was too soft. These problems and many others were hard on the settlers. After three short years, most of them left the fort and went back to Utah.

Potosi Mine

The earliest miners in Las Vegas were looking for lead, not silver or gold. The Mormons wanted lead to make their own tools and bullets. But the lead from the Potosi Mine broke too easily to make good tools. Upset by what they found, the Mormons soon stopped mining. Years later, the mine came to life again when silver was discovered by a group of new miners.

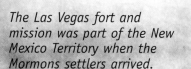

The Las Vegas fort and mission was part of the New Mexico Territory when the Mormons settlers arrived.

Muddy Valley Settlers

Other Mormon families were sent by Brigham Young to settle near the Virgin and Colorado Rivers. They farmed the rich soils of the Muddy Valley. The towns of St. Thomas, St. Joseph, and the port of Callville were a few of the places they settled.

With plenty of river water nearby and mild winter weather, the farmers grew many crops. They planted beautiful orchards and hundreds of acres of cotton. The farms in the area were part of what the settlers sometimes called the "Cotton Mission." They grew cotton and then hauled it to Utah so it could be made into cloth. They sent other crops to communities in Utah as well.

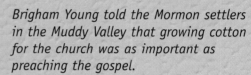

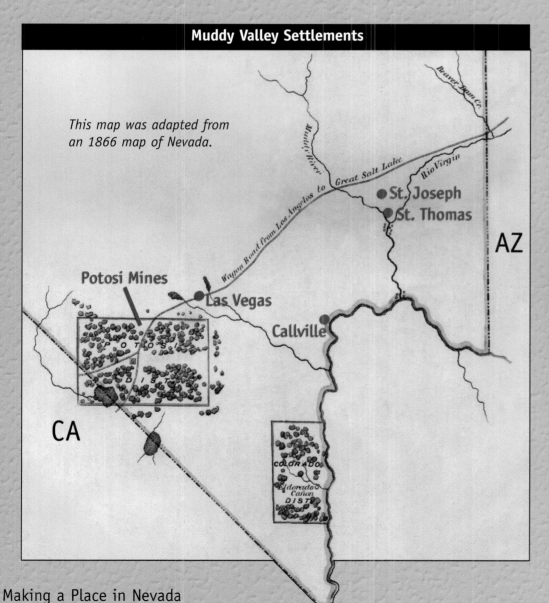

Muddy Valley Settlements

This map was adapted from an 1866 map of Nevada.

Potosi Mines

Las Vegas

Callville

CA

AZ

Brigham Young told the Mormon settlers in the Muddy Valley that growing cotton for the church was as important as preaching the gospel.

Steaming Along the River

The Callville settlement was mostly a steamboat port, named after its founder Anson Call. Mormon leaders hoped transporting supplies and converts by steamboat would be faster and safer than travel by land. The settlers built a landing, a large warehouse, a post office, and many other buildings.

Transporting supplies along the lower Colorado was already happening when the Mormon settlers arrived. Steamboats, paddleboats, and barges made their way up the river from the Gulf of California. They delivered supplies to the miners in El Dorado Canyon and other small ports along the river.

Getting steamboats up the river to Callville, though, was very difficult. Not many could make it through the narrow canyons and white-water rapids of Black Canyon.

One steamboat named the *Esmeralda* used a **steam winch** to get through the dangerous waters. Strong cables clipped to iron rings in the walls of the canyon pulled the boat upstream.

But problems like these kept Callville from becoming the port Mormon leaders and settlers had hoped it would be. Settlers moved away from the towns along the river. Soon the railroads made travel by land safer and faster. Even the U.S. Army who built a fort at Callville, later abandoned it.

Now the towns of Callville and St. Thomas are completely covered by the waters of Lake Mead.

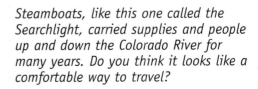

Near the shores of the Colorado River, you can see a few remaining ruins from the old U.S. Army fort. This is also where the settlement of Callville used to be. Today, most of this area is under the waters of Lake Mead.

Steamboats, like this one called the Searchlight, carried supplies and people up and down the Colorado River for many years. Do you think it looks like a comfortable way to travel?

Delivering Mail

Carrying mail across the western *frontier* was a dangerous job. The mail traveled once a month between Salt Lake City, Utah, and Sacramento, California. A pack train of mules and a few brave men made the trip over the Sierra into the Carson Valley. Heavy winter snows and Indian attacks were a problem from the beginning.

One man named John "Snowshoe" Thompson strapped 10-foot boards to his feet to help him cross the snowy mountains. Carrying a heavy pack, he could glide through the trees, reaching Genoa in five days or less.

A **frontier** *is land that lies beyond an established settlement.*

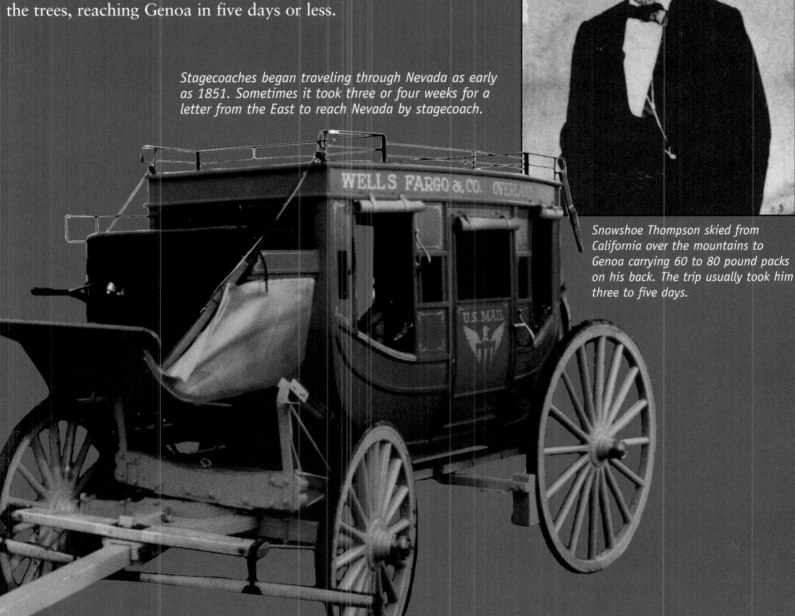

Stagecoaches began traveling through Nevada as early as 1851. Sometimes it took three or four weeks for a letter from the East to reach Nevada by stagecoach.

Snowshoe Thompson skied from California over the mountains to Genoa carrying 60 to 80 pound packs on his back. The trip usually took him three to five days.

The Pony Express

Riding the Pony Express

Sending mail out west took a very long time before trains and airplanes were invented. To speed up delivery, one company started a new service called the Pony Express.

About 80 young men were hired to ride from St. Joseph, Missouri, to Sacramento, California. Riders had to be small. Most weighed less than 125 pounds. They ranged in age from 11 years to just over 40. The company gave each boy a place to stay and food to eat. Riders were also given a small Bible and asked to swear an *oath,* or a promise.

The trip from Missouri to California was over 2,000 miles long. Riders rode from 75 to 100 miles each. They carried a leather mail pouch called a *mochila.* Riders stopped to change horses every 10 to 15 miles at *relay stations* spread out along the trail.

Most relay stations in the East were already being used as stagecoach stops. Out west, many new stations were built. Sometimes tents or dugouts were used as stations. Some stations were built with adobe bricks.

The Ruby Valley Pony Express station now stands in front of the Northeastern Museum in Elko.

This painting by Frederick Remington shows how quickly Pony Express riders changed from one horse to another.

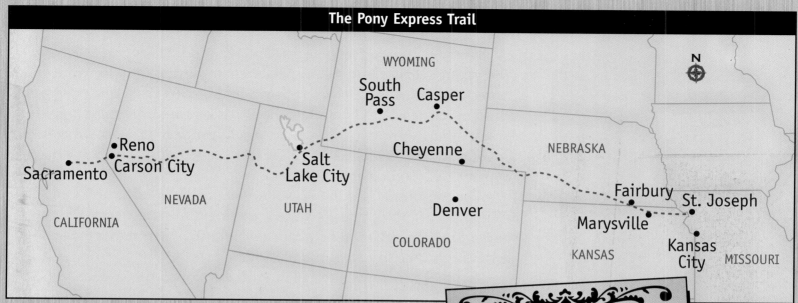

WYOMING

South Pass

Casper

Reno

Carson City

Sacramento

NEVADA

CALIFORNIA

Salt Lake City

UTAH

Cheyenne

NEBRASKA

Denver

COLORADO

KANSAS

Fairbury

St. Joseph

Marysville

Kansas City

MISSOURI

N

Carrying the Mail Through Nevada

There were 29 relay stations across the Nevada desert. William "Billy" Fisher was one of the first Pony Express riders hired to carry the mail through eastern Nevada and parts of Utah. Once he rode 300 miles in 30 hours to warn stations about coming Indian attacks. Another time he got lost while carrying the mail through a snowstorm.

After stopping to rest under some trees, Fisher fell asleep. He awoke when a rabbit began licking his face. Nearly frozen to death, he and his horse made their way toward the light of a distant cabin. When the old man opened the door, Fisher fainted on the doorstep. The old man took him in and let him rest. The next day Fisher got back on his horse and continued on with the mail.

The Pony Express lasted only about 18 months before the invention of the *telegraph* put it out of business. Sadly, the owners lost money, but the Pony Express became an important part of history.

WANTED

YOUNG, SKINNY, wiry fellows not over 18. Must be expert riders, willing to risk death daily. Orphans preferred.

Pony Express riders carried mail and other important papers in a leather saddle called a mochila. It had four pockets, two on each side of the horse.

What do you think?

At first, sending a letter by Pony Express cost $5 for a half ounce. Later, the price went down to $1 for a half ounce. Why do you think the Pony Express charged by the weight of a letter? How does that compare with what it costs to send a letter today?

The Telegraph

The invention of the telegraph made sending messages across the country faster and safer. Men began putting up telegraph wires and poles from town to town and city to city. The telegraph did not carry voices like a telephone. It sent and received tapping sounds that were part of a code. Each group of long or short taps stood for a letter. The short taps were called dots, and the long taps were called dashes.

The tapping was done on something called a telegraph key. When telegraph operators were receiving a message, they wrote down the letter that went with each sound. Then they put the letters together to reveal the message.

Samuel Morse was the man who developed the system. The code used to *translate* messages became known as the Morse Code. People called *operators* were specially trained to send and receive the code. A good operator could tap out 35–40 words a minute. People wanting to send a message had to pay for each word. Because of this, most messages were very short.

Telegraph key pads were small and easy to move around. They were used in many different places. Why do you think this one was mounted on a box?

Workers laid hundreds of miles of telegraph poles and wires from California to Nevada and beyond.

Practicing Morse Code

Do you think you can tap out a message in Morse Code? Here's a fun way to try it out. Go through this chapter and pick out one vocabulary word. Keep it a secret! Write down the word and then translate it into Morse Code using the chart on the right. Pretend you are a spy sending a secret password to another spy. Here are four possible ways you could send your password:

1. Use a pencil to tap out the word on your desk. Make sure the short and long sounds are clear. Allow your partner time to write down each letter.
2. Say the code out loud. Try saying "dit" for the short sounds and "dah" for the long sounds.
3. Clap it out with your hands. Go slow enough for your partner to write down the letters.
4. Use a flashlight and a piece of paper. Keep the light covered: then uncover it quickly for a short sound or slowly for a long sound.

Did you understand what your partner was telegraphing to you? Try another vocabulary word to see if it goes faster! Then try sending your partner a whole sentence in Morse Code. Be sure to tell your partner that when you pause it means you are starting a new word.

Letter	Code	Letter	Code
A	• —	S	• • •
B	— • • •	T	—
C	— • — •	U	• • —
D	— • •	V	• • • —
E	•	W	• — —
F	• • — •	X	— • • —
G	— — •	Y	— • — —
H	• • • •	Z	— — • •
I	• •	1	• — — — —
J	• — — —	2	• • — — —
K	— • —	3	• • • — —
L	• — • •	4	• • • • —
M	— —	5	• • • • •
N	— •	6	— • • • •
O	— — —	7	— — • • •
P	• — — •	8	— — — • •
Q	— — • —	9	— — — — •
R	• — •	0	— — — — —

Samuel Morris shows off the telegraph at the Academy of Music in New York.

LESSON 1

Memory Master

1. Which early town was Nevada's first Chinatown?
2. Name three things settlers did to make a living when they came to Mormon Station.
3. What name did Spanish traders give their resting spot?
4. What does the name mean? What metal did the Mormon settlers mine near Fort Las Vegas? How did they hope to use it?
5. How long did the Pony Express deliver mail?

LESSON 2

PEOPLE TO KNOW

Henry Comstock
Philipp Deidesheimer
James Fennimore
John Mackay
Chief Numaga
Adolf Sutro
Mark Twain

PLACES TO LOCATE

Denver
Pyramid Lake
San Francisco

WORDS TO UNDERSTAND

blasting caps
claim jumper
collapse
Comstock Lode
crib
deposit
dynamite
mineral
ore
panning
patent
placer mining
prospector
sluicing
staked a claim
vein

Mining in the West

News of gold in California brought thousands of gold seekers to the West. Most *prospectors,* or miners, only stopped in Nevada on their way to California. Prospectors look for valuable metals, or *minerals,* in the ground. Minerals are things that are mined, like gold, silver, and salt. They are usually mixed with rock, dirt, sand, or gravel. Miners call this mix *ore.*

Panning for gold was slow, back-breaking work. Prospectors used flat bottom pans to scoop up water, earth, and gravel from the bottom of a stream. As they moved the pan in a circle, the water spilled over the sides of the pan. Then they could see gold dust or gold nuggets mixed in with the dirt and gravel. Many prospectors got sick from standing knee-deep in freezing water day after day.

When they found something valuable, prospectors *staked a claim.* This means they measured the area and then recorded it at the nearest government office. They did this to keep others from stealing it, but it didn't always work. People who stole someone else's claim were called *claim jumpers*.

Prospectors hauled many tools and supplies to Nevada's goldfields.

Trying Their Luck in Nevada

As the rush for California gold began to slow down, miners came to try their luck in Nevada. Most were using *placer mining* methods to gather gold and other minerals from our rivers and streams. Panning for gold was one of the earliest placer mining methods prospectors used. Another method, called *sluicing*, allowed miners to sift through more dirt in less time.

Sluicing was done with a series of wooden boxes. Each box had a downhill slope and was slightly lower than the one before. Gallons of water were needed to sift the dirt and gravel away from the gold. As the water flowed through the box, the dirt, sand, or gravel washed away. The heavier pieces of gold fell into the ridges at the bottom of the box.

One group of Nevada miners had trouble with thick black sand that clogged their sluice boxes. Some prospectors threw the black sand out. Later, they learned the sand was filled with silver ore. The miners soon discovered it was the richest silver ore ever found in the United States. They called it the *Comstock Lode.*

A Prospector's Life

Prospectors were very unusual people. Sometimes they spent their entire lives looking for precious metals, like gold and silver. They often wandered through the mountains or deserts for months at a time with only a few basic supplies. They packed things like food, clothes, blankets, and a pick and shovel.

Most prospectors lived in small, rough cabins built from branches, stones, and sagebrush. They ate simple foods, like potatoes, dried beans, meat, and coffee. They looked for gold from sunup to sundown. Some tried searching where no one else had looked. Some sold or traded every-thing they had for a night of drinking or gambling in nearby saloons. Then their search started all over again.

This illustration shows examples of early placer mining methods.

Henry Comstock was not liked by other miners. He was known as a bully and a liar. Some even called him "Old Pancake" because he was too lazy to cook anything but pancakes. Comstock sold out his share of the Ophir Mine before its real value became known. He made only $10,000.

What do you think?

What do you think about naming the largest silver strike in U.S. history for a man who didn't really discover it?

The Comstock Lode

Many people took part in the discovery of the Comstock Lode. One of them was James Fennimore or "Old Virginny." Fennimore and a few other prospectors found one end of the lode in an area called Gold Hill. What they found was a strip of gold mixed with silver. The biggest part of the strike, though, was found in a place called Six-Mile Canyon.

Two Irish miners digging in the canyon found gold sand in a spring. When they dug under the stream, they hit a large *vein* of gold and silver. A vein is a pocket of minerals found in rock. The names of the men were Patrick McLaughlin and Peter O'Reily. They called their find the Ophir Mine.

After going to town to celebrate their find, McLaughlin and O'Reily came back to find a man named Henry Comstock at the spring. Comstock claimed the land and spring were owned by him. The two Irish miners didn't want problems, so they split their find with Comstock. Later the find was named after Comstock.

Mining towns, like Gold Hill, sprang up all over central and western Nevada.

The Rush to Nevada

With the discovery of the Comstock Lode, miners from California began pouring into Nevada. The rush of people helped create new towns like Virginia City, Gold Hill, and Silver City. As the towns grew, life for the area's earliest miners began to change.

Life in the Mining Towns

Mining towns were rough places in the beginning. There were saloons and gambling houses, where miners spent much of their time and money. Some towns had horse races, concert halls for singers, plays, and dancing animal acts.

Mining towns were also places where people from many different countries came. One man, named J. Ross Browne, wrote about what he saw in the mining towns of Nevada.

> *In the course of a day's tramp we passed parties of every description and color: Irishmen …American, French, and German foot-passengers, … carrying their packs on their backs; …Mexicans, driving long trains of pack mules, … women in men's clothes, … whiskey peddlers, organ grinders, …all stark mad for silver.*

At first, most of the miners were single men. Those from faraway countries worked hard to send money to their families. Later, families with children moved into mining towns too. More homes were built, and schools for the children sprang up. In a few short years, the small tent camp of Virginia City had become a town of more than 5,000 people.

Blasting Caps

Life in the mining towns was often very dangerous. **Blasting caps** were one of the worst dangers. Miners used them to set off sticks of **dynamite.** Dynamite sticks are made from explosive materials. The caps were filled with small amounts of blasting powder. Sometimes children played with blasting caps they found lying around. According to one man, "about one boy per week would scratch off the end of a blasting cap." The cap would explode, and the boy holding it would lose the tip of his thumb or sometimes his whole finger. Gold Hill and Virginia City had many boys with missing fingers.

Virginia City was a very busy place during the peak of the mining boom. Records say over 22,000 people once lived in the city. This photograph shows a stagecoach parked in front of Wells Fargo & Co. on C Street.

Today in Virginia City, in the old saloons on C Street, you can take a walk back in time. Portraits of some of the town's famous citizens line the walls. One famous face on the wall is a man with many names. He was born as James Fennimore. Some people called him Finney or Old Virginny. Finney was one of the earliest miners in the area. He is also credited with naming the town when it was just a tent camp.

The story goes that one night after drinking too much whiskey, Finney broke a bottle over a rock and named the town after his home state of Virginia. From then on, early miners called the settlement Virginia Town. When the word leaked out that silver could be found in the area, the town was soon flooded with fortune seekers. Virginia Town became Virginia City almost overnight.

This is a modern photograph of Virginia City's famous C Street. Compare it to the photograph of C Street on the previous page. In what ways has the street changed?

Sometimes prospectors tried to load their animals with too many supplies.

Life on the Comstock

Virginia City during the Comstock boom was an exciting place to live. It was the most important settlement between Denver and San Francisco. Miners worked day and night. The whole town buzzed with activity. There were shop owners, saloon keepers, teachers, and preachers. The city also had its share of trouble. People fighting, stealing, and breaking the law were just a few of the everyday problems.

There were also many interesting people living in Virginia City. One man named John Mackay found large silver deposits nearby. It was actually one of the biggest silver deposits in all of North

Mark Twain

Some people call Mark Twain one of America's best-loved authors. His real name was Samuel Clemens. He wrote wonderful stories like *The Adventures of Tom Sawyer* and *The Adventures of Huckleberry Finn*. People of all ages have enjoyed his stories.

He first came to Nevada to work as a clerk for his brother, Orion Clemens. For a short time, he also tried his luck as a prospector with the hope of becoming rich. But he never did strike it rich. He began using the name Mark Twain when he was writing for the *Territorial Enterprise*. *Roughing It* is the book he wrote about life in Virginia City. Here is a sample of what he wrote:

There were military companies, fire companies, brass bands, banks, hotels, theatres,...wide-open gambling palaces, ...street fights, murders, inquests, riots, a whiskey mill every fifteen steps,...half a dozen jails..., and some talk of building a church.

America. Mackay used much of his money to help people in need. Later, his fortune was used to help build the Mackay School of Mines at the University of Nevada in Reno.

Two famous writers also lived in Virginia City for a time. Mark Twain and Dan DeQuille were young reporters for one of Virginia City's newspapers. It was called the *Territorial Enterprise*. They wrote about things that happened during the Comstock days. Some of their articles were printed in newspapers across the country and around the world. Both men wrote books about life on the Comstock. Thousands of people learned more about frontier life by reading their books.

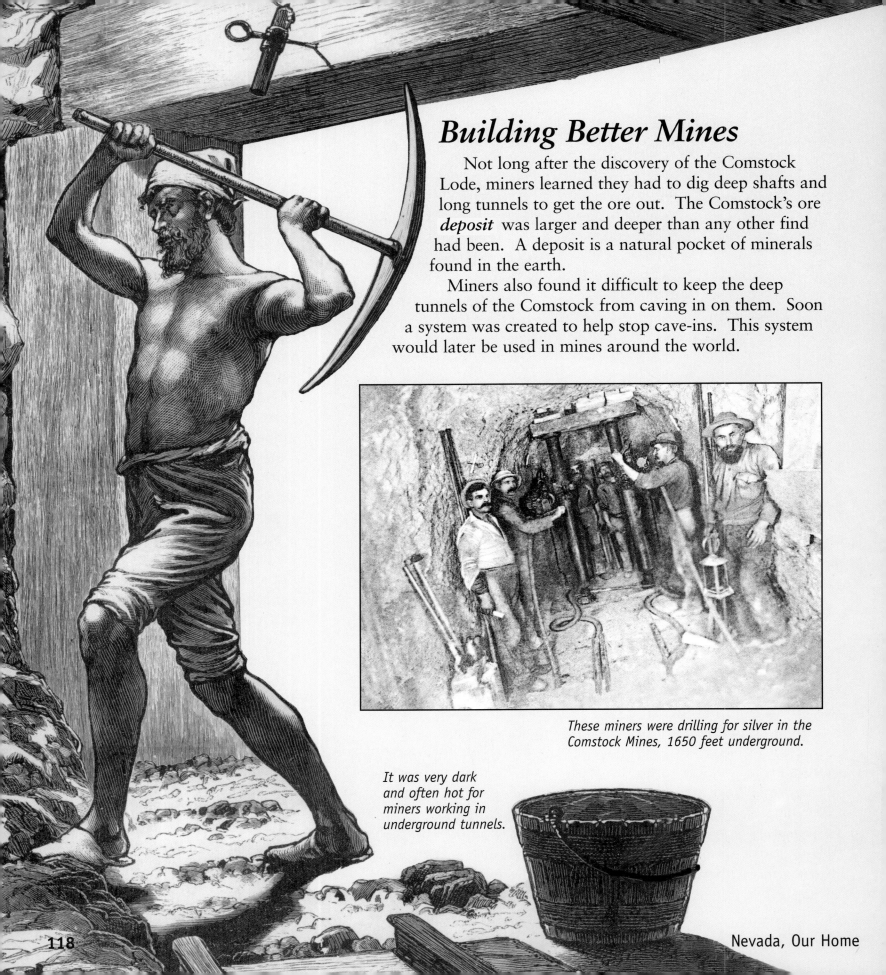

Building Better Mines

Not long after the discovery of the Comstock Lode, miners learned they had to dig deep shafts and long tunnels to get the ore out. The Comstock's ore *deposit* was larger and deeper than any other find had been. A deposit is a natural pocket of minerals found in the earth.

Miners also found it difficult to keep the deep tunnels of the Comstock from caving in on them. Soon a system was created to help stop cave-ins. This system would later be used in mines around the world.

These miners were drilling for silver in the Comstock Mines, 1650 feet underground.

It was very dark and often hot for miners working in underground tunnels.

118

Square-Set Timbering

Early methods used by miners to keep the tunnels from caving in didn't always work. At first, logs about 20 feet long were placed in the roofs of the tunnels. Then posts were used to hold the logs up. Sometimes miners bolted logs together because the tunnels were so long.

The miners soon realized the logs and posts weren't strong enough to prevent cave-ins. There were still too many people who died when a tunnel *collapsed*, or caved-in.

One mining company hired a German man to help solve the cave-in problem. His name was named Philipp Deidesheimer. He was an engineer who began making boxes with 4-6 foot logs, or timbers. He called them *cribs.* The cribs could be stacked on top of each other or placed side by side. They were very strong and could hold up the top and sides of a tunnel. Sometimes cribs were filled with rock to make them more stable.

Deidesheimer's invention was called square-set timbering. It helped make underground mines much safer. Before long, all the Comstock mines were using square-set timbering. This method was used to make mines safer all over the world.

More Dangers

Underground mines had many other dangers besides cave-ins. As miners went deep in the earth the air was hot and hard to breath. It was also bad for their lungs. Pockets of hot air sometimes reached 100 degrees or more.

Falling rocks and explosions from old sticks of dynamite were also common causes of injury or death. Sometimes dynamite left by early miners blew up without warning.

Phillipp Deidesheimer failed to protect his invention of square-set timbering from being stolen by others. Today, inventors can protect their ideas by having them **patented.**

Mining Accidents

Accidents killed many miners in Comstock mines. Here is the accident list for one year:

Falls into deep mining shafts	6
Heat stroke	6
Powder explosions	4
Cave-ins	4
Machinery problems	5
Crushed by cage carrying supplies	1

Sutro's Tunnel

Adolph Sutro was another man with a great idea. He came up with a way to solve the floods in Comstock mining tunnels. Miners working underground in tunnels that were very deep often hit pockets of boiling water trapped in the earth. When hot water flooded the tunnels, the miners had to close the mines to pump out the water.

Sutro's idea was to dig a tunnel that would connect to all the other tunnels. It would serve as a drain to pull the hot water out of the flooded tunnels and onto the desert floor. Sutro would charge the mine owners to use the tunnel.

He also planned to open a mill where the rock would be crushed to help separate it from the silver. With all these services, he hoped to start a new town, called Sutro.

But the tunnel took nine long years to complete. By then, most of the Comstock mines were running out of ore. Sadly, the tunnel wasn't used very much.

Sutro later sold his part of the project and moved to San Francisco, California. He became the mayor of that city and opened his famous Sutro Baths.

Camels in the Desert

It was 1861 when camels were first used to haul salt to the mines outside of Virginia City. The two men who brought them here thought they would do well in Nevada's desert climate. For a while, the men had more than two dozen camels carrying salt and supplies. Later, another group of camels were used to carry other types of freight. But horses didn't like the noise and smell of camels. In the end, camels were banned from public highways.

Today, camels return to Virginia City about once a year. They come back each September with people from all over the world to compete in the International Camel Cup. How would you like to take a ride on a camel?

Sutro's tunnel cost about $3.5 million to build and was more than 20,000 feet long.

Pyramid Lake War

One early spring, problems between Nevada Paiutes and white settlers got worse. It happened when two Native American girls were kidnapped by white men. To get back at the kidnappers, angry Paiutes burned down the local trading post. Three white men died in the attack.

Problems like this continued to create angry feelings between the Paiutes and the white settlers. Soon, fighting broke out at Pyramid Lake. Paiutes led by Chief Numaga killed 76 white men and wounded 29 others. These attacks made nearby settlers even more frightened.

Before the month was out, soldiers and many volunteers went to war against the Paiutes. This time, many Paiutes were killed, and the remaining tribe members backed away from the conflict.

For the next two years, feelings of fear and anger kept native Paiutes and white settlers apart. Then Governor James Nye and two Northern Paiute chiefs came together as a sign of friendship and peace. Even though Chief Numaga led his people against the settlers, he tried to teach them to live in peace. Once when counciling his people, he told them:

You would make war upon the whites. I ask you to pause and reflect. The white men are like the stars over your heads. You have wrongs, great wrongs that rise up like those mountains before you; but can you, from the mountain tops, reach and blot out those stars? Your enemies are like the sands in the bed of your rivers; when taken away they only give place for more to come and settle there. . . . I love my people; let them live; and when their spirits shall be called to the Great Camp in the southern sky, let their bones rest where their fathers were buried.

Chief Numaga was a respected leader of the Northern Paiute people.

Today, Pyramid Lake is part of the Paiute Reservation. It is a very important resource for tribe members. They manage fishing and other water activities at the lake.

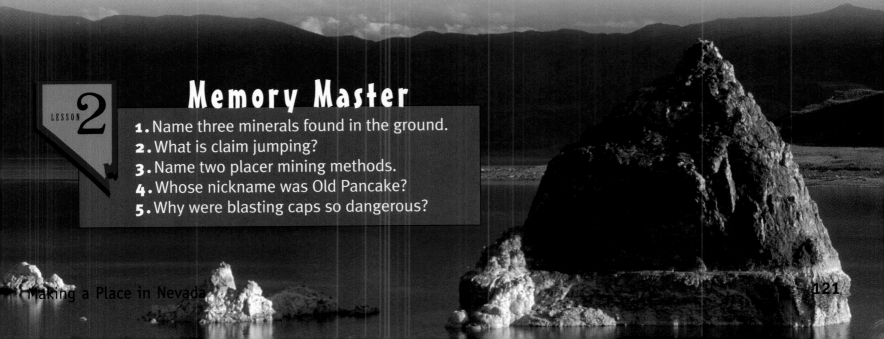

Memory Master

LESSON 2

1. Name three minerals found in the ground.
2. What is claim jumping?
3. Name two placer mining methods.
4. Whose nickname was Old Pancake?
5. Why were blasting caps so dangerous?

Consider ★ Character

Early prospectors and settlers to Nevada faced many difficulties. Crossing the deserts and living off the land took strength and perseverance. There are many examples of people in this chapter who showed these character traits. Now, do some research about another person in Nevada who showed strength and perseverance. Pick someone from history or someone living in Nevada today. Give two examples of how they showed these traits. If you need to, go back and review the character trait definitions at the end of chapter 1.

Geography Tie-In

Do you remember what put the Pony Express out of business? Why do you think this mail system was called the Pony Express? Using the map on pg. 109, answer the following questions:

1. What is the title of the map?
2. Which states are shown on the map?
3. Which city is the farthest western stop?
4. For a letter to go from Marysville to Salt Lake City, which states would it have to pass through?
5. If you lived in Reno, Nevada, which city on the trail is your closest stop?
6. What does this map NOT show?
7. Why do you think the Pony Express is an important part of history?

Technology  Tie-In

Pretend you were a miner living during the Comstock period. Do you think the placer mining methods were the best ways to search for gold? Research other mining methods or see if you can invent a new way to mine for gold. Remember, you have to use the materials and resources found during the 1850s and 1860s. But you can still use the ideas and creativity you have today. What would you call your invention?

Activity

The Comstock Lode Had a Load!

Do you know the difference between the homonyms *load* and *lode*? A load is a group of things, like a load of firewood. A lode is a deposit of valuable ore found in a rock formation. You've probably

never heard the word lode before unless you know a little about mining. What other words in this chapter are words you would know if you were a miner? Maybe you would like to have been a miner during the Comstock days. What other words would you need to understand to be a miner? Using the "Words to Understand" at the beginning of Lesson 2, make a "Miner's Dictionary". For each vocabulary word, write a definition or draw a picture to help you remember what it means. Trade your completed dictionary with a partner to see if you are both ready to stake your claim!

"*Humboldt Station was the name of the station to which we had been looking forward for some hours, simply because it meant "supper." But when we stepped out of the cars, thoughts of supper fled. Four thousand feet above the sea ...there stood a brilliant green oasis. Clover fields, young trees, and vegetable gardens surrounded the little house. In front was a fountain, which sparkled in the sun.*"

—Helen Hunt Jackson, 1887

Timeline of Events

1859
Basques begin settling in Nevada.

1863
Leaders write Nevada's first constitution.

1864
• Nevada becomes our nation's 36th state.
• Abraham Lincoln is re-elected.

1850   1855   1860   1865

1862
Gold and silver are discovered in Austin.

1866
The U. S. Congress adds land to Nevada's eastern border.

1861–1865
The Civil War

1865
William M. Stewart becomes Nevada's first U.S. senator.

A Time of Growth and Change

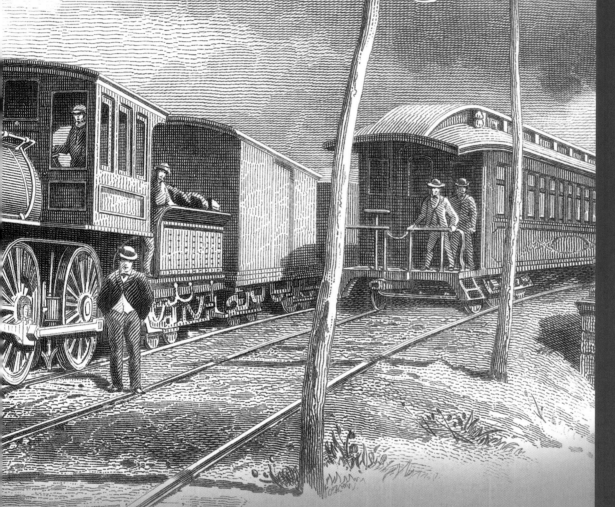

The young Nevada Territory grew very quickly during the last half of the 19th century. New mining towns popped up and then faded away. Citizens began preparing for statehood. Railroads were making it easier for supplies and people in the East to reach the western frontier. A trip across country that used to take months was now possible in less than six days. Ranching became important to Nevada too.

Many Nevada towns began as transcontinental railroad stations.

1867
Land given to Nevada from the Arizona Territory becomes Clark County.

1890 —
Stewart Indian School opens in Carson City. •
U.S. soldiers kill Native Americans at Wounded •
Knee, South Dakota.

1880
Economic hard times hit Nevada.

1905—
Lots sold to create the city of Las Vegas.

1870	1875	1880	1885	1890	1895	1905

1870
• A branch of the U.S. Mint is built in Carson City.
• The Nevada state capitol is built in Carson City.

1881
The Stewarts take over the Las Vegas Ranch.

1887
Wovoka has Ghost Dance vision.

1893
George Washington Ferris Jr. builds the first Ferris wheel.

1869
The first transcontinental railroad is completed.

125

LESSON 1

PEOPLE TO KNOW

James Buchanan
Abraham Lincoln
James W. Nye
William M. Stewart

PLACES TO LOCATE

Aurora
Austin
Fort Churchill
Lander County
Lyon County
Reno

WORDS TO UNDERSTAND

abolish
amendment
boomtown
Civil War
Confederacy
constitution
county seat
elect
Union

Thousands of men were kill or wounded during Civil Wa battles. This battle at Port Hudson, Louisiana, lasted f 48 days.

A Nation in Conflict

Nevada had just become a new territory when our country was beginning to split apart. Citizens across the United States wanted different things from the government. Southern states wanted the right to own slaves to help farmers grow cotton, tobacco, sugar, and rice. Northern states, however, were more focused on business and industry. New jobs were bringing thousands of Europeans to settle in the northern United States. Some citizens in the North were also against slavery.

President James Buchanan tried to keep the country together. But the southern states broke away from the United States after Abraham Lincoln became president. It was the beginning of a ***Civil War*** between the northern and southern states. Southern states began calling themselves the ***Confederacy.*** The northern states were called the ***Union.*** It was a very hard time for our country. Families were also torn apart when fathers and sons fought for opposite sides.

A Country Torn in Half

Work with a partner to complete this activity. See if you can better understand what happened to the United States when the southern states broke away.

Stand opposite your partner, holding a piece of cloth between you. You and your partner represent the North and the South. Now pull on the cloth in opposite directions. Can you feel the strength of the cloth? Cut a small tear in the cloth, and pull again. What happens to the cloth? Think of the cloth as the United States of America. The tear was caused when the southern states decide to break away from the United States. What happened to the strength of the country? Each of you pulled on the cloth just like the North and South pulled away from each other to protect their own interests.

Make a drawing or write a paragraph to show what you learned from this activity.

Nevada Supports the Union

The Nevada Territory supported the northern states, or the Union cause. Union troops in the area were called to help keep Nevada's mining towns peaceful. Territory officials didn't want miners who supported the Confederacy causing trouble in the area. Any troublemakers or supporters of the Confederacy were taken to Fort Churchill to be held or punished.

Miners working the Comstock kept up on the latest war news as it came across the telegraph wires. Some even fired the local cannon to celebrate Union victories. Two Nevada's counties, Lyon and Lander, and the city of Reno were named after Union officers who died during the Civil War.

This uniform was worn by a Union soldier.

Mining Centers

As the Civil War continued in the East, new discoveries of silver and gold brought many small mining towns to the mountains of the Great Basin. They were called *boomtowns.* Boomtowns were places that grew very quickly. Many also faded quickly. However, some are around even today.

More Boomtowns

Like Virginia City, the town of Austin, in central Nevada, started as a boomtown. It was built when silver was discovered near the stagecoach stop in the Reese River Valley. People immediately rushed to the area. Before long, the town had a mayor, schools, churches, banks, and a city hall. Later, it became the *county seat* of Lander County. The county seat is the place where county government meets and works. Today, only about 300 people live in Austin. Many visitors, though, come to the area each year.

Aurora was another Nevada boomtown close to the California border. The winters there were bitter cold, and the summers were hot and dusty. Among the town's many buildings, a few were made of brick. The young Mark Twain tried mining for silver in Aurora. He didn't like the hard work of mining and soon gave up. In fact, most everyone left Aurora when the ore ran out. Today, it is one of Nevada's many mining ghost towns.

When this photograph was taken in 1880, the mines in Austin were beginning to die. The best reminders of the town's past are a few of the original buildings that are still standing today, more than 100 years after they were built.

A Growing Territory

The early mining areas in what is now Nevada had few, if any, laws. Prospectors had to protect themselves and their claims any way they could. As towns and mining communities grew, miners and other settlers began to set up local governments. They wanted rules that would help make prospecting safe.

In towns that grew quickly, like Virginia City, the people wanted more laws. They wanted their own governments. They wanted their own territory, separate from the Utah Territory.

Finally, President James Buchanan created the Nevada Territory. A few days later, Abraham Lincoln became the new president of the United States. Lincoln chose James W. Nye from New York as the territory's first governor.

Once the new governor finally arrived, he started organizing the territory. He called people to serve in the government. He called judges for the courts. He asked the citizens of the territory to vote for, or **elect,** people to help make laws. Governor Nye also wanted to collect taxes that would help pay for new schools and services. He wanted to help the people of the Nevada Territory get ready for statehood.

Abraham Lincoln was our country's 16th president.

When James W. Nye arrived in the new Nevada Territory, he chose to make Carson City the government center.

Beginning the Work of Statehood

Many months after Nevada became a territory, the government began the work of becoming a state. The territory's first job was to create a *constitution,* or set of laws. After the constitution was created, it had to be approved by the voters. It also had to be approved by the United States Congress.

Nevada voters didn't approve the first constitution that was drafted. But Congress and President Abraham Lincoln really wanted Nevada to become a state. President Lincoln wanted more Union votes to help him win the re-election. He also wanted Union votes to help him pass a new *amendment,* or addition to the United States Constitution. This new amendment would *abolish,* or get rid of, slavery. It was called the 13th Amendment.

The Nation's 36th State

Nevadans worked hard and fast to get a second constitution approved before the upcoming November election. In a few months, a new constitution was written and approved by Nevada voters. Then it was then sent by telegraph for approval by Congress. At the time, it was the longest telegraph that had ever been sent.

On October 31, 1864, Congress approved the new constitution making Nevada our nation's 36th state. It happened just in time for Nevada voters to help re-elect President Abraham Lincoln. William M. Stewart became our state's first U.S. senator. Later, that year he met with President Lincoln in Washington, D. C.

This letter was sent by James Nye, governor of the Nevada Territory, to Washington leaders to ask them to approve statehood for Nevada.

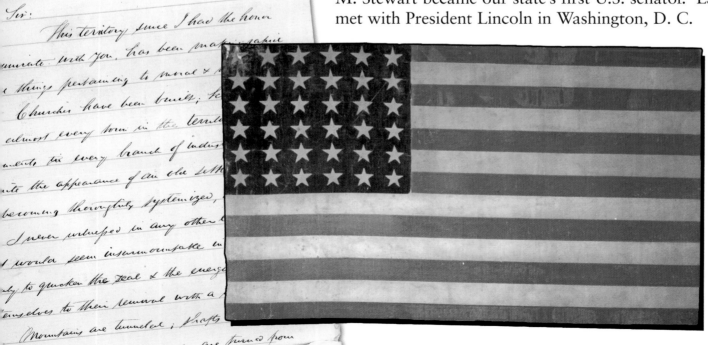

This flag was made after Nevada became our nation's 36th state.

More Land for Nevada

A few years after Nevada became a state, its government asked Congress to consider adding more land to the state. Nevada wanted to create a new county and expand the eastern border toward the Utah Territory. They hoped the new land would add valuable mining resources to the state.

Congress finally agreed to give Nevada the additional land. The change moved our eastern border from 115 degrees latitude to 114 degrees latitude. The following year, another section of land was added to Nevada. Las Vegas was part of this area. Before it became part of Nevada, this small section of land belonged to the Arizona Territory. Years later, it became known as Clark County.

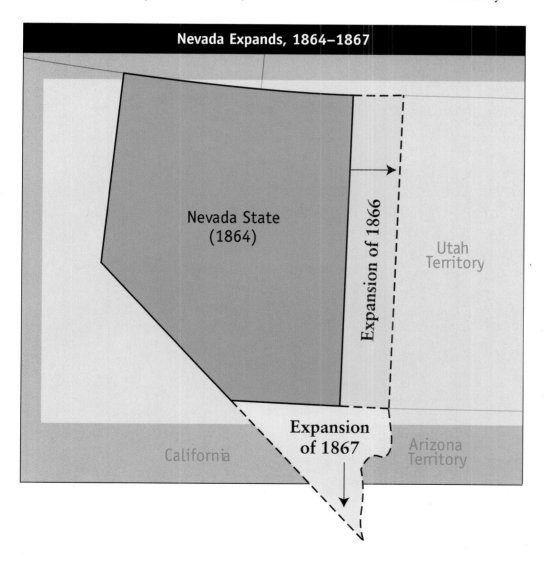

Nevada Expands, 1864–1867

Nevada State (1864)

Expansion of 1866

Expansion of 1867

Utah Territory

California

Arizona Territory

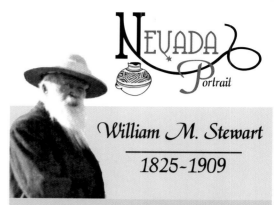

Nevada Portrait

William M. Stewart
1825-1909

William Morris Stewart first moved to Nevada during the Comstock days. He was born in New York and then moved to Ohio with his parents. As a young man, he helped clear the trees from his father's farm. He also received a good education.

Interest in the Gold Rush brought Stewart to the West. He spent time mining in California. Then he studied to become a lawyer. Stewart moved his family to Virginia City, where he became a very powerful mining lawyer.

Later, Stewart became Nevada's first United States senator. He helped write a very important amendment to the United States Constitution. It was the 15th Amendment which said men of all races had the right to vote.

Stewart also made it possible for the U.S. Mint in Carson City to make coins from Comstock silver. He supported projects that helped bring water to Nevada ranches and farms. He worked hard to help people get a good education.

The University of Nevada and the Stewart Indian School both got started with his help. Stewart didn't like the idea of Indian reservations. He believed Native American people needed a good education and a chance to do things for themselves. Stewart served the people of Nevada until he was 77 years old.

Activity

Cause and Effect

In almost every part of your life you experience something called cause and effect. A cause is an action, like turning on a light when you enter a dark room. The effect is what happens because of your action, such as the dark room filling with light. Events in history also have causes and effects.

Look at each pair of sentences below. Decide which sentence is the cause and which is the effect that follows. Write your answers on a separate sheet of paper. Use the letter "C" for cause and "E" for effect.

Cause: An action that causes something else to happen.
Effect: Something that happens because of an action.

Example:
C	Nevada's constitution is approved by Congress.
E	Nevada becomes our country's 36th state.

1. _____ Men of all races had the right to vote.
   _____ The 15th Amendment became part of the United States Constitution.

2. _____ Southern states decide to separate from the United States.
   _____ Northern and southern states fight over the issue of slavery.

3. _____ Gold and silver ore is uncovered in the Reese River Valley.
   _____ The town of Aurora begins to develop.

4. _____ Lincoln wins the re-election.
   _____ President Abraham Lincoln gets Union votes.

Memory Master

LESSON 1

1. Name two cities, counties, or towns in Nevada that were named after Civil War officers.
2. What is a boomtown?
3. Which amendment to the Constitution ended slavery?
4. Nevada became our nation's _____ (which number) state.

Rebuilding Old Mormon Fort

Octavius Gass

Many years after the Mormon settlers left their fort in Las Vegas, Octavius Gass began to rebuild it. Gass was a prospector who came to the area after mining in California and Eldorado Canyon. He was tired of mining and wanted to find a new way to make a living.

Gass and a few of his mining friends started a ranch on the land where the old Mormon fort stood. They tore down some of the old buildings and cleaned up the old fort. They wanted to sell supplies to travelers like the Mormon settlers had done. The fort was renamed Las Vegas Rancho.

Gass and his partners raised cattle and horses. They grew beans, grain, and vegetables. They planted peach, apricot, and apple trees. They used the underground springs to get the water they needed. Tired travelers also stopped to rest at the warm bubbling springs.

After a while, Gass bought out his partners. He and his family worked and lived at Las Vegas Rancho for more than 15 years. Later Gass lost the ranch when he was unable to pay his bills. He and his family moved to California.

LESSON 2

PEOPLE TO KNOW

Pedro Altube
Fred Dangberg
Octavius Gass
Hock Mason
Benjamin Palmer
John Sparks
R.B. and T.B. Smith

PLACES TO LOCATE

Douglas County
Europe
Mottsville
Pyrenees Mountains

WORDS TO UNDERSTAND

Basque
brand
demand
heritage
vaquero

When Octavius Gass owned Las Vegas Rancho, it was still part of the Arizona Territory. Later, Congress added the area to Nevada.

Early Ranching in Nevada

Some of Nevada's earliest cattle ranches began in the Carson Valley. Plenty of water and rich grasslands made it an ideal place to raise cattle. Most of the beef was sold to settlers who were on their way to California. Ranchers in the valley made a good living. Things got even better when the Comstock silver rush began.

As more miners flocked to the region, the *demand*, or need, for food grew. Miners and other newcomers also needed grain and hay for their animals. As the needs of the people changed, so did area ranches. Many new ranches were created, and smaller ones got bigger.

Linking the Past to the Present

Do you think ranches in Nevada today are as important as they were in the 1800s? Do they still help our growing state meet its demand for food like they did during Nevada's early mining days? See if you and your class can learn more about how important ranching is for our state.

Herds like these grazed Nevada's rangelands even during the winter.

Ranching Families

Fred Dangberg, "Hock" Mason, and two men by the name of Smith were a few of the first cattle ranchers in Nevada. Dangberg's ranching and farming operation was just outside of Genoa. It spread across more than 50,000 acres. Later, the Dangberg family started the town of Minden, Nevada.

"Hock" Mason came from California to start a large ranch in what is known as Mason Valley. Just west of Mason Valley, R.B. and T.B. Smith raised their herds. The area became known as Smith Valley.

Ranches spread across many other parts of the state too. In White Pine and Nye counties, ranches provided food for miners and nearby townspeople. Near the Reese River, ranchers helped feed the miners in and around the town of Austin. Other large cattle herds were spread throughout Humboldt and Elko counties.

One man, named "Honest John" Sparks, built a huge ranch in Elko County. For a while, he had more than 70,000 cattle and nearly 500 horses. Sparks became Nevada's tenth governor. He was also the first rancher to bring Durham and Hereford cattle to Nevada. Soon other ranchers began raising Herefords when they learned Herefords provided more meat than longhorns.

Ranching families worked hard to make a living from the land.

Nevada Portrait

Benjamin Palmer
1826~1908

One of Nevada's earliest ranchers and pioneers was a man named Benjamin Palmer. Palmer was one of the first black settlers to the Carson Valley. Not much is known about the early years of his life. One woman who wrote about him said that he and his sister bought their way out of slavery.

When Palmer first came to Nevada, he was not yet 30 years old. He settled on 320 acres of grassland along the Carson River. Later, his sister Charlotte settled next to him on 400 acres.

Palmer was a hard-working cattle rancher and horseman. He drove 1,500 head of cattle from the state of Washington to Nevada's Carson Valley. The trip took him nearly three months.

Virginia City's *Territorial Enterprise*, claimed Palmer was one of the biggest taxpayers in Douglas County. His property and livestock were described as some of the most valuable in the region.

Even though Palmer couldn't read or write, early Mottsville records show he served his community in a number of ways. He was political committee member. He also served on at least one jury. Palmer lived in Douglas County for over 50 years. When he died, he was buried in the Mottsville cemetery.

A Cowboy's Life

Some of the first settlers who came to Nevada from California brought with them Mexican *vaqueros.* Vaquero is the Spanish word for cowboy. Vaqueros were excellent horseman who passed on their unique skills and traditions to others in the region. Over time, vaqueros in the West became known as buckaroos.

Few small ranchers could afford to hire these skilled riders at first. Most families helped each other with common farming and ranching labors. As ranching in the area grew, big companies began buying out some of the smaller ranches. By then, buckaroos were becoming a more permanent part of the landscape. They worked long hours driving the herds and breeding new stock. Nevada even had a few Native American and African American buckaroos.

Branding cattle was another job buckaroos had to do. A brand is a special mark that is burned into the hide of a cow with a hot iron. Only a skilled buckaroo could brand a cow's hide without burning clear through it. Even today, ranches have their own brands or special designs that help others know which animals belongs to them.

Once the cattle are branded, buckaroos drive them out to the range to graze. Sometimes, they move the cattle around so they'll get plenty of grass and water to eat. Ranchers want their cattle to grow fat, so they'll be worth more when they sell them for beef. There are still many working cattle ranches in Nevada today.

These buckaroos worked on ranches in Nevada's Railroad Valley.

Activity
Design Your Own Brand

The history of branding cattle and other livestock in Nevada began over 130 years ago. Some of the old brands that were used in Nevada when branding first began are still around today. The Lye brother's brand, for example, was first used in 1864. It looks like this: 7ᒪ

Today, the same brand is used by Keith and Jean Thomas, who operate the Lye Ranch.

Have you ever tried to read a brand? First, it's good to know a few of the general rules. Then you can try creating your own brands. Use symbols, letters, and numbers that mean something to you. You could use the initials of your name or your favorite number. Be creative. Then share your special designs with your friends and classmates.

Rules for Reading Brands

The first thing to remember is that brands are read from top to bottom, left to right, and outside to inside.

Early brands were usually simple letters or numbers. As more ranchers began branding their livestock, they added other symbols to help them create new brands.

Lazy	Hanging	Combined	Reversed
Connected	Bar	Circle	Slash
Box	Rocking	Flying	Picture

Raising Sheep

Sheepherders were another important group who came to settle in Nevada. At first, most of them only traveled through on their way to California. One man drove 9,000 sheep through the state to sell them in California. In a book about his life, he wrote about the hardships of that trip:

> ...sixteen hundred miles of travel over mountain ranges, across barren plains and still more barren deserts... I knew that there was scarcely a mile of the road which was not beset by savages who were making it their principal business to rob and murder a white man or band of white men whenever opportunity offered.

Up until the Comstock rush began, few people tried raising sheep in Nevada. Then, almost overnight, sheep were being used to feed a growing population. Sheepherders soon learned that Nevada's wide-open spaces, wild grasses, and sagebrush were perfect for raising sheep. A few ranchers even switched from raising cattle to raising sheep. Some ranchers tried raising both.

Many of Nevada's early sheepherders immigrated from Europe. Pedro Altube was a **Basque** immigrant who started a large sheep ranch near Elko. He came from the Basque villages in the Pyrenees Mountains between France and Spain.

Altube invited more Basques to come to Nevada. He gave them jobs and, sometimes, sheep as payment for their work. This helped some of them start their own sheep ranches. Altube became known as "The Father of the Basques in America".

Remember, an emigrant is a person who leaves one country to settle in another.

An immigrant is a person who lives in a country other than where he or she was born.

At one point during the Comstock era, over 200,000 sheep grazed the rangelands of Nevada.

Painting by Don Gray

This mural of a Basque sheepherder in Ely, Nevada, reminds some of its citizens of their Basque heritage.

This is the traditional Basque flag.

Basques in Nevada

The Basque people who came to our state loved the high deserts and mountains of Nevada. It was a good place to raise sheep as their families had been doing for centuries in Europe. Many Basques settled near Elko, Carson City, and Ely.

Many times, the cattle ranchers and sheepherders had trouble getting along. Both wanted control of Nevada's grassy ranges. However, sheep ranchers had a few advantages over cattle ranchers. Sheep adapted to climate changes better than cattle. Market prices for selling sheep didn't go up and down as much either. Ranchers could also make more money from sheep because they could sell their wool.

The life of a sheepherder was a very lonely life. Most of his time was spent alone with the sheep. Sometimes, a faithful dog was his only company for weeks or months at a time. Many Basque families took their herds and spread out across the ranges of Idaho and Oregon too.

Today, many people in Nevada love to attend the yearly Basque festivals. People all over the state get together to celebrate the Basque *heritage,* or way of life. They celebrate with music, dance, and traditional Basque foods.

Linking the Past to the Present

Today, the signs of lonely Basque sheepherders can be seen carved into the aspen trees of northern Nevada. One sheepherder left his name and date carved into this Elko County tree.

This huge field of corn was grown in Nevada's Lahontan valley

Farming in Nevada

When settlers first came to Nevada, they grew only enough food for themselves plus a little to trade or sell. As the mining boom began, Nevada ranches and farms grew to meet the new demands for food.

People in Mason, Smith, Carson, and Washoe Valleys bought more land. They grew alfalfa, potatoes, and wheat. They raised dairy cows to provide people with milk, cheese, and butter. Some farmers planted orchards to provide fresh fruit. Some even planted strawberries and raspberries.

Farm Life

The Crane farm, in Washoe County, was one of the first big alfalfa growers in Nevada. Alfalfa was an important new crop for the area. It could be planted and harvested many times a year—instead of just once like other types of hay.

Early farmers cut the hay with sharp knives until mowing machines pulled by horses came along. Then steam engines took over for horses, and with each new invention, the work got a little easier.

Life on the farm, however, was always hard work. Farmers and their families worked from sunup to sundown. They worked when it was hot and when it was cold. They fought to keep grasshoppers and other pests out of their crops. One farmer wrote about what summers were like in his community:

Moved into a new house....But when warm weather came we were unable to sleep in the house, and were compelled to resort to the sheds and sleep on top of them to keep from scorpions, tarantulas, rattlesnakes, & no escaping mosquitoes. {It was so hot}...chickens at daybreak, hold their wings up and lolling for breath....An egg would roast in short time laying in the sand.

What do you think?

During Nevada's early mining days, farming was just as hard as mining. If you were living then, would you have chosen to mine or to farm? Why?

Memory Master

LESSON 2

1. Which big event in early Nevada history also caused ranching to grow?
2. Who was "Honest John" Sparks?
3. Why do ranchers brand their cattle and livestock?
4. Where did the first Basque sheepherders in Nevada immigrate from?

Building Railroads and Cities

One of the most important events for Nevada was the coming of the *transcontinental* railroad. New cities sprung up around the railway stations. People and goods could be easily transported from station to station and from coast to coast. Cities in the eastern United States were finally connected with the wide-open areas of the West. Life on the frontier was about to change forever.

The Central Pacific

The Central Pacific was the first great railroad in the West. It was organized about the same time the Civil War broke out in the East. For the first few years, *surveyors* studied, measured, and laid out the western route. Then they began to lay the tracks, or rails.

The first tracks laid by the Central Pacific were in Sacramento, California. The job seemed easy at first, but as workers headed east, the job got much harder. Laying track through the Sierra Nevada seemed almost impossible.

Some of the hardest work through the mountains was done by Chinese workers. They blasted and dug through walls of solid granite. The hours were long, and the pay was little. After four years of hard labor and many setbacks, the tracks for the Central Pacific finally crossed the border into Nevada. Laying rails through the Sierra Nevada was one of the most amazing engineering projects of the time.

LESSON 3

PLACES TO LOCATE

Atlantic Ocean
Omaha, Nebraska
Pacific Ocean
Sacramento, California
Truckee

WORDS TO UNDERSTAND

competition
depot
legislature
surveyor
transcontinental

J.H. Strobridge of the Central Pacific Railroad keeps watch over a group of Chinese workers laying track in Nevada.

When railroad depots were first built, they became the center of town. This drawing of Elko was in Leslie's Illustrated Newspaper in 1878.

Railroad Centers

As more tracks and trains made their way across Nevada, many railroad centers, or *depots,* were built. People got on and off the train at these centers. They were also places where people bought and sold things. Many became the main cities of Nevada. Reno, Lovelock, Winnemucca, and Elko were major railroad centers.

Soon, other trains, called short-line railroads, were running in parts of Nevada. These trains were used to transport ore from Nevada's mines to the mills. Some carried supplies to the miners. Short-line railroads like the Virginia and Truckee, the Nevada Central, and the Pioche and Bullionville, became very famous in our state. Most were in operation until the mines closed down. After that, most short-lines and their tracks were simply abandoned.

The Great Train Robbery

It was a dark November night when eight masked men robbed a passenger train outside of Verdi, Nevada. At gunpoint, the bandits locked the engineer, two brakeman, and a few others inside the mailroom. Then they broke open the Wells Fargo strong box and made off with over $40,000 in gold coins. The money they stole was the payroll for the Yellow Jacket Mine at Gold Hill.

Three rewards were offered for the capture of the masked men. Together, the rewards totaled $30,500. Washoe County's undersheriff, James H. Kinkead, visited the scene of the robbery the very next morning. He followed a set of footprints and soon caught up with one of the men. Kinkead took the man to the Truckee jail, where the man confessed to the crime and gave the names of the other men involved.

Before long, the rest of the men were captured and put in prison. Most of the missing money was also recovered. This Central Pacific hold-up is reported to have been the first train robbery in the West.

This newspaper article was written the day of the robbery.

[From our Evening Edition of Yesterday]
THE GREAT TRAIN ROBBERY—All th
upon Streets to-day is of the great robber
the railroad, between Reno and Verdi, la
night. It is believed here that the robber
got in the vicinity of $150,000. Chief D
Sheriff Cummins, Officer Lackey and ot
and detectives left this city early this f
the scene of the robbery. Wells Fargo &
$10,000 reward For the recovery of th
or any part of it, and the arrest and co
robbers. Under the head of telegraphi
an account of the robbery, as sent us f
It is probably correct, though it diffe
the stories told on the streets. We ar
near a hundred men are out is pursu

THE GREAT RACE

It was a big dream to imagine that one day a railroad could travel across the United States from the Atlantic to the Pacific Ocean. With help from President Lincoln, however, two companies took on the challenge.

The Central Pacific Railroad began in California and traveled east. It began nearly two years before the Union Pacific Railroad. The Union Pacific's job was to build the line going west from Omaha, Nebraska. Each company got money from the government and 6,400 acres of land for every mile of track they laid.

By 1865, both companies were racing toward each other. Both had problems of every kind. During one summer, the Union Pacific had 45 men killed by Indians, 10 were shot during fights or robberies, and dozens of mules died from the heat.

Central Pacific workers had even more problems. Some of their trains crashed. Hundreds of Chinese workers died in the mountains, and it was nearly impossible to get enough water to the workers and livestock each day.

The **competition,** or desire to win, drove both companies to push their workers harder and faster than ever. When one company laid six miles of track in a day, the other company pushed their workers to lay seven.

Cheating was also a problem, so Congress stepped in to help. At last, a meeting place where the tracks would come together was decided upon. The place was Promontory, Utah.

On May 10, 1869, the first transcontinental railroad was complete. Thousands of people came to watch the last tracks laid. A golden spike was used to connect the joining tracks that had these words engraved on it: "May God continue the unity of our Country as this Railroad unites the two great Oceans of the world."

Promontory, Utah was the spot where the two railroad companies finally came together.

Progress in Nevada

New growth and challenges came flooding into Nevada with the coming of the railroad. In Carson City, a branch of the United States Mint was built. Congress had decided it would cost too much to send Comstock silver to the mint in California. Coins from Comstock silver could be made cheaper and easier right in Nevada. Nearly $50 million in silver coins were produced in Nevada's mint in its 23 years of operation.

Another stately addition to Carson City was the two-story sandstone capitol building. At first, many people were unhappy about the ugly spot where the capitol would be built. They called it the Plaza, but it had no trees or grass. Nevada's lawmakers, or *legislature* were the first to use the building. Later, the governor and others had their offices their too.

Since Nevada's capitol building was completed in 1871, two new wings have been added.

Working Toward Women's Rights

In the Nevada legislature, a bill, or proposed law, was introduced to give women the right to vote. At this time, women of the United States could not vote. Men were the only lawmakers.

A legislator from Storey County introduced the Nevada bill by saying, "The women of our land are human beings. They are, I presume, intelligent human beings. Moreover, sir, they are citizens of the United States."

You would think that all women would have supported this idea, but there were many who did not. Since there were so many men and women who opposed the bill, it did not become law. Women were not allowed to vote in state or national elections until the 20th century.

Women fighting for their right to vote, traveled through Nevada from town to town.

Mining in Eastern Nevada

Good fortune came to a few mining areas of eastern Nevada too. The small town of Eureka turned tons of ore into silver and lead bars. Hundreds of men were hired to bring wood down from the mountains to heat the smelting furnaces. A beautiful red brick courthouse, an opera house, and newspaper building were also built in town.

But the little town wasn't without problems. When trouble broke out between the Italian woodcutters and the owners of the furnaces, five men were killed. Luckily, the conflict ended peacefully, even though no one was ever blamed for the murders.

The town of Pioche, near the Utah border, also had its ups and downs as a result of mining. At first, a great deal of wealth came out of its mines. The local government spent much of it on its now famous Million Dollar Court House. But sudden riches caused problems for the town too. It brought gunfighters and others who didn't respect the law into the area. The small town had at least 40 murders in less than two years. Worst of all, no one was ever punished for these crimes. When silver prices began dropping and the mines flooded with underground water, people began to leave. The boom in Pioche ended after only five years.

Banks in early Nevada used to print their own money.

This stagecoach is stopped at the corner of Main and Gold Streets, in Eureka. The Bureau Hotel is in the background.

Memory Master

LESSON 3

1. What was the name of the first great railroad company in the West?
2. Name three Nevada towns that began as early railroad centers.
3. Name the place where the nation's first transcontinental railroad came together.
4. Why was a branch of the United States Mint built in Carson City?
5. Name one reason the mines in the boomtown of Pioche closed.

PEOPLE TO KNOW

Hannah K. Clapp
William Clark
George Washington Ferris Jr.
Charles P. Squires
Archibald Stewart
Helen Stewart
Wovoka

PLACES TO LOCATE

Los Angeles, California
Chicago, Illinois
Lovelock
National Statuary Hall
Stewart Indian School
Washington, D.C.

WORDS TO UNDERSTAND

auction
economy

The Stewart Ranch

Archibald and Helen Stewart were living in Pioche when they heard Octavius Gass needed help. Gass was in danger of losing his Las Vegas Ranch. The Stewarts helped by loaning him money. But when Gass couldn't repay the loan, the Stewarts ended up with the ranch.

Helen Stewart didn't like the ranch at first. It was too quiet and far away from the city life she loved. She wanted to be around other women. She wanted her children to have friends to play with. The Las Vegas Ranch was a very lonely place.

One day when Archibald was out of town, a ranch hand came to the house. He told Helen he was quitting. He also told her he wanted his pay. Mrs. Stewart refused to pay him. She told him he would have to wait until her husband returned. The ranch hand was very upset. He said many unkind things to Helen. When Archibald returned, she told him what had happened.

The Stewart Ranch was an important rest station for travelers.

Archibald Stewart was a successful miner, rancher, and businessman when he took over the Las Vegas Ranch.

The First Lady of Las Vegas

Archibald Stewart went after the ranch hand. The man had gone to a neighboring ranch where outlaws were often seen. When Stewart got there, a fight began. Stewart was shot and killed. No one was ever blamed for his murder. Helen had his body buried at the ranch. Even though she had once hated living there, she and her children stayed there for another 20 years.

Helen had to work hard to feed the travelers who stopped there to rest. She served as post mistress and supplied miners in the area with food. She hired ranch hands to help her manage the large, 1,000-acre property. Years later, Helen married one of the ranch hands. She also hired someone to come to the ranch to teach her five children.

Selling the Ranch

Years later, Helen sold the Las Vegas Ranch to William Clark, a wealthy Montana senator. He bought the property for the railroad. Later, the railroad divided the land into smaller lots and *auctioned* them off. An auction is a public meeting where something is sold to the person willing to pay the most money. The lots were the beginning of the city of Las Vegas.

Helen Stewart loved to collect local artifacts, especially Indian crafts and baskets. She had one of the largest basket collections in the state.

Helen Stewart is often called the "First Lady of Las Vegas" because it was her land that was sold to start the city of Las Vegas.

Las Vegas, a Major Railroad Town

Western railroad owners also soon realized that Las Vegas was the perfect desert rest stop. As soon as William Clark bought the Stewart ranch, he began to lay out his plans. Clark was the head of a new railroad company called the San Pedro, Los Angeles, and Salt Lake Railroad. The company hoped to build a line connecting Utah's capital city with the West Coast. Las Vegas was to be a major supply point along the route.

Las Vegas also became an important link to the new mining towns of Rhyolite and Bullfrog. Clark then built another railroad line to connect Las Vegas with these new towns. The line made it easier for miners to receive their supplies by train.

At first, the town grew quite slowly. The summer heat and constant winds were hard on people's nerves. Then a major fire caused even more problems. Businessmen didn't stay long once they saw the dusty little town. To make matters worse, hundreds of railroad workers lost their jobs after a nation-wide strike.

About 3,000 people came to William Clark's two-day land auction in the spring of 1905.

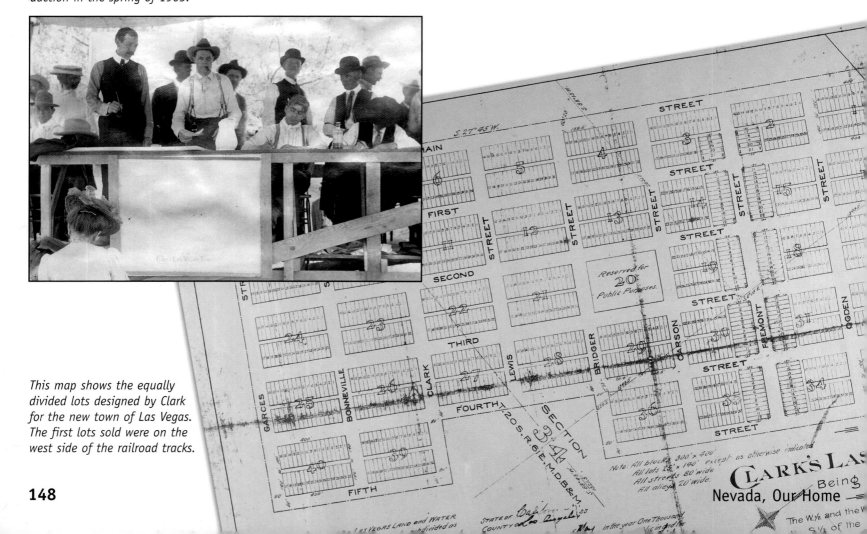

This map shows the equally divided lots designed by Clark for the new town of Las Vegas. The first lots sold were on the west side of the railroad tracks.

Nevada, Our Home

Back in Time

Charles P. Squires was an early Las Vegas citizen who was asked to buy the town newspaper. The paper was called the *Las Vegas Age*. This was Squires reply:

"What on earth would I do with a newspaper? I have troubles enough already.... But something had started a train of thought which I was unable to sidetrack. Now just suppose I had a newspaper in Las Vegas; perhaps I could help revive the poor, sick little town."

Squires did buy the newspaper and ran it for 40 years. He also built the first hotel in Las Vegas—in a tent.

Many people who came to the land auction stayed in Squires Las Vegas hotel. It was located on Main and Stewart Streets.

Las Vegas School

Plans were made by town officials to hold the first Las Vegas school in a tent near Las Vegas Creek. However, these plans soon changed, and the old Salt Lake Hotel was moved from 2nd and Stewart to 2nd and Lewis. It soon became the town's first school.

Students of all ages went to the school together. Miss Schultz and Miss Tuttle were its first teachers. Even in Nevada's earliest days, parents believed education was very important.

How do you think these children felt about attending the first school in Las Vegas? Do they look happy to be there?

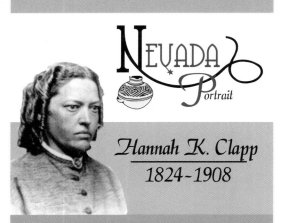

Adapting to New Ways

By the late 1800s, Nevada's Native Americans knew that their traditional ways of live were quickly disappearing. Some tried hard to keep their traditions alive. Others, however, gave up or became very sad. They did not like how they were treated. They did not like being forced into a new way of life.

The Fight for Fair Treatment

In Chapter 3, you read a little about a Nevada Paiute woman named Sarah Winnemucca. She spoke out many times about the problems Nevada's Native Americans had. She wrote a book about these problems with the help of some of her white friends. The book was called *Life Among the Piutes: Their Wrongs and Claims.*

Sarah also tried to teach her people the importance of a good education. She believed the white man was successful because of education. Sarah opened an Indian school in Lovelock. The school helped many Native American people. Later, the school was closed because there wasn't enough money to keep it open.

Did you notice the two different spellings of the word Paiute on this page? Do you think there is more than one right way to spell a word?

Linking the Past to the Present

In March of 2005, a statute of Sarah Winnemucca was honored in our nation's capital. The beautiful bronze piece was placed in Statuary Hall inside the capitol building in Washington, D.C. Sarah worked hard for the rights of the Paiute people. Her desire to see her people treated with respect will be forever remembered. She is the eighth woman and fourth American Indian to be honored with a statue in this famous hall.

This beautiful bronze sculpture of Sarah Winnemucca was created by 25-year-old Benjamin Victor. A copy of it also stands in our state capitol building.

The Stewart Indian School

Nevada's government also decided to help educate its Native Americans. It created the Stewart Indian School just outside Carson City. However, in the beginning there were many problems with the school.

Native American students from all over the West were forced to leave their homes to go to the school. When they arrived, they were forced to give up most of their cultural ways. Brothers and sisters hardly ever saw one another. Students were even punished for speaking their native language. This caused many hard feelings and more unhappiness among the Native American people.

Years later, the school was asked not to strip students of their cultural heritage. School leaders learned that teaching students basic trades and skills was a more positive way to help them. Students were taught things like ranching and cooking, mechanics and sports. Many Native American athletes earned honors during their time at the school. After 90 years, the school finally closed. Today, it is on the National Register of Historic Places.

"The first thing they did was cut our hair. . .[after] we'd lost our hair and our clothes; with those two, we'd lose our identity as Indians."

—Asa Deklage, 1855

This photograph shows the first graduating class from the Stewart Indian School. It was taken in 1901.

Wovoka and the Ghost Dance

Another famous Nevada Paiute Indian was a man by the name of Wovoka. As a teenage boy, he spent much of his time with a white ranching family named Wilson. Sometimes Wovoka even went by the name of Jack Wilson. For many years, he lived the life of a rancher in Nevada's Mason Valley.

When he was about 30 years old, he had a vision or dream. Wovoka said he talked with God in his dream. He said God told him there would one day be a world set aside for native peoples. God told him his people would not suffer or die of starvation in the new world. He was also told the new world would only come if his people practiced a certain dance. It became known as the Ghost Dance.

Word of Wovoka's vision soon spread to other Indian nations. Chiefs and leaders from other tribes visited him to learn more about his dream. Many believed Wovoka's dream meant that all Indian lands would be given back to native peoples. Some Lakota tribes believed that they would be protected by wearing a special shirt called a ghost shirt. They thought ghost shirts would protect them from the bullets of white settlers and soldiers. They wore ghost shirts as they danced.

The ghost shirts, however, didn't really have special powers. They didn't protect the dancing tribes from the battle that soon broke out. Nervous white settlers called for help when they thought the tribes might turn violent. U.S. soldiers attacked the Native Americans at a place called Wounded Knee, South Dakota. Nearly 300 Native Americans were killed.

Wovoka was not with those tribes dancing in South Dakota. In fact, he hardly ever left his home in Mason Valley. He was a peaceful man and always taught his followers to get along with others.

Wovoka was hardly ever seen without his wide-brimmed black sombrero.

Nevada's Boom Goes Bust

By the late 1800s, Nevada's mining riches had finally run out. Mines closed, and thousands of people left the state to find work in other places. Farms and ranches suffered too. As people moved away, fewer people needed crops or beef. Hard times swept across the state.

Nevada was in need of new ways to use its resources. The state needed new jobs to help keep people from leaving. Our state was forced to look at new ways to build its *economy.*

Ferris Wheel

The man with the idea for the Ferris wheel was George Washington Gale Ferris, Jr. He moved with his family to Nevada's Carson Valley when he was five years old. His family began farming and planting crops. They planted a garden and orchards filled with different kinds of trees. As a young boy, Ferris loved to watch waterwheels bring water out of the Carson River. He even dreamed about riding on the bucket of a waterwheel.

After attending military school, Ferris became an engineer. One day, Ferris and some other engineers were asked to build something unusual for a celebration in Chicago, Illinois. The celebration would be called the World's Columbian Exposition.

Ferris had a wonderful idea for the project. He wanted to build a large wheel that could carry people. At first, no one thought his idea would work. They called him "The Man with Wheels in His Head". Ferris worked hard, though, and didn't give up.

When the wheel was finally finished, it stood 250 feet tall. Each of the 36 cages could carry 60 people. It took close to 20 minutes for the ride to go around twice. One ride cost just 50 cents. Soon it became one of the fair's most famous rides.

The first Ferris wheel was built in 1893. Here we see it at the 1904 World's Fair in St. Louis.

Memory Master

LESSON 4

1. Why was the Stewart Ranch important to Nevada history?
2. In what Nevada town did Sarah Winnemucca start a school?
3. Name two of the skills or trades that were taught at the Stewart Indian School.
4. What was a ghost shirt? Why did Native American's wear them?
5. For what event did George Washington Ferris build the first Ferris wheel?

CHAPTER 7 REVIEW

Consider  Character

What would Nevada be like today if its citizens had given up before statehood? Would you be living in a territory? This chapter shows how the people of Nevada faced hard challenges but didn't give up. They showed a character trait that is necessary for survival. We call this trait perseverance! Find three examples of people in this chapter who persevered even when problems came. Think about how their perseverance helped make Nevada what it is today. In small groups, discuss with your classmates what you are doing in your life to persevere. What will Nevada be like in 50 years because of your actions?

Technology Tie-In

Imagine you and your family will be moving to a new city or country. You have been given the job of deciding where your family will go. It would be helpful before you make your decision to know certain things about your family. For example, does your family like the city or the country? What does your dad do for a living? What kinds of things does your family like to do for fun? Will some of the things you need and want be nearby?

Ask your family questions like these. The answers will help you choose a place where your family can be happy. Do a little research on the Internet to help you choose your imaginary new home. Prepare a poster of pictures and reasons why you have chosen a certain place. Share your decision with your family or class members.

In this chapter you have learned about a few groups of immigrants who came to live or work in early Nevada. You've read about the Basque sheepherders, a group of Italian woodcutters, and some Chinese railroad workers. Now see if you can locate on a map or globe the original country these groups came from. Work with a group of your classmates to make a list of what these immigrant groups did to help build Nevada.

Activity

Read a Population Chart

Nevada's population went up and down for many reasons during the last half of the 1800s. Study this chart, and then answer the following questions:

1. Which three areas had the largest periods of growth between 1875 and 1880?
2. Which areas experienced the most growth after Nevada became a state?
3. Name the two areas where the population suffered the most between 1880 and 1900?
4. Name the area that experienced the biggest population ups and downs during this period.
5. Pick one area and describe the things that made its population grow or decline.

	1861	1870	1875	1880	1890
Carson City	2,076	3,668	3,222	5,412	4,883
Elko	---	3,447	3,602	5,716	4,794
Eureka	---	---	5,029	7,086	3,275
Esmerelda County	2,299	1,553	1,318	3,220	2,148
Storey County	4,581	11,359	19,528	16,115	8,806
White Pine County	---	7,189	2,557	2,682	1,721

"*Instead of trying to make people to fit into a certain mold, we should encourage them to furnish their own mold.*"

—*Maude Frazier*

Timeline of Events

1900
- Jim Butler finds silver at Tonopah.
- Copper is discovered near Ely.

1902
Gold is discovered in Goldfield.

1900   **1905**   **1910**

1903
Newlands irrigation project begins.

1911
Nevada begins building public roads and highways.

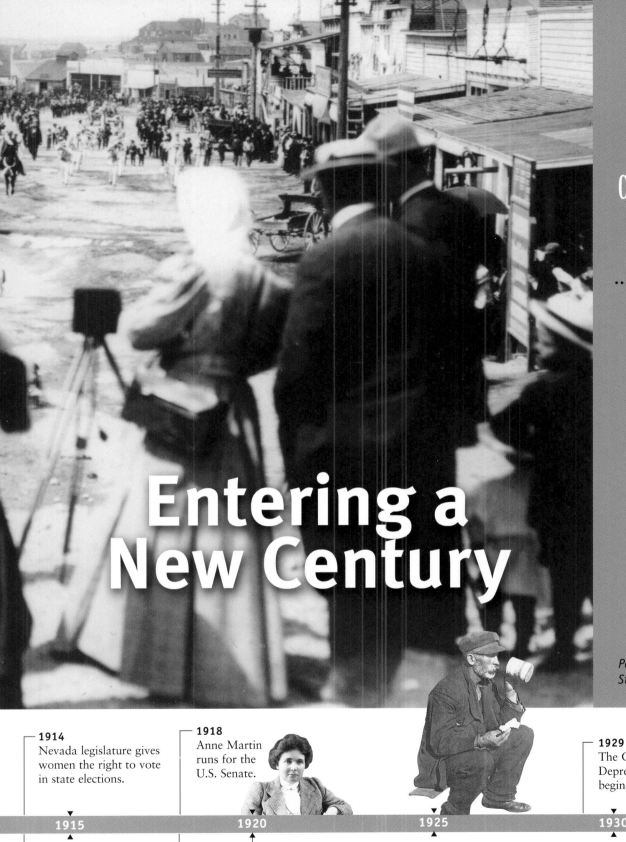

As the 20th century began, Nevada was becoming a busy place. New mining and railroad towns were springing up. Roads and other forms of transportation were also improving. Education and voting rights for women were becoming important issues.

Entering a New Century

People lined Tonopah's Main Street for this 1907 parade.

1914
Nevada legislature gives women the right to vote in state elections.

1918
Anne Martin runs for the U.S. Senate.

1929
The Great Depression begins.

1935
President Roosevelt dedicates Boulder (Hoover) Dam.

BOULD
Canyon Proje
[HOOVER
DAM
Las Vegas, Nev

1915

1920

1925

1930

1935

REMEMBER!
E FLAG OF LIBERTY
SUPPORT IT!

1914–1918
World War I
The U.S. enters the war in 1917.

1920
The 19th Amendment gives women in the United States the right to vote.

BAR
Apache
Casino
COCKTAIL LOUNGE

1931
• Gambling becomes legal.
• Six-week divorces are granted in Nevada.

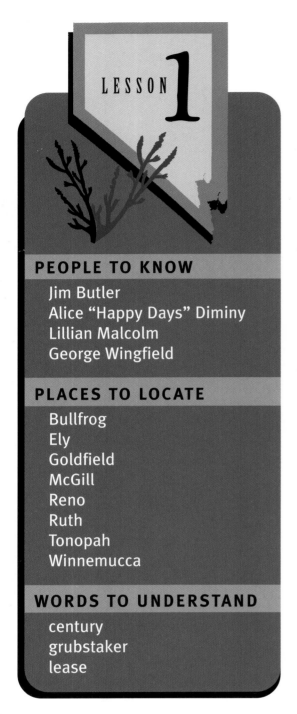

*A **century** is a period of 100 years. Do you know what century you were born in? What century do you live in now?*

Mining Moves South

By the turn of the **century,** many Nevada mines had closed. Still, a few prospectors searched the deserts looking for riches. One man, named Jim Butler, discovered an area of rich silver ore in southwestern Nevada. A new mining camp soon developed around his find. It was called Tonopah.

Butler made a great deal of money without having to do much of the work. He decided to **lease,** or rent, part of his land to other people. The people he leased to had to agree to give him part of whatever they found. They sealed their deal with nothing but a handshake. Luckily for Butler, the men he leased to kept their word.

Jim Butler was a farmer and rancher before he discovered a large vein of ore that came near the surface of the ground.

A Challenging Life

Bullfrog, Goldfield, and Rawhide were some of the other mining districts that brought new prospectors to central and southern Nevada. Many prospectors were *grubstaked* by others. Grubstakers paid for the supplies of miners in return for a share of their profits. Some of these prospectors made rich strikes in southern Nevada.

Living conditions in these small mining towns, however, were not very good. Most miners and their families lived in houses that were slapped together quickly. One woman described life in Tonopah this way:

> *The problems of housekeeping on the desert were very real. During the bitter cold winters the wind moaned and whistled through the cracks in the board-and-batten houses. In the terrific summer heat, you had to cook over a wood stove with one eye always watchful for insects....Have you ever turned suddenly to look at your baby on the floor and found a scorpion on his arm? Have you ever found a bedbug on your pillow and faced the task of getting rid of the pest? The women used to say that it was no disgrace to get bedbugs, but it was certainly a disgrace to keep them.*

Life in Nevada's early mining towns was especially difficult for women and children.

Female Prospectors

Although mining in Nevada attracted mostly men, a few daring women were there too. Lillian Malcom came to the Bullfrog mining district fresh from her adventures in Alaska. She thrilled miners with stories of dog sleds and jumping across floating sheets of ice. Sometimes she wore a skirt with boots and sometime she wore men's pants. After leaving Bullfrog, she was off to try prospecting in Death Valley.

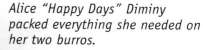

Alice "Happy Days" Diminy packed everything she needed on her two burros.

Other women tried their luck as miners in Goldfield. Alice "Happy Days" Diminy was one of them. She worked her claim alone with only two burros for company. Her husband was in Alaska searching for gold. Diminy lived in a little stone house she built by herself. She lived in Nevada for many years and planted a garden every spring.

George Wingfield
1876~1959

George Wingfield spent his early days as a cowboy, working for ranches in California, Oregon, and Nevada. He was also a gambler and owned a saloon for a while. Like so many others, he followed the rush to Tonopah when gold was discovered there.

Later, when gold was found in a place called Goldfield, Wingfield joined with a man named George Nixon. They bought many mines and banks in Goldfield. They also owned and operated a large mill that processed the ore. As time went on, the two were owners of entire city blocks. Wingfield had become a multi-millionaire by the age of 30. He became a powerful man in Nevada.

After the boom in Goldfield was over, Wingfield started a ranch and dairy farm in Fallon. He built a creamery and gave the city of Reno a piece of land for a park.

Wingfield also became involved in Nevada politics. He supported efforts to legalize gambling and quick divorce in the state. But he didn't think women should be allowed to vote.

In the end, Wingfield had big financial problems. He was no longer the powerful or popular man he had once been. He lived out the rest of his life in Reno.

Queen of the Mining Camps

It didn't take long for the small tent town of Goldfield to become Nevada's largest city. Once the word got out that rich gold deposits had been found there, thousands of people rushed to the area.

A millionaire named George Nixon sent his young partner, George Wingfield, to Goldfield to help him make even more money. Nixon and Wingfield bought the claims of many miners. Soon they were in control of most of the mines in Goldfield.

All the wealth coming out of the mines brought other mining companies to the area too. A beautiful, four-story hotel was built in Goldfield. Banks, saloons, newspapers, libraries, theatres, and churches lined the streets. The people of Goldfield also enjoyed baseball games, circus performances, and even major sporting events.

One Labor Day event brought lightweight championship boxing to Goldfield. Oscar "Battling" Nelson and Joe Gans fought for the $30,000 prize money. More than 8,000 people came to see the fight. Joe Gans was the winner.

As Goldfield grew, big labor unions were formed by the miners. Members of the Industrial Workers of the World (IWW) were sometimes called "Wobblies". There were many problems between mine owners and labor unions. After a strike broke out, Governor Sparks sent the state police to Goldfield to keep the peace.

After 10 years, Goldfield's boom began to die. Then a fire destroyed most of the town's buildings.

Autos in the Boomtowns

Tonopah and Goldfield were the first Nevada boomtowns to use automobiles. They also were some of the first towns in our state to have speed limits for cars. In Tonopah the speed limit was 4 miles per hour. In Goldfield it was 6 miles per hour. The new laws also made it clear that "vehicles drawn by horse" always had the right of way.

This 1906 photograph shows Oscar "Battling" Nelson arriving in Goldfield just before the big fight.

A Need for Roads and Highways

As Nevada's silver, gold, and copper booms came and went, so did its population of people. By the early 1900's many of those who came to Nevada came by automobile. They had to drive across the deserts because very few roads linked the new mining towns with larger cities. Some people thought trips like this were exciting. Others had a difficult and often dangerous journey.

Driving in the Desert

As travel by automobile became more popular, travel companies tried to get people to go on automobile adventures through the desert. They took out ads in the newspapers. One ad read like this:

Go automobiling in Death Valley with Alkali Bill.... Alkali Bill himself meets every train and whizzes you over the desert 45 miles by way of Death Valley and the famous Amargosa Canyon...

Soon, our government realized that better roads were needed. However, they didn't have much money to spend. There was no money to pay workers, so the government ask for volunteers to help build our roads. They also looked for new ways to earn money for road building. One way they raised money was by making a law that people needed to have drivers licenses. With the money made from these licenses, Nevada was able to begin building roads.

What do you think?

How do you think transportation has changed since the automobile was invented?

How would your life be different today if there were few roads for you to travel on?

Early automobiles had a hard time making their way through the sandy deserts of Nevada.

Copper in Nevada

Just west of Ely, two prospectors searching for gold found a strip of red metal just barely under the ground. The red metal turned out to be a large copper deposit. Soon, a new mining rush in Nevada had begun.

A little while later, the Nevada Consolidated Copper Company was formed. The company built a mill and smelter to separate the copper from the ore. A new railroad line took the ore from the mines to the smelter. As more people took jobs in the area, new towns like McGill and Ruth popped up.

The owners of Nevada Consolidated Copper also organized company towns for their workers. These towns were much nicer than most mining towns. The company towns were planned communities with many services, like reading rooms, a fire department, and a hospital. Company towns were more orderly than most Nevada mining towns and not as violent.

The copper coming out of mines in the area was used to make wires that carry electricity. Big open copper pits gave jobs to many people. Copper actually made more money for our state and its miners than all the silver from the Comstock Lode.

Not far from Ely, miners in Ruth dug large copper deposits out of big, open pits. Each pit was dug one level at a time.

Memory Master

LESSON 1

1. Who was Jim Butler? What is he famous for?
2. What is a grubstaker?
3. Which big labor union members were some times called "Wobblies"?
4. How did Nevada's government make money to help pay for building roads?
5. What was a company town?

Bringing Water to the Desert

Far away from Nevada, in Washington, D.C., President Theodore Roosevelt talked about supporting new projects in the West. Nevada's Senator Francis Newlands hoped to get *federal*, or U.S. government, money for water projects. He knew one of our state's most important needs was to bring water to the desert. He wanted people to be able to farm the western and central deserts of Nevada.

The first part of Newlands's project was to dig canals and ditches and to connect the Truckee River with the Carson River. The new U.S. reclamation service wanted to irrigate more than 400,000 acres of land. A booklet was printed to attract settlers to the area. Settlers were promised cheap land and water.

Hundreds of settlers came, but there were still many problems to overcome. During dry years, farmers couldn't get enough water to their crops. Many frustrated settlers gave up and left their farms. Others decided to stay and keep trying. In time, other water sources were developed. Finally, farmers were able to grow successful crops in the desert.

LESSON 2

PEOPLE TO KNOW

Edna C. Baker
Clara Crowell
Ann Martin
Francis Newlands
President Theodore Roosevelt

PLACES TO LOCATE

Carson River
Lahontan Dam
Rhyolite
Rye Patch Dam
Truckee River

WORDS TO UNDERSTAND

Allied forces
permanent
ration
suffrage

Many ditches and canals were dug to flood Nevada's deserts with much-needed water.

Storing the Water

Digging ditches to carry water into the desert was only one part of Newlands's plan. Another important part of the plan was to build **permanent,** or lasting ways to collect and store water. Federal money was used to build the Lahontan Dam and reservoir on the Carson River.

Reservoirs are places where large supplies of water are stored. After the reservoir was built, the town of Fallon attracted many farming families and businesses. Newland's project was one of the first federal water projects in the western United States. It helped Nevada become one of the nation's leading growers of alfalfa.

This photograph shows the Lahontan Dam just before it was completed in 1914. It was built so farmers could have enough water to get through the hot Nevada summers.

Activity

Research an Event in the 20th Century

Look at the timeline at the beginning of this chapter. It shows important events that happened during the 20th century in both the United States and Nevada. Read through the events and see which ones you already know about. Choose one event you want to know more about. What would you like to learn? Write down three questions. Then try to find the answers in books, on the Internet, or by asking family members or people in your community. Once you finish your research, you can present what you've learned in one of many ways. You can write an essay or song, make a poster, perform a skit, or give a speech to your class.

Nevada Votes for Women

Women's *suffrage,* or the right to vote, was one of our country's biggest issues in the early part of the 19th century. Many times efforts to give women the vote in Nevada failed. Finally, male voters gave Nevada women the right to vote in state elections.

It took six more years before all women in the United States could vote in national elections. Right away, women began running for important government offices. Anne Martin was one of them. She ran for a seat in the U.S. Senate twice. Even though she never won the senate seat, her work in support of women's suffrage was very successful. She became president of Nevada's suffrage group and worked with other women across the world.

Edna C. Baker was the first woman in Nevada to be elected to a state office. She was elected to be a member of the University of Nevada's Board of Regents. She also supported Nevada's suffrage movement.

Anne Martin
1875~1951

Anne Martin was a very important leader in the fight for women's rights. She was born in Empire, near Carson City. She attended a school for girls in Reno and later graduated from the University of Nevada. Her father had been a state senator.

Martin was in her 30's when she became involved in the women's suffrage movement. She even became president of Nevada's Equal Franchise Society. She drove all over the state, meeting with women and men who supported the cause.

Many people in Nevada's small mining towns supported the movement. However, people in places like Reno and Carson City did not.

Eventually, the votes of miners, ranchers, and railroad workers were enough to give women in Nevada the vote.

Martin also fought for women's suffrage across the nation and in Europe. Once, while she was in England, she was arrested for protesting.

Lady Sheriff

When George Crowell, the Lander County sheriff died, his wife Clara was selected to replace him. Clara had already proved she was well suited for the job. One night, she ran a stranger off her property when he came to her door demanding money.

After becoming sheriff, Clara chased horse thieves, bank robbers, and cattle rustlers. She broke up brawls, ran criminals out of the mountains, and demanded people respect the law.

When Clara's term was up, she went to work for the county hospital. She was the matron there for the next 20 years.

A Nation at War

Far across the Atlantic Ocean in Europe, World War I was raging. Sometimes it was called the Great War or the War to End All Wars. On one side were the countries of Germany, Austria-Hungary, and Turkey. On the other side were the *Allied forces* of Great Britain, France, Italy and Russia.

Even before the United States joined the war, many American businesses sold supplies to the Allied countries. Most Americans did not want to get involved in the war. However, the pressure for the United States to step in and help the Allied troops increased. Soon men all over the country, between the ages of 21 and 30, had to sign up for military service.

The island of Great Britain included the countries of England, Scotland, and Wales.

When WWI broke out, it was the headline in almost every newspaper.

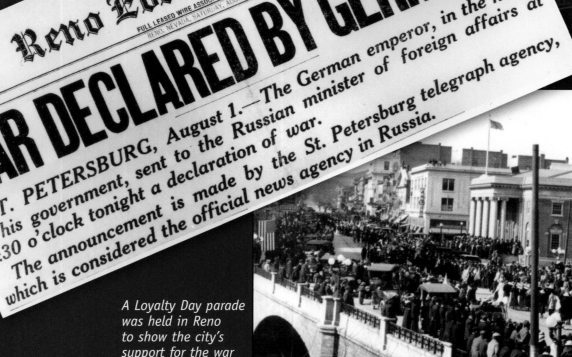

Reno Evening Gazette

FULL LEASED WIRE ASSOCIATED PRESS REPORT
RENO, NEVADA, SATURDAY, AUGUST 1, 1914

TODAY'S NEWS TODAY
Full Associated Press Service Night and Day. Clean both in news and advertisements.

WAR DECLARED BY GERMANY

ST. PETERSBURG, August 1.—The German emperor, in the name of his government, sent to the Russian minister of foreign affairs at 7:30 o'clock tonight a declaration of war. The announcement is made by the St. Petersburg telegraph agency, which is considered the official news agency in Russia.

A Loyalty Day parade was held in Reno to show the city's support for the war effort.

Everyone else, including women and children, supported the war efforts from home. Women worked as nurses, secretaries and drivers. Families tried to help by eating less food. That way, more food could be sent to those fighting overseas. This food-saving effort was called *rationing*. Americans also bought war bonds to help pay for the war.

When the war finally ended, the Allied troops had won. People celebrated, and returning soldiers marched in parades. Many fathers and brothers from Nevada fought in the war. Some of them never made it home.

Even though the war made life very difficult for a while, World War I helped our state's economy. There was an increased need for copper, silver, and lead. Because of this, mines in Nevada were busy and people had jobs.

This war poster asked Americans to buy war bonds. It was aimed at immigrants. Why would the government try to get immigrants to support liberty?

REMEMBER! THE FLAG OF LIBERTY SUPPORT IT!

BUY U.S. Government Bonds 3rd. LIBERTY LOAN

LESSON 2

Memory Master

1. What natural resource made Las Vegas a good choice for a railroad rest stop?
2. Why was the Newlands project so important for Nevada?
3. Who was arrested in England for taking part in a women's suffrage protest?
4. What is rationing? How did it help the war effort?

Healing the Wounds of War

Soon after World War I ended, new industries created more jobs. People were able to buy telephones and radios. Families in small towns got electricity for the first time. Now they had light with the flip of a switch. They could also keep their food cool in refrigerators.

Many families bought their first car during the 1920s. Owning a car gave people the freedom to go wherever they wanted. Buying a car cost about $290. Airplanes were another new invention that would bring many changes over the years.

Another thing that changed was how women dressed. They began wearing their skirts and hairstyles much shorter than before. Women that dressed in these new styles were called flappers. This period was a lively time that became known as the Roaring Twenties.

Compare the way the women in this photograph dressed with the women in the photograph at the beginning of the chapter. How have styles and fashions changed since the 1920s?

Can you guess what this funny-looking machine does? If you guessed that it played music, you guessed right! It was called a wind-up phonograph. How has modern technology changed the way we listen to music today?

Life

Let Me Entertain You

Listening to nightly radio programs was something families came together to enjoy. They loved listening to comedy acts and detective stories. They listened to the new sounds of jazz music. Another thing many people enjoyed was going to the movies. The first films were called silent movies because they didn't have sound. Sometimes theater owners hired a piano player to play music for the movie. Later, when sound was added, people called them talkies.

The Great Depression

As the end of the Roaring Twenties drew near, Nevada and the rest of the United States fell into a *depression.* A depression is a time when there isn't enough work for the people. When people can't work, they can't buy food or clothing for their families. Many families were starving. Some even lost their homes.

It was a very hard time for our country. Hundreds of businesses closed. Banks closed, and many people lost their life savings. Workers all across the country lost their jobs. This was the worst depression the United States had ever known. It was called the Great Depression.

Depression Cycle

- Factories lay off workers.
- People lose their jobs.
- People cannot buy things.
- Stores go out of business.
- Stores do not order from factories.
- Factories do not get orders.

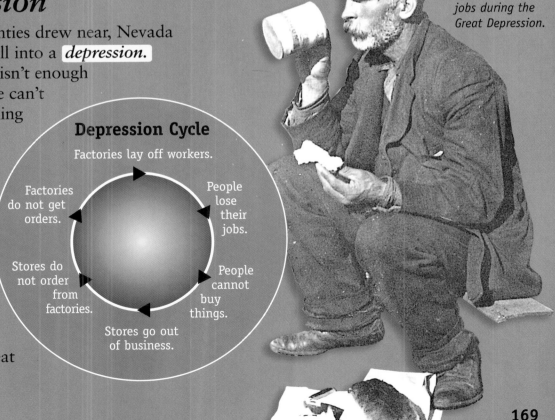

Thousands of men lost their jobs during the Great Depression.

During the depression, many people lost their jobs. The only way they could eat was to go to a soup kitchen.

Hanging On to Hope

People tried to help each other as much as they could during the depression. Soup kitchens were opened to serve meals to hungry people. Local police and firemen collected food and gave it to families who had no money. The Salvation Army, Red Cross, and many churches helped too. People began wondering if the depression would ever end. Many people thought our government should do more to help.

People in Nevada were better off than people in other parts of the country. A new project was about to help our state. The U.S. Congress approved the plans to build Hoover (Boulder) Dam. The project soon brought thousands of jobs and people to the state.

This federal employment office in Las Vegas became a busy place after the government decided to build Hoover Dam in Nevada.

Taming a River

When the Colorado River flooded the farmlands of southern California, a huge lake formed where many farms used to be. People frustrated by the problem needed help. The Southern Pacific Railroad stepped in to help get the river back on course. People wanted to prevent a flood like this from happening again.

Proposals to dam the mighty Colorado River began a few years after the flood. However, plans to build it didn't come together for almost 20 years.

There were many good reasons besides flood control to dam America's wildest river. The dam would also help slow the flow of the river, making it easier for boats to travel along it. But the biggest reason to build the dam was the millions of gallons of water that could be used to generate electricity for farms and homes in the area.

Workers Pour into Nevada

Once the construction of the dam was approved by President Coolidge, it took four years to build. Thousands of people who could not find work near their homes came to Nevada.

The first workers who came lived in nothing more than camps in the desert. McKeeversville and Ragtown were two of these early camps. The camps had rustic-looking tents, shacks, and houses.

Summer heat in the desert was over 100 degrees, and there was no air conditioning. Men, women, and children lived in very rough conditions. Later, the camps were replaced when the government built a new city.

Booklets, like this one, were designed to attract tourists to the site.

BOULDER
Canyon Project
[HOOVER]
DAM

Las Vegas, Nevada

Why do you think one of the camps was called Ragtown? Does this photograph give you a clue?

Bill Tomiyasu
1882~1969

Yonema (Bill) Tomiyasu was one of the best early farmers in all of Nevada. He grew acres and acres of fruits and vegetables. He supplied area restaurants with fresh tomatoes, melons, peppers, lettuce, asparagus, onions, carrots, and more. He also supplied food to the workers eating in the Boulder City mess halls.

Tomiyasu was born near Nagasaki, Japan. His father was a sugar cane farmer and the family was very poor.

When Tomiyasu was about 16, he left Japan and came to the United States. Later, he moved to Nevada because it was against the law for Japanese people to own land in California.

He bought 40 acres in Las Vegas and began to find the best way to grow fruits and vegetables in the hot, dusty climate.

He and his family spent all their time working in the fields. Even during World War II, when most Japanese Americans were sent to prison camps, the Tomiyasus just kept growing crops. They supplied food for the gunnery school in Las Vegas, where pilots were trained.

Tomiyasu later lost the farm because of a bad business deal. Today, there is a street in Las Vegas and an elementary school named in honor of Yonema "Bill" Tomiyasu.

Boulder City

The new city built for Hoover Dam workers was called Boulder City. It was a lot like living in the company towns that were built by Nevada mining companies. Single men lived in long buildings called **barracks.** Families were given small wooden houses to live in. Rose Lawson talked about the first houses that were built in Boulder City:

> We didn't have any plumbing; we didn't have any water. We did have electricity—one outlet in each room and a light hanging from the ceiling. … The house was built exactly like a shoebox: two rooms with a little porch…. Every house was exactly alike…. Men coming home from work—if they weren't thinking, they'd come into the wrong house.

Workers living in the city bought their goods at a company store and ate at a company mess hall. Later, there was even a public school. When workers returned too late from a weekend in Las Vegas, they often found the gates to the city closed. The city's **curfew** meant workers would sometimes have to sleep in their cars. A curfew is a set time for people to be off the streets. Workers were expected to be well rested and ready for work each morning.

Men working on Hoover Dam were fed in this dining hall that was part wood and part tent.

Hard Labor

More than 13,000 men worked to build the Hoover Dam. Some carried water, and some climbed the cliffs high above the river. Men working in the tunnels had to deal with unbearable heat. Much of the work was very dangerous, and things didn't always go well.

Many men were hurt and over 100 men died. No one had ever built a dam this big before. Building a cement wall between two steep canyon walls was an engineering marvel. Tons of steel and concrete were used to make the dam.

Today, the wall of the dam stands 726 feet high and 1,244 feet across. The highway that runs across the top of the dam connects Arizona with Nevada.

When the dam was almost finished, President Franklin Roosevelt came to Nevada to dedicate it. One of the workers said this about the president's visit:

Everybody was excited…. That was quite impressive, hearing him dedicate that dam. After that we went right back to work, moving that pipe again.

—Dean Pulsipher

Finished at Last

Six months after the dam was dedicated, it was finally complete. Today, the dam brings thousands of visitors to Nevada each year. Inside the dam, large generators pull water from the Colorado River to produce electricity. The electricity is sent to homes and businesses in Nevada, California, and Arizona. Behind the dam are the waters of Lake Mead. People go there to boat, fish, and swim.

Working as a high scaler on the walls of the canyon was a dangerous job.

Boulder or Hoover Dam?

Sometimes people get confused about whether to call it Boulder or Hoover Dam. Actually, the name has changed so many times that it's a little hard to know. At first, the planners wanted to name the dam after Boulder Canyon, where the dam would be built. Later, when the dam was moved to a different canyon, they named it Hoover Dam, after President Herbert Hoover.

Then, when Franklin Roosevelt became president, the name of the dam was changed back to Boulder Dam. But that was not the end of the name battle. The name was changed back to Hoover Dam one more time, and so it remains today.

The waters of the Colorado River back up behind Hoover Dam to form Lake Mead.

Nevada, Our Home

Nevada's New Economy

Families weren't the only ones having trouble as a result of the depression. The state was running out of money for its much-needed public projects. Building dams and reservoirs was very important, but improving and building state highways was important too. There just wasn't enough money to pay for everything Nevada needed. Soon, the state had to begin looking for new tax sources. One answer was to make gambling *legal* and then tax it. To make something legal means it's no longer against the law.

Gambling had always been a part of frontier life. Different groups tried outlawing it now and then, but people usually found ways to get around the new laws. Somewhere in Nevada, people were always betting on cards, dice, horses, or sporting events.

Building a Tourism State

Nevada became the first state in the nation to make gambling legal. In the beginning, though, it didn't seem to help the state's economy much. But soon people from California began coming to Nevada for a weekend of fun. All the money they spent on gambling was money the casinos had to pay in taxes. Gambling taxes soon began to help our state pay for things like schools, highways, health care, and other public services.

Another law Nevada passed that brought many people to our state was its new divorce law. People could get easy divorces after living here for only six weeks. Once our state started offering quick weddings, Nevada became the wedding and divorce capital of the United States.

The Apache Casino was one of the many downtown Las Vegas casinos that used an Old West theme to attract tourists.

LESSON 3

Memory Master

1. Name two new things that families enjoyed following World War I.
2. Name two things that happened to families because of the depression.
3. What river was dammed to build the Hoover Dam?
4. Where did the people who worked on the dam live before Boulder City was built?
5. Which two new laws helped build Nevada's tourism industry?

CHAPTER 8 REVIEW

Consider ★ Character

Honesty

At the beginning of this chapter, you read about a man named Jim Butler. He leased land to prospectors who promised to give him part of the gold or silver they found. Because they kept their word, these prospectors showed the trait of honesty. How important is it to be honest today? Do you keep your promises? For one week, try keeping an honesty journal. Write down when you choose to be honest and when you don't. Did you notice when others were honest or not honest? Did you find it hard to be honest? Why?

Technology 🔬 Tie-In

Taking the heat out of desert life in early Las Vegas was very difficult because of high summer temperatures. Sometimes it reached 105 degrees or more, just as it does today. Many of the early settlers lived in tents that got very hot. In those days, tents had a "fly cover", or section of cloth above the tent, that helped protect the tent from the heat of the sun.

Hoover Dam workers living in early tent towns cooled their tents at night in creative ways. They hung wet sheets in front of the doors and windows. A breeze blowing through the wet sheet helped to cool the tents. Later, when homes were built in the area, similar cooling systems were created to cool them. They were called evaporative coolers. Some homes still use them today. But for very hot climates like those in southern Nevada, most people cool their homes with air conditioning. Without it, Las Vegas may not have become the major city that it is today.

Activity

Be an Inventor!

Reread the section on mining towns, especially the report by the woman in Tonopah (Lesson One). What technology could you develop to keep insects out of the house? Remember you only have the materials available to mining towns in the early 1900s. Draw a picture, or write a description of what you would invent to keep pests out. Be creative, like the settlers who cooled their tents at night by hanging wet sheets in front of the windows!

Geography 🌍 Tie-In

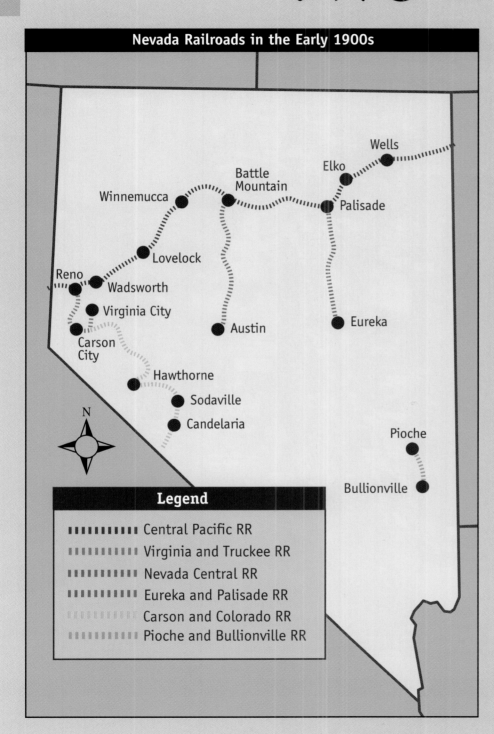

Nevada Railroads in the Early 1900s

Wells
Elko
Battle Mountain
Winnemucca
Palisade
Lovelock
Reno
Wadsworth
Virginia City
Austin
Carson City
Eureka
Hawthorne
Sodaville
Candelaria
Pioche
Bullionville

N

Legend

⦚⦚⦚⦚⦚⦚⦚ Central Pacific RR
⦚⦚⦚⦚⦚⦚⦚ Virginia and Truckee RR
⦚⦚⦚⦚⦚⦚⦚ Nevada Central RR
⦚⦚⦚⦚⦚⦚⦚ Eureka and Palisade RR
⦚⦚⦚⦚⦚⦚⦚ Carson and Colorado RR
⦚⦚⦚⦚⦚⦚⦚ Pioche and Bullionville RR

Expanding Railroads

Railroads helped our state's economy. They provided a faster, easier way for people to ship things to places around the state. Study this map of railroads in Nevada. Answer the following questions:

1. Which railroad owned the most track?
2. Which railroad had the shortest route?
3. Why were so many railroads built during this time?
4. Which railroads had the same names as the routes they traveled?
5. Which railroad traveled through Sodaville?
6. Are any of these railroads still used in Nevada today? If so, which ones?

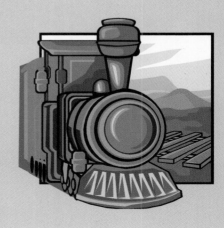

Modern Nevada

"*I will show these people [those outside Nevada] that Nevadans are like everybody else, maybe better than some other people. We are not the riffraff that they make us out to be!*"

—Governor Grant Sawyer

Timeline of Events

1930
U.S Army Munitions Depot is built in Hawthorne.

1941
• Pearl Harbor is bombed by Japan.
• Las Vegas Army Air Corps Gunnery School opens.
• El Rancho Las Vegas is first hotel built on the Strip.

1941-1945
World War II

| 1930 | 1935 | 1940 | 1945 |

1933
Adolf Hitler takes power in Germany.

1942
The town of Henderson, Nevada is created.

1945
Allied forces defeat Germany and Japan.

178

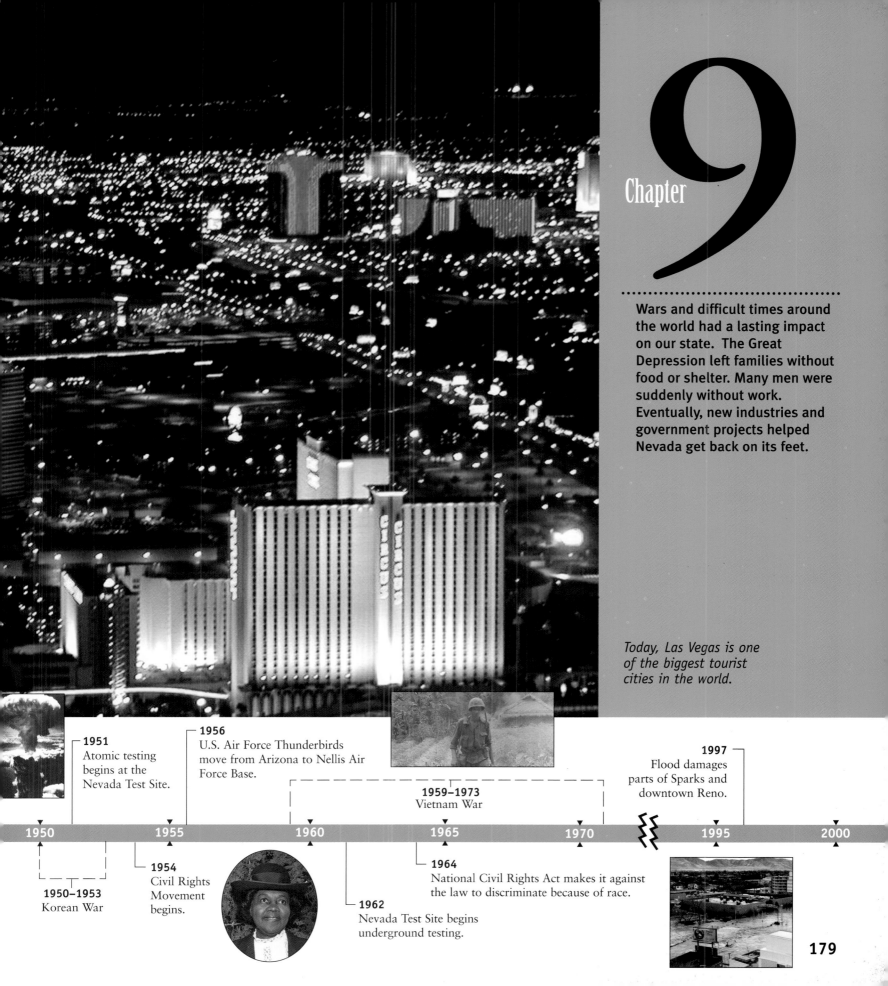

Wars and difficult times around the world had a lasting impact on our state. The Great Depression left families without food or shelter. Many men were suddenly without work. Eventually, new industries and government projects helped Nevada get back on its feet.

Today, Las Vegas is one of the biggest tourist cities in the world.

1951
Atomic testing begins at the Nevada Test Site.

1956
U.S. Air Force Thunderbirds move from Arizona to Nellis Air Force Base.

1959–1973
Vietnam War

1997
Flood damages parts of Sparks and downtown Reno.

1950   1955   1960   1965   1970   1995   2000

1950–1953
Korean War

1954
Civil Rights Movement begins.

1964
National Civil Rights Act makes it against the law to discriminate because of race.

1962
Nevada Test Site begins underground testing.

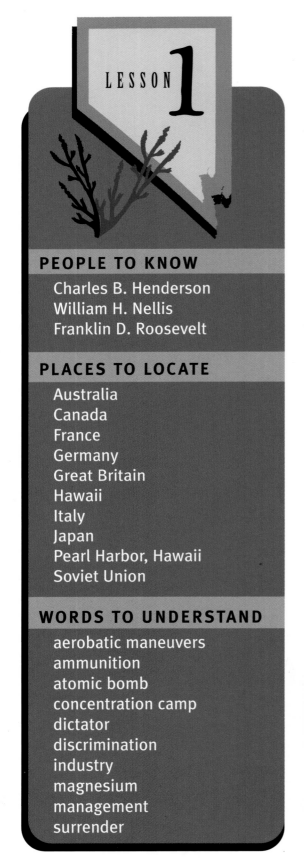

PEOPLE TO KNOW

Charles B. Henderson
William H. Nellis
Franklin D. Roosevelt

PLACES TO LOCATE

Australia
Canada
France
Germany
Great Britain
Hawaii
Italy
Japan
Pearl Harbor, Hawaii
Soviet Union

WORDS TO UNDERSTAND

aerobatic maneuvers
ammunition
atomic bomb
concentration camp
dictator
discrimination
industry
magnesium
management
surrender

Problems Around the World

While people in Nevada and the rest of United States were trying to recover from the Depression, countries in Europe were having problems too. Both Germany and Italy let *dictators* control their governments.

Soon, Germany and Italy began attacking their neighbors. The attacks turned into war. Then Japan joined the war with Germany and Italy. The three countries became known as the Axis powers. This was the beginning of World War II.

A dictator is the sole ruler of a country. Everyone must follow his orders. There is little freedom in a country ruled by a dictator.

The United States Joins World War II

At first many people in the United States didn't want to worry about the growing problems in Europe. President Franklin D. Roosevelt asked the Japanese to agree to peace. The Japanese never answered. Instead, they attacked the U.S. naval base at Pearl Harbor, Hawaii.

It began early one Sunday morning as Japanese planes flew a surprise attack. They bombed United States airplanes and battleships. More than 2,000 people were killed, and almost that many were wounded. After the attack, the United States joined the Allied forces of Great Britain, France, Canada, Australia, and the Soviet Union. Together, they fought against the Axis powers.

Pearl Harbor was attacked on December 7, 1941.

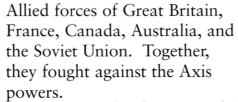

Pearl Harbor

Pacific Ocean

Pearl Harbor

Hawaiian Islands

0   200 Miles
Scale of Miles

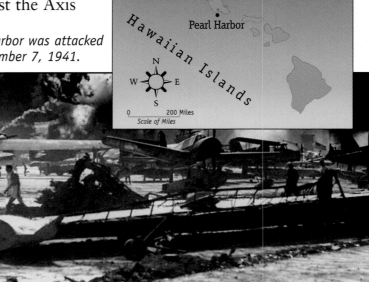

For the United States, the war began quickly. Factories hurried to make supplies. Our country needed airplanes, tanks, and bombs. Factories also made *ammunition,* such as bullets, grenades, rockets, and missiles. Millions of men and women were called to serve in the army, air force, and navy. People were training to go to war on bases all over the United States. In Nevada, there were bases where people were trained and factories where war supplies were made.

Training Pilots in Nevada

Leaders in the United States Air Force thought Nevada was a great place to build an air base. The sunny weather and cloudless skies made the conditions perfect for pilot training. An area north of Las Vegas was chosen because it was far from crowded cities. It was called the Las Vegas Army Air Corps Gunnery School.

The base was very good for southern Nevada's economy. Building the base cost more than $2.5 million and gave jobs to more than 6,000 people. It was a great success, and thousands of pilots were trained there. Later, the school's name was changed to Nellis Air Force Base in honor of Lt. William H. Nellis who was killed during the war.

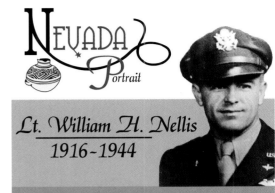

NEVADA Portrait

Lt. William H. Nellis
1916-1944

Young Bill Nellis spent most of his early life in Searchlight, Nevada. He lived with his grandmother and helped her run the local hotel. Then Nellis moved to Las Vegas to attend high school. He worked after school to pay the rent and even found time to play football. Nellis also loved to dance.

Later, he worked for a gas station in Las Vegas. He wore a crisp, white uniform and hat while he checked the oil, washed the windows, and pumped gasoline for the station's customers.

After high school graduation, Nellis got married. He and his wife moved back to Searchlight, where he worked in the mines for $5 a day.

When the war broke out, Nellis joined the air force. At the age of 24, he signed up for flight school. The day after graduation, Nellis was made an officer and was soon off to war.

As a World War II fighter pilot, Nellis was one of the oldest in his group. He flew in 70 combat missions and was shot down three times.

Two days after Christmas, his plane was hit by ground fire. It burst into flames and Nellis was unable to get out. Almost six years later, the Air Force honored him by renaming the gunnery school Nellis Air Force Base.

Many well-trained pilots graduated from the Las Vegas Army Air Corps Gunnery School.

More Bases for Nevada

Because of Nevada's wide-open spaces, the military built other types of bases in Nevada where supplies could be stored. An ammunition warehouse, or depot, was built near the town of Hawthorne. Here, the navy stored ammunition to keep it far away from enemy attacks on U.S. coastlines. These explosive supplies were also placed away from homes and people in case of an accident.

The ammunition was stored in deep holes lined with concrete. Many people in Nevada had jobs because of this project. Fallon, Tonopah, and Reno also had bases that helped bring money and jobs to Nevada towns.

The Thunderbirds

Today, Nellis Air Force Base is home to the famous Thunderbirds. These highly trained pilots perform air shows all over the world. They are especially famous for their special tricks, or **aerobatic maneuvers.**

The Thunderbirds got their name from an Indian legend. The legend said the wings of the Thunderbird made the earth tremble, and lightening shoot from its eyes.

Pilots thought Thunderbirds were a good symbol for their team. Can you guess why?

A Hawthorne Army Ammunition Depot worker takes out the inside of an old artillery shell. Sadly, the government may end up closing the base.

From Minerals to Miracle Metal

Military bases were an important part of bringing money and jobs to Nevada during World War II. But turning ore into a silvery white metal called *magnesium* was even more important for Nevada. Magnesium was used to build airplanes and bombs. The United States needed more of both when it entered the war.

Soon the government asked a company by the name of Basic Magnesium Incorporated to build a factory in the desert near Las Vegas. The factory needed large amounts of electricity to keep it running. Since Hoover Dam was close by, they could get all the electricity they needed.

Basic Magnesium was able to hire thousands of workers. In fact, there were so many workers that a town had to be built nearby. The first community built was called Basic Townsite. Later, the name of the town was changed to Henderson, in honor of Nevada's Senator Charles B. Henderson.

Many people working for Basic Magnesium chose to stay in Nevada after the plant closed.

Modern Nevada

Black Workers at Basic Magnesium Industries

Many of the workers at Basic Magnesium were African Americans. Most of them had come from southern towns in Arkansas and Louisiana. They came west to Nevada when jobs were hard to get in the South. Entire families moved to Nevada because they could earn a good living in the Henderson factories. Some brought their aunts, uncles, and cousins too. The African American population in the southern part of our state rose from just under 200 to more than 4,000 in just ten years.

Even though the African Americans were very hard workers, they were forced to live on the west side of Las Vegas. They had hoped to escape the *discrimination,* or unfair treatment, of the South. In the western parts of the United States, discrimination was usually less violent than in the South, but it still happened.

Black workers were forced to live apart from white workers. Basic Magnesium workers lived in an area called Carver Park. Homes there, however, had no running water or electricity. Dirt roads made the area hot, gloomy, and dusty. It was not a very nice place to live compared to the houses for white workers.

Conditions at Basic Magnesium were difficult for African American workers too. They were never given *management* jobs. They were also forced to use separate restrooms and washrooms from white workers.

When the war ended, many Henderson plants closed, and workers lost their jobs. Some African Americans stayed and went to work in Las Vegas hotels. Later, the state helped new companies take over the factories. The new plants began producing chemicals and other products. Before long, Henderson was a booming place for business, or *industry,* in Nevada.

This was the first African American family to move to Carver Park.

*Having a **management** job means you are one of the people in charge of running the business.*

Carver Park

DEVELOPED BY
THE HOUSING AUTHORITY OF THE
COUNTY OF CLARK · NEVADA

A VICTORY HOUSING PROJECT OF THE

FEDERAL PUBLIC HOUSING AUTHORITY

The homes built in Carver Park were one example of discrimination in Nevada.

The End of World War II

After years of fighting and millions of deaths, World War II finally ended. At last, the Germans **surrendered,** or gave up. But the war against Japan was still going on. Then the United States decided to drop an **atomic bomb** on the city of Hiroshima, Japan. When Japan didn't surrender, the United States dropped a second bomb on another city. Finally, the Japanese surrendered. World War II ended almost six years after it had begun.

The atomic bomb that finally ended World War II was dropped on the city of Nagasaki, Japan.

An **atomic bomb** is a very destructive bomb. When it explodes, it gives off an enormous amount of energy.

The Enola Gay dropped one of the bombs on Hiroshima, Japan.

THE HOLOCAUST

"...the time will come when we'll be people again and not just Jews!"

—Anne Frank,
*A Jewish girl
who died during
the Holocaust in
Europe*

One of the worst things that happened during World War II was something called the Holocaust. The German dictator, Adolf Hitler, hated Jewish people. He captured as many Jewish men, women, and children as he could find and sent them to *concentration camps.*

Most of the people in these camps were killed. Others were forced to work very hard. They were given few clothes to wear and little to eat. When the war ended, Allied soldiers freed the people still living in the camps. Many soldiers cried when they saw how the prisoners had been treated. About 6 million Jews were killed in these camps.

Linking the Past to the Present

In this lesson you've read a little bit about what it might be like to live under the rule of a dictator. Do you know of any dictators in the world today? See if you can learn more about what it might be like to live in a country where the leader is a dictator.

Jewish men in the camps were forced to live in terrible conditions.

LESSON 1

Memory Master

1. What major event happened to get the United States to join the Allied forces?
2. What is a munitions depot?
3. Name two things magnesium is used for.
4. How did the town of Henderson begin?
5. What finally brought World War II to an end?

HOTEL EL RANCHO VEGAS
"Western America's Finest"
LAS VEGAS, NEVADA

EL RANCHO
Round-Up Roo

STOP AT THE SIGN OF THE WINDMILL

The Beginning of the Strip

El Rancho Las Vegas was the first hotel and gambling resort to be built along the famous Las Vegas Strip. It was about three miles outside of town along Highway 91, on the road to California. The western motel and casino had a swimming pool, riding trails, and a few small shops. Hollywood stars often came to entertain the guests. At first, no one thought El Rancho would survive because of its location. Soon, however, the resort had actually doubled in size.

The next hotel to come on the scene was the Last Frontier Hotel. It, too, was built with the Old West in mind. Even the bar stools were made to look like saddles. Because it was built just after World War II, getting materials and supplies was very difficult. Every resource had gone to the war effort.

When the hotel first opened, it was not yet finished. Maxine Lewis, the entertainment director, said this about the hotel's very first night:

I'll never forget opening night. [All] the town's leading citizens attended, stepping over the rugs as the carpet men were putting down the last tacks. I will also never forget the crowd shaking their heads and saying it would never be a success as the hotel was too big and plushy for Las Vegas.

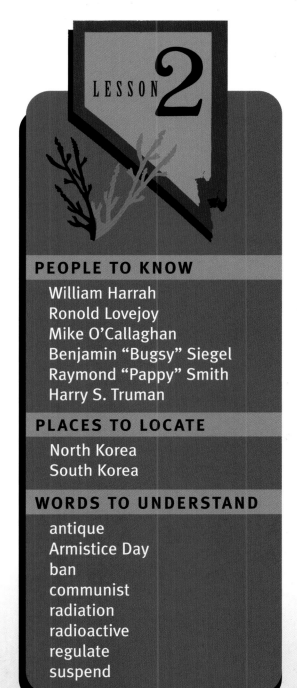

LESSON 2

PEOPLE TO KNOW

William Harrah
Ronold Lovejoy
Mike O'Callaghan
Benjamin "Bugsy" Siegel
Raymond "Pappy" Smith
Harry S. Truman

PLACES TO LOCATE

North Korea
South Korea

WORDS TO UNDERSTAND

antique
Armistice Day
ban
communist
radiation
radioactive
regulate
suspend

Gangster Casinos

Almost four years passed before another hotel joined El Rancho Vegas and the Last Frontier. The Flamingo Hotel and Casino was the third hotel to be built on the Strip. The project was started by a man named Billy Wilkerson. But it became famous because of a young New York gangster named Benjamin "Bugsy" Siegel.

By the time Siegel was 18, he had already been involved in murder, drugs, and many other lawless activities. With Siegel's help the Flamingo became a big, flashy place with lots of neon lights. It had rows of palm trees and beautiful gardens, a waterfall at the front entrance, a health club, tennis courts, and more. All that luxury cost about $6.5 million, and Siegel's gangster friends paid for it all. The hotel opening, however, did not go well. Few people in the area came. Weeks later, Siegel was murdered, and others moved in to manage the hotel.

Not long after that, other casinos with mob connections opened along the Strip. Most of them hid millions of dollars, so they wouldn't have to pay taxes. In time, Nevada governors and other officials worked hard to *regulate,* or control, this growing industry.

Siegel's Flamingo Hotel and Casino, with its bright pink sign, opened for business on December 26, 1946.

More Gambling Centers

Reno was also becoming a big gambling center. "Harolds" Club was the first modern casino in that city. The owner of the club was Raymond "Pappy" Smith. One of Smith's ideas changed the gambling business in Nevada. He put up signs all around the United States and beyond. The signs told people how many miles they needed to travel to reach "Harolds" Club in Reno. Some of the signs were in very unusual places. There were signs in Alaska and on the islands in the South Pacific. "Harolds" Club signs became famous. Some were even seen in movies.

Another way Smith brought customers to his casino was by allowing people to bet with pennies and nickels. He hoped average people would gamble too.

Harrah's Hotel and Casino was another famous gambling hotel built in Reno. Owner William Harrah started with a small bingo parlor. He was well known for running an honest game. Harrah's *antique* car collection also brought many tourists to Reno. Today, more than 150 of Harrah's antique cars can be seen in Reno's National Automobile Museum.

Lake Tahoe has become a large gambling center too. Many hotels and casinos provide tourists with year-round gaming. But just as many visitors come to the area to enjoy summer or winter activities. Some have built homes in the mountains to get away from city life. Others come to relax in the lake's crystal-clear waters. Winter activities, like skiing and snowboarding, are wildly popular as well.

Bill Harrah bought his first car at the age of 16. Over his lifetime, he restored about 1400 antique automobiles.

In the early days of Harolds Club, "Pappy" Smith gave every gambler who lost a free meal and money for a bus ride home.

These planes bombed targets in North Korea.

The Korean War

Only five years after the end of World War II, the United States went to war again. This time the war was in Korea. President Harry S. Truman and 15 other nations sent troops to help South Koreans protect themselves from invading North Koreans.

The United States didn't want to get involved in the war at first. Later, President Truman agreed to send troops to the region. The war lasted three years. More than 35,000 American soldiers lost their lives, including 34 from Nevada.

War in Vietnam

The Vietnam War, fought in Southeast Asia, was the longest war in American history. U.S. troops were sent to help the South Vietnamese protect themselves from North Vietnamese invaders. The North Vietnamese wanted everyone in Vietnam to live under a **communist** government. But the South Vietnamese wanted their own government.

Many people in America were angry when our government sent troops to Vietnam. They held protest marches and spoke out against the war. Other Americans believed our country should help other countries fight communism. More than 58,000 Americans died in the war. About 151 of them were from Nevada.

When the war finally ended, many soldiers were missing in action (MIAs). Others were held as prisoners of war (POWs). Today, there is a long, black, stone wall in Washington, D.C., that honors the Americans who died in Vietnam.

The idea behind communism is that everyone is the same. There are no poor people and no rich people. The people have all things in common. So far, however, the idea hasn't worked very well. Communist leaders have refused to follow the plan. They get rich while the rest of the people remain poor.

Nevada Soldiers

Many soldiers from Nevada fought bravely during these wars in Asia. One man who lost his leg during the Korean war later became the governor of Nevada. His name was Mike O'Callaghan. Another man, named Ronald Lovejoy, was a prisoner of war in North Korea. At a reunion many years after the war, Lovejoy told of trying to help a fellow prisoner stay alive. He said one day his friend just gave up and died.

Vietnam is a country with a hot, moist climate. Many people there were simple rice farmers before the war destroyed their land and crops.

Days of Honor

Our country has many holidays when we pause to honor someone or something special. One of these is called Veterans Day. Every year, on November 11, we honor those people who have gone to war.

In the beginning, Veterans Day was called *Armistice Day.* Armistice means to stop fighting or to declare a truce. President Woodrow Wilson named the first Armistice Day right after World War I. Later, it became known as Veterans Day.

Memorial Day is another day our country honors special people. It first began after the Civil War, when many people visited and decorated the graves of fallen soldiers.

No one is really sure how or where this tradition got started, but soon people began calling it Decoration Day. Today, it's a national holiday we call Memorial Day. It has also become a day for honoring all of our dead, not just those who died because of war.

Citizens line Las Vegas streets for this 2005 Veterans Day parade.

Modern Nevada

Bombs in Our Backyard

Nevada
Test Site
●

It was January of 1951 when the government started testing atomic bombs in the deserts of Nevada. After World War II, atomic testing had taken place in the Pacific Ocean. Then testing was moved to scientific labs closer to the United States. Government leaders hoped moving the testing closer to home, would make it cheaper and easier.

Nevada was chosen to be the site of future atomic tests for many reasons. First, the area north of Las Vegas had very few people. Good weather conditions and miles of government-owned land were also reasons Nevada was chosen. Las Vegas officials thought the test site would help bring jobs and government money to the area. They supported the government's decision to open a test site in Nevada.

Sometimes an atomic cloud was easily visible from downtown Las Vegas.

It wasn't long before the citizens of Las Vegas began to feel the ground shake and see mushroom-shaped clouds in the sky. Although strange at first, the tests soon became part of everyday life. Reporters were invited to come and watch the explosions. Businesses began advertising "Great Atomic Bomb Sales" and "atomic hairdos". Movies, like the *Amazing Colossal Man*, told make-believe stories of how *radiation* might change people and animals.

Radiation is a type of energy wave. Its effects on people and animals can range from mild sickness to death.

The Fallout

Atomic bombs that exploded at the Nevada Test Site left behind large clouds of *radioactive* dust and sand. Sometimes radioactive dust is called fallout. When a bomb went off, clouds of dust traveled east, blown by the wind. Radioactive dust blew into many of the small towns and communities in southern Utah. As it fell to the earth, radiation came in contact with animals, people, and the land.

At first, local people were told no one would be in danger from the fallout. Government officials didn't listen when people reported stories of goats turning blue. They didn't respond when farmers told them thousands of sheep died shortly after an explosion.

Years later, large numbers of people in small Utah towns began to die of cancer. These people became known as "downwinders". Today, the federal government gives money to the families of some of the people who died from cancer because of the testing.

Atomic Tests in Nevada

The *Atomic Tests in Nevada* booklet was given to people who lived near the test site. It provided them with information about atomic testing and public safety tips. Here is a small sample of what was inside:

You people who live near Nevada Test Site are in a very real sense active participants in the Nation's atomic test program. You have been close observers of tests which have [helped] greatly to building the defenses of our country and of the free world.

ATOMIC TESTS IN NEVADA

BULLETIN
ATOMIC TEST
SHOT SCHEDULED
FOR 5 AM
TOMORROW

Every Test Is Evaluated

The End of Testing

A little more than 10 years after atomic testing began, governments across the world voted to *ban,* or outlaw, above ground testing. For the next 30 years, explosions at the Nevada Test Site were done in underground shafts and tunnels. Not until 1992 was all testing *suspended,* or stopped. By then, over 900 atomic tests had taken place at the site.

Memory Master

LESSON 2

1. What did gangster casino owners do that prompted government officials to begin regulating the industry?
2. How did Raymond "Pappy" Smith attract all kinds of gamblers to his casino?
3. Decoration Day later became which national holiday?
4. What is radiation? How does it affect people, land, and animals?

A Diverse State

Since the early mining days of Nevada, many different cultures, or ethnic groups, have settled in our state. Virginia City and other Nevada mining towns were settled by people from England, Wales, Germany, Ireland, Mexico, Spain, Italy, and many other countries of the world. A *diverse* place includes people from many different countries and cultures.

Some of these people were accepted by those already living here, but many others were not. For example, after World War II, it was difficult for Americans to trust Japanese people. That was because of the Japanese attack on Pearl Harbor. Not even those Japanese people born and raised in the United States were safe from *prejudice.* Prejudice is judging people based on their race, religion, whether they are male or female, or whether they are rich or poor.

Kay Fujii ▶

When Pearl Harbor, Hawaii was attacked, Japanese Americans were treated very poorly by our government and other Americans. The Fujii family of Reno, Nevada had their home searched by the FBI. The family camera, radio, and other things were taken from them. Kay Fujii, who owned a gardening business in the area, was sent to jail. Bud Fujii, who was nine, had to protect himself from attacks by students and words of hatred from his teachers.

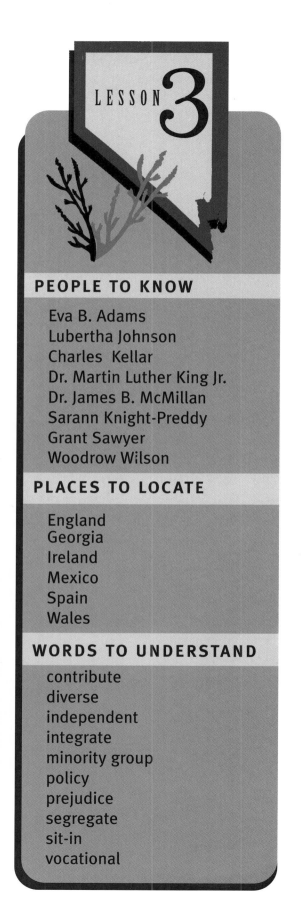

LESSON 3

PEOPLE TO KNOW

Eva B. Adams
Lubertha Johnson
Charles Kellar
Dr. Martin Luther King Jr.
Dr. James B. McMillan
Sarann Knight-Preddy
Grant Sawyer
Woodrow Wilson

PLACES TO LOCATE

England
Georgia
Ireland
Mexico
Spain
Wales

WORDS TO UNDERSTAND

contribute
diverse
independent
integrate
minority group
policy
prejudice
segregate
sit-in
vocational

The Civil Rights Movement

Even though many good things were happening around the country, minority groups had a hard time getting good jobs. There were other problems too. Hotels, theaters, and restaurants were segregated. Segregation separated white people from black people. Cities and neighborhoods were segregated too. So were schools, hospitals, and swimming pools. Many people wanted to change this in Nevada and around the United States. African Americans began to work together to make changes. They wrote letters and talked to leaders. They wanted new laws that would stop segregation and discrimination. They wanted better jobs and fair and equal treatment

Minority groups are those whose race or religion is different from most of the people in the region.

What is written on this coke machine that you would not see today?

Dr. Martin Luther King Jr.

Dr. Martin Luther King Jr. was a minister in Georgia. He worked hard to end segregation, especially in southern states. He led peaceful marches and protests. He reminded everyone that our nation was built on the belief

that "all men are created equal." Dr. King spoke in cities all across the country. Both black and white people joined in his marches. Over 200,000 people took part in a march in our nation's capital. Dr. King gave his famous "I Have a Dream" speech there. He told people that only a person's character should count, not his or her color. Sadly, a few years later, Dr. King was murdered. But his death didn't stop the struggle for civil rights. Others across the nation worked hard to continue the fight.

Civil Rights in Nevada

After Basic Magnesium Inc. closed its doors, most African American families got only low-paying service jobs at hotels and casinos. Casinos didn't let African Americans gamble, eat, or attend shows. They couldn't even watch black entertainers.

In fact, African American entertainers weren't allowed to stay in the hotels they performed in. After their shows were over, they were quickly asked to leave. They were told to look for lodging in black boarding houses on the west side of town.

The Moulin Rouge

The Moulin Rouge was the first *integrated* hotel in Las Vegas. This meant that it was open to both blacks and whites. Black entertainers not only performed there, they were also allowed to gamble and stay the night. Many white entertainers, after their own shows were over, came to the Moulin Rouge to gamble with their black friends.

The Moulin Rouge was also the first to hire black workers to do more than clean rooms and wash dishes. They hired a black hotel manager. They also hired black dealers, chorus girls, waitresses, and hosts. However, the hotel stayed open only about six months. Years later, it opened and closed again and again under many different owners.

In 1960, another historic civil rights event took place at the Moulin Rouge. A meeting was held to talk about changing the segregation policy of Las Vegas hotels and casinos. It came about because a large group of African Americans had decided to hold a peaceful protest along Las Vegas Boulevard. They wanted hotel owners to know they were against hotel and casino segregation. They promised to hold a protest march along the street if something wasn't done to change the *policy,* or rule. The group also promised to invite lots of newspaper reporters.

But the march never took place. State and local officials got together with African American leaders and hotel and casino owners. They worked out an agreement that would finally put an end to hotel and casino segregation in Las Vegas.

Listen to a Speech

Search the Internet, library, or reference books to find a copy of Martin Luther King's "I Have a Dream" speech. See if you can find a recording of the speech. If you can't find a recording, have the people in your class read the speech out loud. Listen to the words of the speech. As a class, talk about what the words mean. How does the speech make you feel about civil rights?

Dr. James McMillan, the mayor, and other important members of the Las Vegas community were present at this historic meeting.

This protest was held in Carson City in 1961.

---

*A **sit-in** was something protesters did to try to change things. They sat peacefully in a public place and refused to leave until they were treated fairly.*

More Work to Do

Gaining civil rights for African Americans was a slow process. Government officials in Nevada were slow to create laws against discrimination. Black citizens in Carson City marched on the state capitol in protest. In Reno, they held peaceful **sit-ins.**

Finally, in 1964, the United States passed The Civil Rights Act. This made it against the law to discriminate against people based on their race or color. Still, problems continued, especially in Nevada schools. Black children were bused into white schools and neighborhoods. Fights broke out in many junior highs and high schools. Things didn't improve much until more laws were passed to stop discrimination.

Nevada, Our Home

Civil Rights Leaders in Nevada

Many African American leaders have had important roles in the fight for civil rights in Nevada. **James B. McMillan,** the first African American dentist in Nevada, was one of them. When he first came to Las Vegas, all African Americans were forced to live and work on the west side of the city. He asked black Nevadans to join together in a peaceful protest against Las Vegas hotels and casinos. He helped bring about the Moulin Rouge Agreement. His efforts and those of many others made it possible for blacks to get better jobs in hotels and casinos.

Woodrow Wilson was also involved in Nevada civil rights issues. Wilson became Nevada's first black legislator. He helped push Nevada to adopt fair housing laws. He helped pass laws that required black workers be treated fairly on the job. He also made it possible for Nevada's African Americans to receive better *vocational,* or work-related, training.

Lubertha Johnson was already well educated when she came to Nevada. She helped fight discrimination in our schools, theaters, hospitals, and housing. She also worked hard to help stamp out poverty in Las Vegas.

Charles Kellar was probably the first African American lawyer to move to southern Nevada. He did not receive a warm welcome when he arrived. He fought hard to make it possible for black lawyers to practice law in Nevada. He fought against many unwritten policies of discrimination in other areas too. Kellar helped our state stamp out segregation in the schools and in housing.

Grant Sawyer, our state's 21st governor, was one of many white Nevadans to fight for civil rights. Sawyer believed in civil rights for all African Americans. He was the first Nevada governor to hire minorities for state jobs. He helped African American leaders and casino owners work out the Moulin Rouge Agreement.

Sawyer fought for what he believed in, even when it made him unpopular.

Other Groups Fight for Rights

Other groups of people in Nevada worked for fair and equal treatment too. Asian, Hispanic, and Native Americans had trouble getting good jobs. All these groups have worked to bring about important changes.

Many organized groups have helped Nevada's Native Americans become more *independent,* or self-sufficient. They have been encouraged to become more involved in state politics. All of Nevada's minority groups play an important part in improving our state. Each group has something to *contribute,* or give.

The Women's Movement

Minority groups weren't the only ones working for equal rights. Women were also looking for equal treatment. Many wanted to continue working outside the home like they had during World War II. They wanted better paying jobs. Women wanted more opportunities for education. They wanted jobs that in the past had only been given to men.

Women in southern Nevada wanted good jobs in casinos. They wanted to be able to work as dealers, like women in Reno and Lake Tahoe were doing. They wanted to be paid like men were. Women across the state fought for equal pay and to change state laws.

They also began running for government offices and starting their own businesses. Eva B. Adams became the director of the U.S. Mint in Nevada. Sarann Knight-Preddy was the first African American and first woman in the state to have a gaming license.

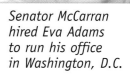

Senator McCarran hired Eva Adams to run his office in Washington, D.C.

Linking the Past to the Present

Because of the hard work by minority groups and others, we now have laws to protect the rights of different types of people. Laws are important, but they do not always make people think differently. Change usually happens slowly, and there is still much work to be done. How can you help?

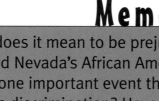

Memory Master

LESSON 3

1. What does it mean to be prejudiced?
2. Why did Nevada's African Americans fight against segregation?
3. Name one important event that happened at the Moulin Rouge in Las Vegas.
4. What is discrimination? Have you ever experienced it?
5. Pick one person from this chapter, and write down what they did to help the fight for civil or equal rights.

Modern Immigrants

During the 19th century, many immigrants came to live in Nevada. The same is true today. There are groups living in our state from India, Russia, Thailand, Ethiopia, Tonga, Israel, Greece, Puerto Rico, Argentina, and many other countries.

These immigrants bring to Nevada a rich cultural heritage. To celebrate these diverse traditions, Folklife Festivals are held around the state. They feature dancing and ethnic foods. They showcase many traditional arts and crafts, such as Hawaiian lei making and cowboy or Navajo silversmithing. They share unique customs, such as Polish papercutting, Ukrainian Easter egg making, and the Chinese lion dance.

Some immigrants have opened restaurants or other small businesses in our state. Many have also become American citizens.

LESSON 4

PLACES TO LOCATE
Sparks
Truckee River
Yucca Mountain

WORDS TO UNDERSTAND
decade
mercury
microscopic
nuclear waste
tungsten

Reno's Cinco de Mayo celebration is a popular cultural event. Today, Hispanics are Nevada's fastest growing ethnic group.

Nevada Civil Rights Calendar of Events

January	Martin Luther King Jr.'s Birthday
February	Black History Month
March	Women's History Month
April	Take Our Children to Work Day
May	Asian Pacific American Month
	Cinco de Mayo (May 5)
June	Gay Pride Month
August	Women's Equality Day (August 26)
September	Hispanic Heritage Month
	(September 15 - October 15)
October	Disability Employment Awareness Month
November	Native American Heritage Month
	Veterans Day

Newmont Mining Corporation operates this open-pit mine in Twin Creeks, Nevada

Nearing the End of the Century

Nevada continued to grow and develop during the last few **decades** of the 20th century. The state's rapid growth came with many problems and challenges too. Mining, water, industry, and storing nuclear waste were all important issues.

*A **decade** is a period of ten years.*

Return of the Mining Boom

Mining has been an important part of Nevada since its beginning. In fact, you may remember that one of our state nicknames is the Silver State. New mining methods during the last half of the 20th century helped mining in Nevada boom once again.

For over 30 years copper was the most valuable metal mined in Nevada. It brought many people and jobs to our state. Later, new discoveries of *microscopic* gold were found near Elko. These goldfields have also had a positive impact on our state. Some people claim these gold deposits are the richest in the Western Hemisphere. Most of them are located close together along a 50-mile strip of land known as the Carlin Trend.

Other Nevada mines are some of the nation's leading producers of *mercury* and *tungsten.* Cement, gypsum, lime, salt, sand, and gravel are a few of the important nonmetals Nevada produces.

__Microscopic__ gold is too small for your eyes to see. It can only be seen using a microscope. __Mercury__ is a silvery metallic element used in batteries and thermometers. __Tungsten__ is a hard, brittle element that handles high temperatures. Its most common use is in electrical equipment.

Golden Nevada

Gold is a very important mineral to Nevada. The mines in our state produce more gold than any other state in the nation. The gold coming from Nevada also makes the United States the second largest producer of gold in the world. Only South Africa produces more.

Nevada, Our Home

Water Resources for Nevada

The need for water has always been an important part of life in Nevada. As more people began moving to the southern part of our state, new water resources had to be found. The government began to think about pulling Colorado River water out of Lake Mead. It would have to be piped into Las Vegas.

Once the project began, it took about 10 years to complete. Today, the project is part of the Southern Nevada Water System. It includes six pumping stations, a reservoir, a 4-mile tunnel, and 31 miles of pipe. This new water system made it possible for the area to support more people than ever before.

Managing a River

The Truckee River is another important water resource for our state. It provides irrigation for farmlands. It feeds livestock and is also used for recreation and industrial supply. The Truckee runs from Lake Tahoe, through parts of California, Reno, and Sparks, and into Pyramid Lake.

Heavy rains have caused the Truckee to run over its banks now and then. The last big flood was in 1997. Seven inches of rainfall near Lake Tahoe caused mudslides and the worst floods in over 30 years. Hundreds of businesses were hit, and thousands of people were out of work.

Since then, state officials and many citizens have worked to find ways to prevent future floods. The Truckee River Whitewater Park has improved water flow. It has also provided new opportunities for recreation.

Governor Mike O'Callaghan and others watch the first water flowing from Lake Mead in 1971.

Photo by Peter Goin

The heavy rains of 1997 flooded much of downtown Reno.

This photo shows members of the Northern Nevada Development Authority touring the Yucca Mountain Project.

What do you think?

Why do you think Yucca Mountain was chosen as a spot for nuclear waste? What do you think should be done with nuclear waste?

Yucca Mountain

For almost 20 years, the U.S. government has wanted to store **nuclear waste** at Nevada's Yucca Mountain. Nuclear waste is the material that is left over after nuclear energy is made. Most of the people in our state don't want radioactive material stored here. They believe it's too dangerous.

The government has spent millions of dollars to get Yucca Mountain ready for shipments. If the site is approved, steel cans of nuclear waste will be shipped starting in 2010. The waste is harmful to humans, so it would have to be moved by machines. State officials and thousands of citizens are fighting to keep Yucca Mountain from becoming a nuclear waste dump.

The designs for Caesars Palace follow an ancient Roman theme.

Theme Resorts

As things all over Nevada changed, so did hotels and casinos on the Las Vegas Strip. Hotel owners spent more and more money. Each hotel promised to be bigger and more beautiful than those built before.

Caesars Palace was one of the first luxury resorts built with a theme in mind. It was copied from the designs of ancient Rome. Huge stone pillars line the walkways. Graceful statues shoot streams of water into the air. The Olympic-sized pool is lined with marble tiles from Italy. Caesars was also the first to add many shops alongside the hotel. Hundreds of top entertainers have performed there. Caesars has also hosted many important sporting events.

Since that time, hotels and casinos along the Strip just keep getting bigger and more expensive. The Mirage caught the eye of visitors by bringing in tigers, sharks, and huge aquariums. Treasure Island has an outdoor pirate show for guests and people passing by. Circus Circus, the Bellagio, New York-New York, the Luxor, Excaliber, the Stratosphere, and the MGM Grand are just a few of the other theme hotels on the Strip. In fact, the 10 largest hotels in the world are all located in Las Vegas.

LESSON 4 — Memory Master

1. Name three immigrant groups that live in Nevada today.
2. Which ethnic group is the fastest growing group in our state?
3. What is a decade?
4. Why did the government pull Colorado River water out of Lake Mead?
5. What is nuclear waste? Why doesn't our state want to store it?

Consider ★ Character

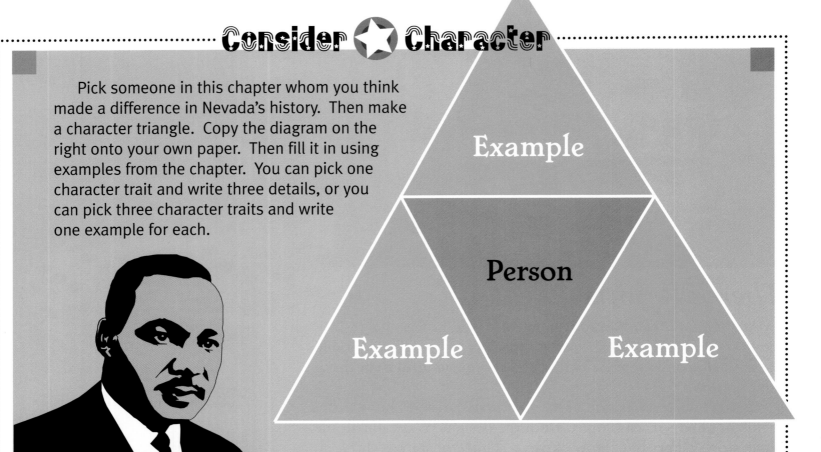

Pick someone in this chapter whom you think made a difference in Nevada's history. Then make a character triangle. Copy the diagram on the right onto your own paper. Then fill it in using examples from the chapter. You can pick one character trait and write three details, or you can pick three character traits and write one example for each.

Example

Person

Example   Example

Technology 🔬 Tie-In

How important is technology in war? How does war affect technology? How does war affect the technology industry? To answer these questions, compare war weapons from World War II, Korea and Vietnam. An interesting comparison would be to research aircraft used in these wars. Use the pictures in this chapter as well as other sources, like the encyclopedia. Then discuss with your class how technology changes and how it affects the results of war.

Locate the biggest map of the world in your classroom. A wall map or globe will work best. Send one person at a time up to the map. Then have the teacher or another student read off the "Places to Locate" lists from Lessons 1–3. Have the student at the map locate one place from the list. Then have another student take a turn. Keep going until each student has had a turn or all the places have been located on the map or globe. Were the students near the end of the list faster than those at the beginning of the list?

Activity

New Ideas Make Life Better

Imagine what your life would be like today if there were no airplanes, telephones, automobiles, or electric lights. Important inventions like these make our lives better and easier in many ways. Read through the following list of important inventions and the people who invented them:

- A Scottish immigrant by the name of Alexander Graham Bell invented the telephone.
- Thomas Edison was the inventor of the electric light bulb.
- The Wright brothers, Orville and Wilbur, were the first to fly a powered airplane.
- An industrial-strength rubber for tires was accidentally created by Charles Goodyear.
- An engineer named Thomas Moore was the first to name his invention the refrigerator, or ice box.
- Stuart Cramer called his new climate control invention air conditioning.

Choose one invention from the list. On a separate piece of paper, write five ways your life would be different without the invention. For example, "If there were no automobiles, I would have to find another way to get to soccer practice. I could walk, ride my scooter, take my skateboard, run, ride a horse, or miss practice."

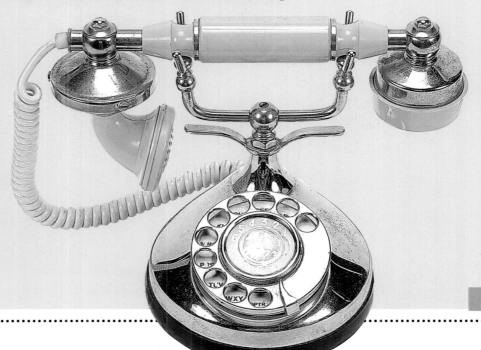

"*I think it's good that we get a chance to choose our leaders instead of just being told who they are.*"

—*Sarah Hatch,*
a fourth grader

10

It wasn't long after our country became a new nation that the people created a standard for government. The Constitution of the United States gave the power of government to the people. Today, it still gives people the power to elect their national, state, and local governments. In Nevada, we can elect those who we think will serve best. We can decide how we want to use our resources to meet the needs of our people.

Governing Nevada

Nevada's capitol building, in Carson City, is one of the oldest capitol buildings west of the Mississippi.

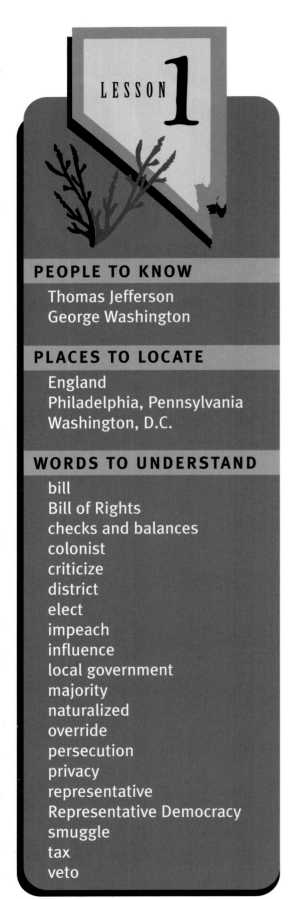

PEOPLE TO KNOW

Thomas Jefferson
George Washington

PLACES TO LOCATE

England
Philadelphia, Pennsylvania
Washington, D.C.

WORDS TO UNDERSTAND

bill
Bill of Rights
checks and balances
colonist
criticize
district
elect
impeach
influence
local government
majority
naturalized
override
persecution
privacy
representative
Representative Democracy
smuggle
tax
veto

Birth of a Nation

More than 100 years after Columbus discovered the New World, *colonists* began settling the eastern coast of America. Many came to the new land to escape religious or political *persecution.* Persecution is when people cause others to suffer because of their beliefs. Colonists came from all over Europe and England. By 1733, England had 13 colonies along the eastern coast of North America. But the people in the colonies were unhappy with the King of England. They thought his laws and rules were unfair. They wanted to form a new and independent nation.

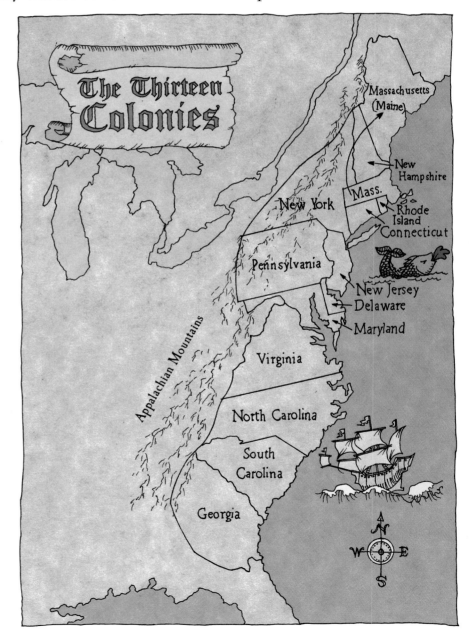

The Thirteen Colonies

The Declaration of Independence

Men from the 13 colonies got together to write a statement to the world. They listed all the unfair things the king had done. They wrote about how the king had taken away some of their rights. They called this document the Declaration of Independence. Here is a list of other things the colonists wrote about:

- All people are equal.
- All people are born with basic rights.
- Governments exist to protect these rights.
- Government power comes from the people.

England and the colonies went to war over these problems. It was called the Revolutionary War. George Washington was the leader of the American soldiers. The fighting lasted almost six years. When the war finally ended, the colonies were free to make their own laws and rules. They formed the government of the United States of America.

People in England are sometimes called British.

Thomas Jefferson was the main author of the Declaration of Independence, but many men helped. Today, its famous words are engraved in stone on a wall of the Jefferson Memorial in our nation's capital.

Taxing the Colonists

The colonists became angry when England began raising their **_taxes._** A tax is money collected by the government. It helps pay for things like government workers, the army, and the police. England thought the colonists should help pay for these things and more. In the Declaration of Independence, the colonists said they did not like being taxed without their consent. Here are a few of the taxes the colonists were forced to pay:

- The **Sugar Act** taxed sugar and molasses. Colonists used sugar in their tea and molasses for baking.
- The **Stamp Act** forced colonists to buy stamps and place one on every piece of paper they read or used. Letters, newspapers, and even playing cards had to have stamps.
- The **Townsend Acts** were taxes on glass, tea, paper, and paint. After the colonists rebelled against them, England dropped all of the taxes except the one on tea. To rebel against something means to refuse to do it.
- The **Tea Act** taxed British tea. It also said colonists could not buy tea from other countries. The colonists were very unhappy, so they **_smuggled_** tea from France and Spain. To smuggle means to bring goods into a place even though it is against the law.

Government for a New Nation

After the United States became a new country, Americans had a very big job to do. They needed to create a government. They didn't want a king or queen. They wanted to be able to choose their government leaders. Important men from each state met in Philadelphia, Pennsylvania. Sometimes we call these men our nation's Founding Fathers. They talked about the kind of government the United States should have. They wrote our country's constitution.

The words of the Constitution are still the basis for our government today. What do the first three words say? What clues do they give you about our government?

A constitution is a set of rules and ideas for the government. It is the basic law of the land. It tells us how good government should work. Our Founding Fathers wanted to be sure that no one group would have all the power. One of the ways they did this was by dividing the government into different levels and branches.

Levels of Government

There are three different levels of government in the United States. Each level of government has a different job. **Local government** is the government that directs things closest to home. State government is responsible for things all around the state. National government is sometimes called the federal government. It directs things for the whole United States. Take a look at the chart below to see examples of the different jobs for each level.

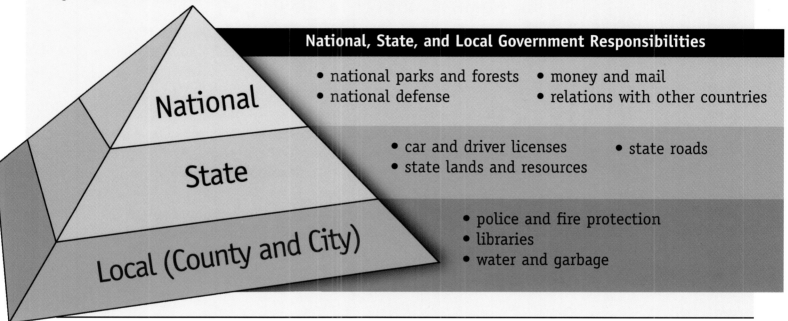

National, State, and Local Government Responsibilities

National
- national parks and forests
- national defense
- money and mail
- relations with other countries

State
- car and driver licenses
- state lands and resources
- state roads

Local (County and City)
- police and fire protection
- libraries
- water and garbage

Branches of Government

The Constitution gives power to three branches of government. Each branch has duties and powers of its own. Each branch also shares powers with the other branches. This way one branch cannot become too powerful or make laws alone. This is called the system of **checks and balances.** Let's learn a little more about the duties and powers of these branches.

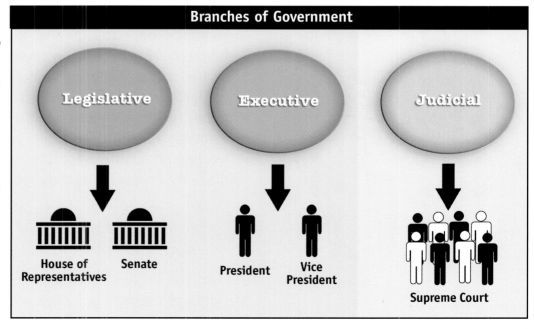

Branches of Government

Legislative
House of Representatives   Senate

Executive
President   Vice President

Judicial
Supreme Court

Our Legislative Branch

The legislative branch of our government is responsible for making the laws. The men and women who serve in this branch research, write, and talk about laws. They are our *representatives.* Each of the 50 states sends its representatives to Washington, D.C., to make laws for the whole country. They serve in Congress.

Representatives of the People

The government of the United States is what we call a *representative democracy.* Democracy means the people rule by vote of the *majority,* or the greatest number of votes.

A representative democracy works a lot like picking one person from your class to go to your school's student council meetings. The person you select represents the whole class. He or she takes your class's ideas and concerns and shares them with other council members. Then all the representatives vote for things that concern the whole school.

In government and at school, when representatives don't vote the way you would vote, you can choose someone else the next time. In this way, the government gets its power from the people.

This is the United States capitol, located in Washington, D.C.

What do you think?

Imagine that more than half of the students in your school want to start school at 7:00 a.m. instead of 8:00 a.m. Do you think it's fair to make everyone go to school an hour earlier? What happens to the rights of those who don't want to go to school an hour earlier? Because there are not as many of them, they represent the minority. What rights does the minority have when choices are made by a majority rule? Do you think our founding fathers worried about this important question? Think about this statement made by President Thomas Jefferson:

> *All ...will bear in mind ...that though the will of the majority is in all cases to prevail [win] ... the minority possess [have] their equal rights, which equal law must protect ...*

Can you think of examples in our state or in our nation when the rights of the minority have not been protected? In what ways are you part of a minority?

The president of the United States gives his State of the Union address to the nation and the members of Congress.

States Send a Voice to Congress

Each state elects senators and congressmen to serve in Congress. Both the Senate and the House of Representatives are parts of Congress. Senators serve in the Senate and represent the needs of their entire state. Congressmen, or representatives as they are often called, serve in the House of Representatives. They speak for the interests of certain *districts* within their state. A district is a small group of people that live close to one another. The House of Representatives is sometimes called "the people's house".

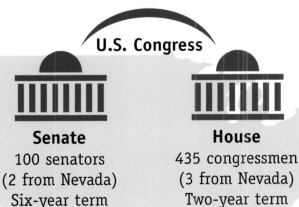

U.S. Congress

Senate
100 senators
(2 from Nevada)
Six-year term

House
435 congressmen
(3 from Nevada)
Two-year term

The Senate

- The Senate has 100 members.
- Each state elects two senators.
- Senators serve for six years, which is one term. They can also serve more than one term if reelected by the people.
- Senators must be at least 30 years of age.

House of Representatives

- The House of Representatives has 435 members.
- The number of congressmen from each state is based on the state's population. This means larger states, like California and Texas, elect more congressmen. Each state elects at least two. For example, Nevada has three members of the House of Representatives while California has 53.
- Congressmen serve for a 2-year term. They, too, can serve longer when reelected.
- Congressmen must be at least 25 years of age.

Both senators and congressmen must have been U.S. citizens for at least seven years. They must also live in the state they represent. In Nevada, we elect two senators and three congressmen to serve in Congress.

(Left to right) Senator Harry Reid, Congressman John Ensign, Congressman Jim Gibbons, Senator Jon C. Porter, Congresswoman Shelley Berkley.

······· Activity ·······

Get Involved!

These people are your senators and congressmen. Go to **www.congress.org.** to learn more about these representatives. While you are there, see if you can also learn which state sends the most representatives to Congress. Which state sends the fewest?

As a class, talk about questions you would like to ask your representatives. Is there something important you would like them to do for Nevada or for the nation?

Write a letter or send an e-mail to your representatives.

Impeach *means to be accused of doing something wrong.*

Congressional Powers

Making laws isn't the only thing Congress does. The U.S. Constitution gives Congress power to:

- Pass tax laws
- Approve the printing of money
- Send the country to war
- Set the nation's budget
- Borrow money for the nation

Each part of Congress also has things only it can do. For example, only the House of Representatives can *impeach* our president. Only the Senate can remove the president from office.

The president of the United States and his family live in the White House.

Our Executive Branch

The executive branch of our government is in charge of making sure laws are obeyed. The president of the United States is the head of this branch. Because this branch is so large, the president has lots of help from the vice president and others.

Some of the president's other duties are to meet with governments from other countries, head the military, and approve *bills* from Congress. A bill is a written idea for a law. If the president likes a bill, he can sign it and make it a law. If he doesn't like a bill, he can *veto,* or reject, it.

The president of the United States is elected for one term, which is four years. If re-elected, the president can serve no more than two terms or eight years. The president must also be a born in the United States and have lived in the country for at least 14 years. He or she must be at least 35 years of age.

When a bill is vetoed, it goes back to Congress. Congress then chooses to rewrite the bill, drop it completely, or vote against the president's veto. To pass a bill the president has vetoed, two-thirds of Congress most vote to **override,** *or go against, the president's veto.*

A natural-born citizen of the United States is someone who was born in this country. A **naturalized** *citizen of the United States takes a test to become a citizen after moving here from another country.*

Our Judicial Branch

The courts of the United States are part of our judicial branch of government. They decide what laws mean and what the punishments should be for people who break the law. They try to settle problems in a peaceful way. They make sure our laws are in line with the Constitution and the *Bill of Rights.*

The Supreme Court

The Supreme Court is the highest federal court in our nation. Once a decision is made in the Supreme Court, no other court in the country has the power to change it or reverse it. The court is made up of one chief justice and eight associate justices. It is the only court that was created by the U.S. Constitution. All other federal courts were created by Congress.

Judge and Jury

A judge and jury are also important parts of our judicial system. Judges serve at all levels of government and in different types of courts. There are county judges, juvenile judges, federal judges, district judges, and many more.

A judge's duties include directing courts of law, listening to testimony, instructing juries, and informing citizens of their rights. Sometimes judges question witnesses, do research, and even perform marriages. Most judges are lawyers too. State and local judges are elected to the court. Federal judges are selected by the president.

A jury is a group of people chosen to decide what is true in a court. Serving on a jury is something citizens are asked to do. They must be able to give fair and equal treatment to all kinds of people. They must also follow the law when making their final decisions. Serving as a jury member is an important part of being a responsible citizen. Jury members must be at least 18 years of age.

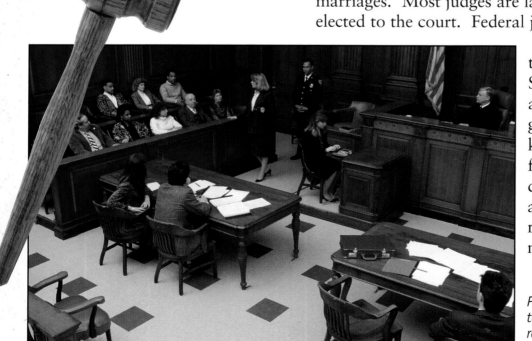

Many of the walls and floors of the United States Supreme Court are made of lightly colored marble.

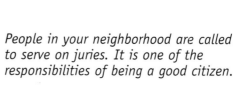

People in your neighborhood are called to serve on juries. It is one of the responsibilities of being a good citizen.

The Bill of Rights

Like the Constitution, the Bill of Rights is another important document for our country. It protects the rights of the people. It states that our government cannot make laws that take away our basic freedoms. Some of those rights include the freedoms of speech and religion. The Bill of Rights is made up of 10 amendments. These laws are additions to our Constitution.

After the Bill of Rights was created, other important amendments were added to the Constitution. The 13th Amendment ended slavery in our country. The 14th Amendment gave people protection under the law. The 18th Amendment changed the voting age from 21 to 18. Are there other amendments you remember reading about?

1st Amendment

Freedom of religion: You can worship as you wish, or not at all. The government cannot choose one religion for the whole country.

Freedom of speech: You can express your opinion about any subject without being arrested. You can even criticize the government. But what you say can't cause danger or harm to others.

Freedom of the press: The government cannot tell people what they can or cannot print in newspapers or books.

Freedom of assembly: You have the right to join and meet with any group. However, you cannot commit crimes with the group.

2nd Amendment

Right to bear arms: You can own guns for hunting and other legal activities.

3rd Amendment

Right to not have soldiers in your home during peacetime: In the past, kings had made people feed and house soldiers not only during wars but in times of peace.

4th Amendment

Freedom from improper search and seizure: You have a right to privacy. But if the police have a reason to think you have something illegal in your home, they can get a search warrant and search your home.

5th, 6th, and 7th Amendments:

These have to do with rights people have if they commit crimes. They include the right to a speedy trial and a trial by a jury.

8th Amendment:

No cruel or unusual punishment is allowed.

9th Amendment:

People have other rights not named in the Bill of Rights.

10th Amendment:

A great deal of power will remain with the states. The people did not want the federal government to have all the power.

What do you think?

Does freedom of speech mean you can write graffiti on public property? Can you tell lies that harm others? How can we use our freedoms so they don't hurt anyone else?

Political Parties

Political parties are groups of people who have a lot of the same ideas about government. Most people in the United States choose either the Democratic party or the Republican party. They are the two main parties in Nevada and in the rest of the United States, but there are other parties too.

Political parties want members of their party to get elected to government jobs. The people in each party choose candidates and help them run for office. The parties raise money to pay for TV and radio advertising, make and hand out posters, and help in many other ways. The candidates gives speeches to try to win votes. At election time, people vote for the person they think will do the best job.

During elections, look for these two animals on signs and badges:
*The **elephant** is the symbol for the Republicans.*
*The **donkey** is the symbol for the Democrats.*

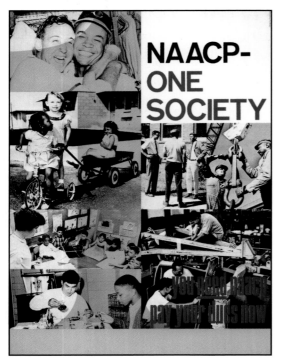

There are many different kinds of special interest groups that speak for the needs of people.

Interest Groups

Sometimes people who share common interests get together to try to make changes. Have you ever heard the saying, "There is strength in numbers"? Instead of having just one voice, interest groups combine their single voices into large groups of voices. The more members there are in the group, the more *influence,* or power, the group has to sway government decision makers.

Many important interest groups have played a part in Nevada history. One group is the National Association for the Advancement of Colored People, or the NAACP. This group works in states all across the country to fight racial discrimination. Black leaders, like Charles Kellar and Dr. James McMillan, served as presidents of our state's NAACP. Their work helped fight prejudice, segregation, and discrimination in Nevada.

LESSON 1

Memory Master

1. What is the Declaration of Independence? Who wrote it?
2. Name the three levels of government.
3. What is a representative democracy?
4. Name something other than making laws that Congress has the power to do.
5. Why is the Bill of Rights an important document for our country?

Our State Government

Nevada's government is a lot like our national government. We have our own state constitution that directs our leaders. Our government is also made up of legislative, executive, and judicial branches. These branches help balance power in our state government—just like they do in the federal government.

The Legislative Branch

Nevada's legislative branch consists of an assembly and senate. Together they are called the legislature. There are 42 members of the assembly and 21 members of the senate. Each member represents a certain area of our state. Just like in national government, the biggest population centers have the most representatives.

Las Vegas and Reno have the most representatives in our legislature because they have the largest populations. Some people in *rural* Nevada think this system does not fairly represent them. The rural parts of Nevada are those less-populated areas away from cities. Sometimes we call rural areas the country.

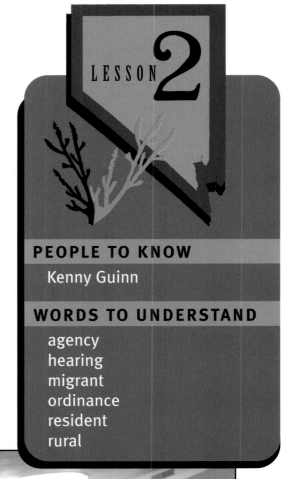

LESSON 2

PEOPLE TO KNOW
Kenny Guinn

WORDS TO UNDERSTAND
agency
hearing
migrant
ordinance
resident
rural

Governor Guinn gives the State of the State address to members of the legislature.

Making Laws

Our state legislature meets every two years in Carson City at the state's capital. The legislative session begins in January. It takes our legislature about 120 days, or four months, to make the laws for our state. Sometimes legislators are unable to finish all their duties in that amount of time. When this happens, a special session is called. Special sessions gives legislators time to complete their work.

Legislators in Nevada make many kinds of laws. They make amendments to the state constitution, just like those made to our U.S. Constitution. Legislators also make tax laws that help our government pay for services.

Business and fishing licenses and license plates are just a few of the licenses sold by the state of Nevada that help pay for services.

What do you think?

Have you ever thought about how the laws in our state affect you? Did you know that people who operate a business or provide a service in our state need a license? Your teachers have to have a license to teach you. The person who cuts your hair has to have a license. Carpenters, plumbers, and electricians have to be licensed by the state. Your dentist and doctor have to pass a test before they can practice medicine in our state. Why do people need a license to do certain jobs or businesses in Nevada? Does knowing these people are well-trained make it easier to trust them to do a good job for you?

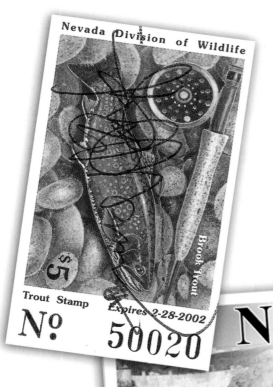

222

How a Bill Becomes a Law

All Nevada laws begin as bills. You already know that a bill is a written idea for a new law. An idea may come from any *resident* of our state. But it can only be presented to the legislature by one of its members. To see how it works, let's follow a bill as it becomes a law.

Suppose that you and your classmates want to propose a new law. You would begin by writing a letter to one of your state legislators. If your legislator likes the idea, he or she will put the idea in written form. This is called drafting a bill. Now the bill is ready to be introduced into the senate or assembly. This step is called the first reading. From here, the bill goes to a committee for review. Sometimes the committee just passes the bill along to the next step. But, most of the time, the committee keeps the bill, so they can study it carefully. They hold public meetings, or *hearings,* to discuss the bill. They talk to other people interested in the bill. Sometimes they make changes to the bill as a result of talking to others.

Then the bill goes back to be read a second time. It can also be amended again if necessary. When this is complete, the president of the group schedules a third reading of the bill. Then it is ready for a vote. If a majority of the voters vote for the bill, it then makes its way to the other legislative group. A bill goes through all the steps in one house of the legislature before moving on to the other. Sometimes it takes a long time for a bill to get through both houses before reaching the governor.

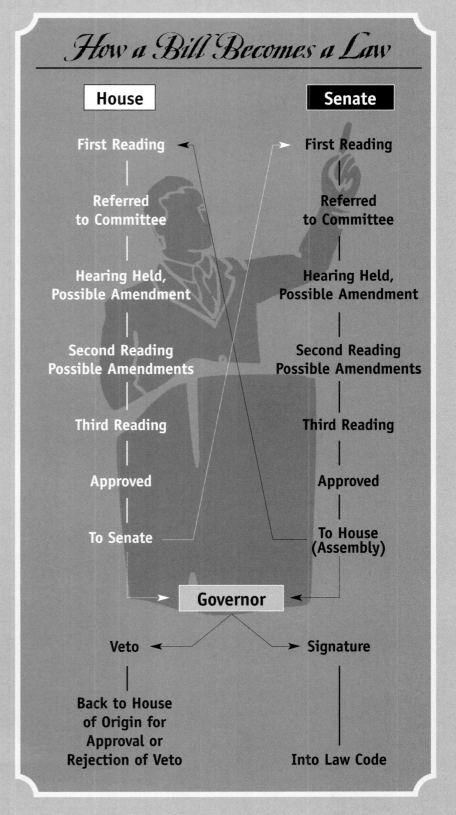

How a Bill Becomes a Law

House	Senate
First Reading	First Reading
Referred to Committee	Referred to Committee
Hearing Held, Possible Amendment	Hearing Held, Possible Amendment
Second Reading Possible Amendments	Second Reading Possible Amendments
Third Reading	Third Reading
Approved	Approved
To Senate	To House (Assembly)

Governor

Veto — Signature

Back to House of Origin for Approval or Rejection of Veto — Into Law Code

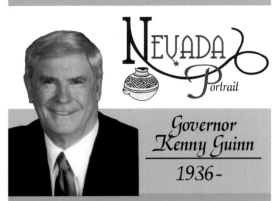

Nevada Portrait

Governor Kenny Guinn
1936~

Governor Kenny Guinn had a very simple beginning. He was born in Arkansas and then moved with his family to California. His father was a *migrant* farm worker who didn't know how to read. As a boy, Guinn lived in a farm labor camp with about 100 other migrant families. He worked hard picking cotton, grapes, and peaches. He also gathered nuts and laid irrigation pipe.

Education was very important to the Guinn family. Young Kenny studied hard. Later, his football skills helped him get a college education. After college, he worked as a coach and teacher. In 1964, Guinn and his family moved to Las Vegas. He worked for the Clark County schools. After five years, he was named superintendent of county schools. The Kenny C. Guinn Middle School in Las Vegas is named after him.

Before becoming governor, Guinn also served as the president of Southwest Gas Corporation and as a temporary president of UNLV. His first term as governor was in 1999. In 2002, he was re-elected. After the state received money from tobacco lawsuits, Governor Guinn started the Millennium Scholarship Program. This program gives state college scholarship money to any Nevada students who keep a B average throughout high school.

The Executive Branch

The executive branch enforces laws made by our legislature. The governor is the head of this branch. The governor and many other elected leaders, agencies, and state workers are in charge of collecting taxes, suggesting budgets, giving help to schools, and many other things. Just like the president does for federal laws, our governor signs Nevada bills into laws.

Capitol Building

The Nevada state capitol building is over 130 years old. With marble from Alaska and windows made from French crystal, it is a very beautiful building. It is one of the oldest buildings in Nevada. Originally it was built to provide offices for both the governor and the legislature. Before long the growing legislature needed more space, so they moved to a new building. Today our state capitol is still used by the governor and his staff.

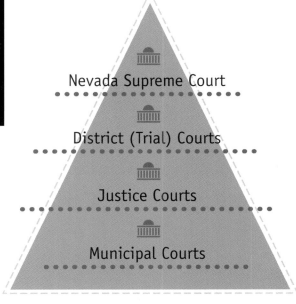

Nevada Supreme Court

District (Trial) Courts

Justice Courts

Municipal Courts

The Judicial Branch

This branch of government includes our state courts and judges. Nevada courts settle arguments about what laws mean. There are many different types of courts in our state. The highest is the Nevada Supreme Court. Seven justices serve in this branch of government. They also manage all other courts in our state judicial system.

District or trial courts are the next type of courts in Nevada's judicial system. Today there are nine district courts and over 60 district judges. This court deals with things like juvenile and abuse problems, and family law.

Justice courts handle small crimes and cases under $10,000. We call these judges, **justices** of the peace. At last count there were 48 justice courts in Nevada and 63 justices of the peace.

Municipal courts are the courts in our cities and towns. These are the courts most people visit when they get a traffic or speeding ticket. They handle cases that happen within the city limits. Today, there are 17 municipal courts and 27 municipal judges.

The Pershing County courthouse in Lovelock, is one of the few remaining round courthouses still in use.

County and City Governments

There are many regions with different needs in our state. Each region has local governments that provide services to all the people. County and city governments also help spread government power all around the state. That way, no one group can become too powerful.

Our state is divided into 17 small regions called counties. Counties have government leaders and laws called *ordinances.* Each county has its own government building in a city known as the county seat. Can you find your county and county seat on the map?

County governments are in charge of keeping all kinds of records. They keep land records and local tax records. They keep birth records and death records. They make laws for the county and hire sheriffs to enforce them. County laws deal with things like pollution and parks. They also decide where houses, stores, and other businesses should be built.

City Governments

City governments are another important part of Nevada local governments. They help protect the people. They hire the police departments, fire departments, and people to keep the streets clean and safe. City governments also provide things like clean drinking water and garbage collection. They give licenses to local businesses. You even buy a license for your pet from your city government.

The city council and the mayor are elected by the people. Their job is to make laws that keep things running smoothly.

What do you think?

Do you know who your local government leaders are? Are there problems in your town that you would like the city council to discuss? How can you become involved in your community?

Nevada Counties and County Seats

HUMBOLDT
Winnemucca

ELKO
Elko

PERSHING
Lovelock

Battle Mountain

WASHOE
Reno

CHURCHILL
Fallon

LANDER   EUREKA
Eureka

WHITE PINE
Ely

LYON
Yerington

Minden
DOUGLAS

MINERAL
Hawthorne

NYE

Carson City

STOREY
Virginia City

ESMERALDA
Goldfield

Tonopah

Pioche

LINCOLN

CLARK
Las Vegas

N
W   E
S

What's in a Name?

Many of Nevada's counties have very unusual names. Some were even named after famous people. Did you know that Lincoln County got its name from one of our most famous presidents? Abraham Lincoln was the president when Nevada became a state.

Clark County was named after a senator from Montana, William Clark, who built the railroad through southern Nevada. Douglas County was named after a U.S. senator from Illinois by the name of Stephen A. Douglas.

We even have counties that were named after some of the natural features in Nevada. White Pine County got its name from the many trees growing in the area. Esmeralda comes from the Spanish word for emerald. The word Elko comes from an Indian word that means beautiful. Mineral County got its name from the many minerals found there. The name of Eureka comes from a Greek word that means "I have found it." Some people say this is what Nevada miners said when they discovered silver and gold.

Many Nevada counties were named after important military heroes. Storey County was named after a soldier who died in the Pyramid Lake Indian War. The counties of Pershing, Lyon, Lander, and Churchill were all named for U.S. Army generals.

Senator Stephen A. Douglas

Other Local Governments

Nevada has one more type of local government. It is even smaller than county or city government. These special kinds of governments make rules and provide services for the citizens in their community. These community groups include school boards, health districts, library boards, and water districts. Sometimes people are elected to serve on these boards. Other times they are chosen by city or county councils.

As citizens, it's important for us to let government leaders know how we feel about current issues. When you are old enough, voting is one of the best ways you can do this. Voting gives you a voice and allows you to participate in government.

City or county council members meet monthly to discuss the needs of their citizens.

Government Services

We have learned a lot about how our federal, state, and local governments work. Each level of government has special jobs and provides necessary services for the people. Our state and local government manages many public services for Nevadans. There are services for children and for senior citizens. We have a national guard set up to protect us. Our state highway department builds and cares for the roads. Other departments, or state *agencies,* work to make our lives better too. They work to improve things like education, health care, and our environment.

Taxes Pay for Services

Tax money helps pay for most of the services people use. In Nevada, there are many different kinds of taxes. They help pay for schools and textbooks. They pay for programs to protect our land and water. They help pay for all kinds of public services like job training, fire protection, and library services. How many public services can you find in this town?

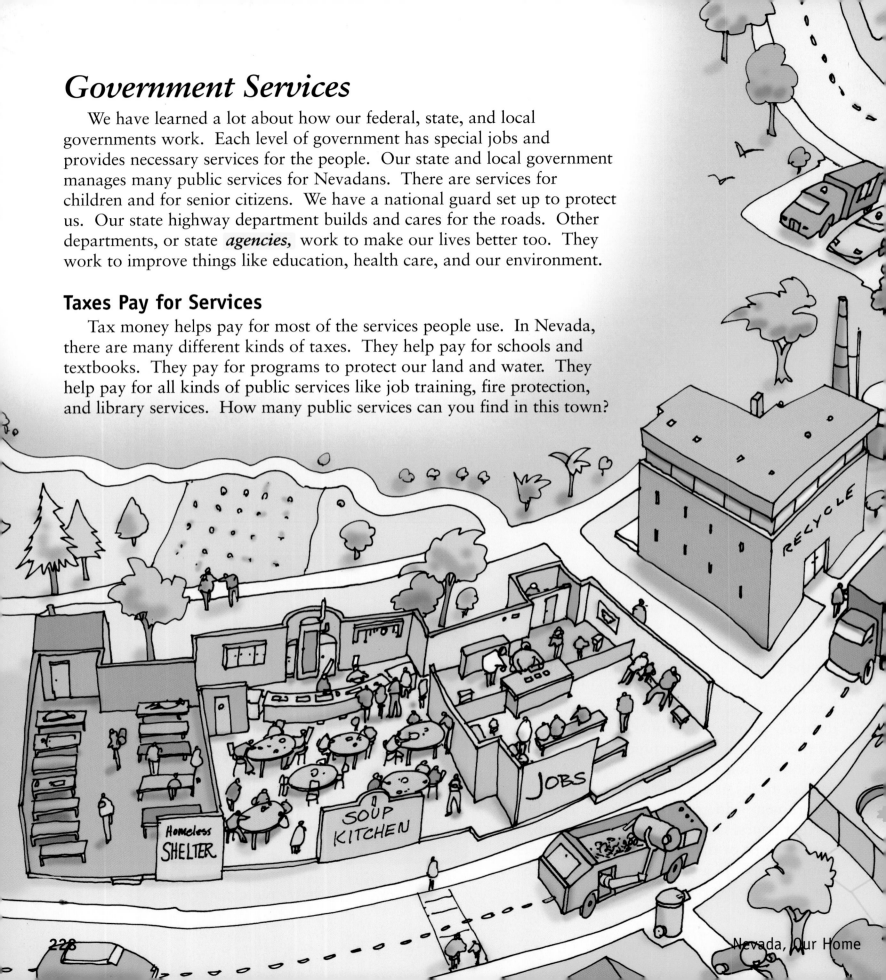

RECYCLE

JOBS

SOUP KITCHEN

Homeless SHELTER

Memory Master

1. What are the two groups that make up our state legislative branch?
2. What is a hearing?
3. Who is the head of Nevada's executive branch of government?
4. Which court includes judges we called justices of the peace?
5. Name two services that taxes pay for.

Consider ★ Character

It takes courage to speak out for what you believe in, run for office, and give speeches to large audiences. Over the decades, many people have shown courage in trying to shape Nevada into a successful state. Many Nevada leaders want a strong Nevada today and for the future. Go through this whole book and find an example of a leader who showed courage. Find an important decision this person made that showed courage as a leader. Would our government be different today without this leader?

Technology 🔬 Tie-In

Have you ever thought about how technology changes law? Does new technology mean new laws? Sometimes the government has to make laws on how to use new technology. Think about some of the legal issues that come from new technology like computers, cell phones, and the Internet. Discuss them with your class. Can you think of others?

- Should you be allowed to talk on your cell phone while driving a car?
- Are there any places that cell phones should be turned off?
- Is Internet information free? Should you be able to copy any words or pictures from websites?
- What should happen to people who send e-mails that can mess up your computer?
- Should you pay sales tax on things you order from the Internet?
- Does everyone have free speech when they write things for the Internet?

Go back to the drawing on the page before to answer these questions about the town:

- How many public services can you find in this town?
- How does the government pay for these services?
- Who makes decisions about these local services?
- Cover up one service. What would happen to the town without it?
- Do you have any of these services near you?

Activity

Your Fair Share of Taxes

Kids, it's time to pay your taxes again! Did you know that every time you buy something you are giving money to the government? You are a citizen paying sales tax. Taxes help keep our state running.

Do you know how much sales tax people pay in Nevada? Look at the map on the right to see how much tax people pay in each county. Then choose three counties with different tax rates and figure out how much sales tax you would have to pay if you bought something that cost $1, $10, or $200.

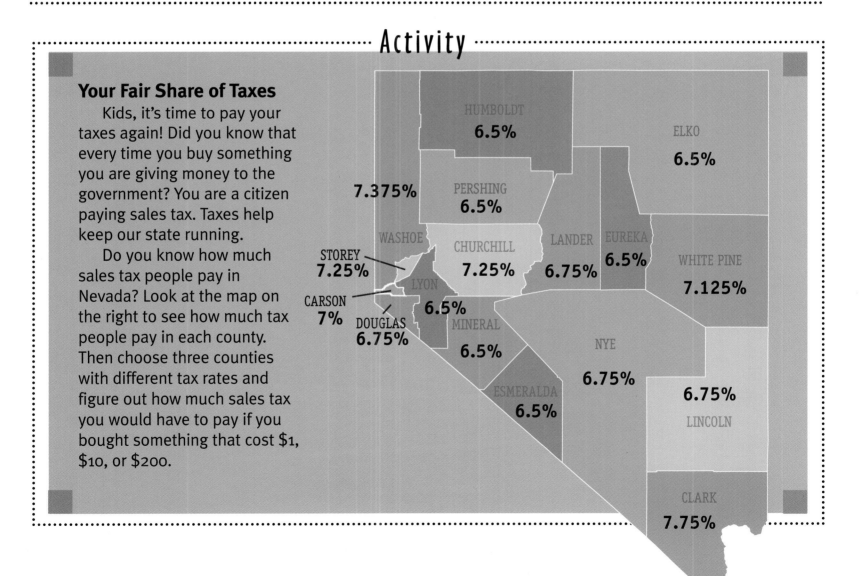

HUMBOLDT 6.5%

ELKO 6.5%

7.375%

PERSHING 6.5%

WASHOE

CHURCHILL 7.25%

LANDER 6.75%

EUREKA 6.5%

WHITE PINE 7.125%

STOREY 7.25%

CARSON 7%

LYON 6.5%

DOUGLAS 6.75%

MINERAL 6.5%

NYE 6.75%

6.75%

LINCOLN

ESMERALDA 6.5%

CLARK 7.75%

Making a Living in Nevada

"With 50,000 new jobs in 2004, Nevada remains a place where dreams can be fulfilled. We are creating these new jobs at a faster rate than any other state in the Union. And these are good jobs, quality jobs, jobs that offer livable wages and benefits for our working families. Given this news, it's no surprise that so many people want to come here and enjoy the wonderful opportunities and lifestyle that Nevada has to offer."

—Governor Kenny Guinn,
2005 State of the
State Address

Our economy is an important part of life in Nevada. It affects the quality of our homes, our schools, and our work. During our history, there have been many times when it was hard to earn a living here. But there have also been periods of enormous growth. Today, Nevada continues to be the fastest-growing state in the nation. There are now nearly 2.5 million people living here.

Construction companies build homes for Nevada's growing population.

233

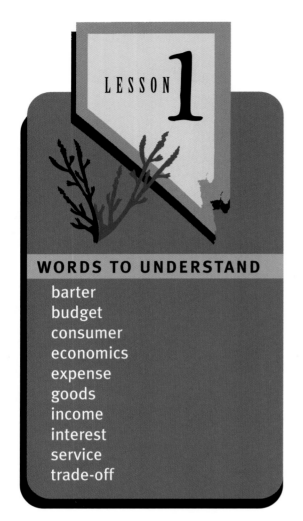

WORDS TO UNDERSTAND

barter
budget
consumer
economics
expense
goods
income
interest
service
trade-off

Economics for Everyone

Economics is the study of how people get the goods and services they need and want. People need food, clothing, and shelter. Sometimes people need medical care from a doctor or nurse. They may also need to have their leaky roof or a broken window fixed. People who help us with the things we need provide *services.*

After people's basic needs are met, there are also many things they want. People want books, games, and bicycles. They like to buy nice stereos, TVs, and cars. Things like these are called *goods,* or products.

When we are children, adults usually make sure our needs and wants are met. When we grow up, we have to take care of our own needs and wants. We have to decide what we want to do to earn a living. Many adults take care of not only themselves but children and relatives too. Later in this chapter, we will learn how people in our state earn money for their wants and needs.

Can you tell what this woman does for a living? Does she provide a good or a service?

······ Activity ·······

Goods and Services

Goods are usually things that are made by people in factories, workshops, or even at home. Services are things that people do for others.

On a separate piece of paper, number from one to five. Read the list of jobs below. Write "G" next to the ones that relate to goods. Write "S" next to jobs that relate to services.

1. Fixing the plumbing
2. Teaching students
3. Making engines for cars
4. Delivering cheese to stores
5. Checking people into hotel rooms

The Role of Money

Today we use money to buy what we need, but that was not always so. Native Americans used to trade for things they wanted and needed. Fur traders also traded, or **bartered,** furs for food and supplies. Sometimes they bought things with gold or silver coins from their native countries. As time went on, banks in towns and cities printed paper money called bank notes. The holder of a note could trade it for silver or gold or use the note as money to buy things. These notes were good only as long as the bank stayed in business.

Later, governments began printing their own money. But people in other states didn't always trust the worth of that money. Finally, the federal government made coins and paper money that could be used almost everywhere in the world.

Spending Money

Most people want to spend their money wisely. They want to get the most for their money. They compare prices from different stores and look at different brands. Everyone spends money on things they need. People who buy things are called ***consumers.*** What kinds of things do you choose to buy?

People all over the world use paper money. Which two countries does this money come from? Can you find them on a globe?

Consumers spend their money on all kinds of goods and services.

How Much Money Does It Cost?

You and your parents need money to buy goods and services. How much money do you need? What can you buy with a dollar? You can probably buy an ice cream cone, a small notebook, or a box of crayons.

Look at the list below of things people buy with their money. Do some research to find out how much money these things cost. Go to the store, look in newspapers, or search the Internet. Most of these things will have more than one price. On a separate piece of paper, list the lowest and highest price you see for each item.

1. a car
2. a house
3. a couch
4. a television
5. a pound of hamburger
6. a pound of oranges
7. a pair of shoes
8. a large pizza
9. a bike
10. a music CD

Cash, Checks, and Cards

Today, personal checks are an easy way to pay for things. But a consumer must put money into the bank before writing a check. Debit cards are another way to subtract money from a bank account.

When people buy something with a credit card, they get the item now, but they have to pay for it later.

Credit card companies also charge card users a fee to use the card. They call the fee *interest.*

Paying interest actually means a consumer pays more for an item than it costs. But interest isn't always a bad thing. Consumers can also earn interest from the bank when they put money into a savings account.

Making Choices

Whenever you buy something, you are making a choice. Sometimes you have to make a trade-off. A ***trade-off*** is choosing not to buy one thing so you will have enough money to buy something else.

Pretend you have $10 to spend. You want to buy a book and a video game, but you don't have enough money for both. Which would you choose to buy? What trade-off would you make?

Adults have to think about trade-offs a lot. Sometimes they have to make ***budgets.*** A budget is a plan you make to help manage your money. Budgets can help people make better spending choices.

Understanding a Budget

Creating a budget is one good way to practice your math skills. Don't forget that **income** is how much money you have, and **expenses,** or bills, are things you need to pay for. Look at this example of a budget and then answer the questions.

1. How much money does it take to make the house payment?
2. Add up all of the expenses. How much money is left over after all the expenses are subtracted from the income?
3. Is there enough left over to buy a $300 TV? What trade-off could be made?
4. Can you think of other expenses that should be included in this budget?

Monthly Budget	
Income:	$2,500
Expenses	
House payment:	$1,200
Food:	$500
Clothes:	$150
Savings:	$100
Electricity/water:	$100
Car payment:	$250
Gasoline:	$50

Saving and Planning

Money is important to people. Without it, people aren't able to take care of their own wants and needs. Money also gives us a way to plan ahead for things we may want or need in the future. Suppose you get an allowance from your parents. Maybe you earn money for walking the dog or mowing lawns. If you earn $10 each week and you want to buy a scooter that costs $100:

- How long would it take you to get the scooter if you saved $10 each week?
- How long would it take if you saved $5 a week?

Most people who save money put it in a bank. Banks are businesses that help people manage their money. Sometimes they loan money to people when they want to open a new business or buy a house or car.

Sometimes people save money in a piggy bank. Is this a smart place to keep a lot of money?

LESSON 1

Memory Master

1. What is economics?
2. What is the difference between goods and services?
3. Give an example of a trade-off.
4. Give one important reason for saving money.

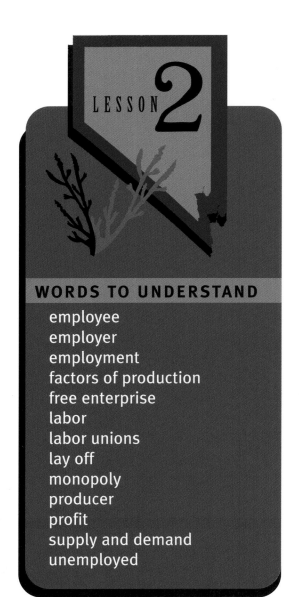

LESSON 2

WORDS TO UNDERSTAND

employee
employer
employment
factors of production
free enterprise
labor
labor unions
lay off
monopoly
producer
profit
supply and demand
unemployed

The Free Enterprise System

Different countries in the world have different ways of producing and selling their goods and services. In the United States, we use what is called a *free enterprise* system. In this kind of system, the people, not the government, own most of the companies. Company owners decide what to produce and sell or what service to provide. They also decide where their company should be located, how much they will charge, and who they want working for them.

Company or business owners are called *employers.* They hire people called *employees* to work for them. Employees earn a wage or salary for their work. Are the adults in your family employers or employees?

Making a Profit

Business owners hope to make a *profit* from selling their goods or services. Profit is the money left over after a company pays all of its expenses. Business owners have many different kinds of expenses. They pay for the materials to make their products. They pay workers to make their products. They might also have to pay rent on their factory or building. These are all different kinds of expenses.

How a Business Makes a Profit

EXPENSE $30
The coat company pays for the cloth and the zipper. It also pays an employee to make the coat. These are expenses.

PRICE $45
The company sells the coat for more money than it costs to make it.

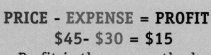

PRICE - EXPENSE = PROFIT
$45- $30 = $15
Profit is the money the business has left after all expenses are paid.

Supply and Demand

Another important part of selling goods or services is something called *supply and demand.* Suppose you are a company who makes and sells toys. Sometimes a toy becomes so popular that a company cannot make enough for everyone who wants one. The demand for the toy becomes higher than the supply. When this happens, demand for the toy often drives the price of the toy higher. People who really want it are willing to pay a higher price to get it.

What happens if the demand for a product or service goes down? Companies with too many dolls sometimes lower the price to get people to buy them. Supply and demand can also have an effect on jobs. For example, if the demand for scooters goes up, a company may decide it needs more workers. They begin looking for people who need work, or *employment.* Likewise, when the demand for scooters goes down, the company may have to *lay off,* or get rid of, some of its workers. When people don't have jobs, we say they are *unemployed.*

Competition

There are other reasons a company may decide to lower its prices. There may be more than one company trying to sell the same product or service. Companies compete with one another to sell the best product for the lowest price. What happens when one company lowers its price on an item both stores sell? People usually buy from the store or business with the lowest price. That's what competition is all about.

What happens when only one company produces a product or service? That company has what is called a *monopoly.* Companies that have a monopoly on something have no one to compete with them. This means they can sell an item or service for whatever price they like. There is no one else who will sell it for a better price.

$1.50

$1.25

Competition is part of a free market system.

Producers are the people who make goods or products. They make things like basketballs, airplanes, books, clothes, candy, and more. Consumers are the people who pay money for goods and services. They buy things like bagels, computers, and cars.

What do you think?

Do you think someone can be both a producer and a consumer? Explain how.

Activity

Competition in Your Community

Are there companies in the community where you live that compete for your business? Does the shopping center nearby have more than one toy store, bicycle shop, or restaurant to choose from? Check the yellow pages of your phone book to see how many stores sell the same product or service. See if you can learn how they get their customers to choose them over the competition.

Factors of Production

There are at least three types of resources that go into the making of any product or service. They are natural resources, capital resources, and human resources. Sometimes we call these things the *factors of production.*

Natural Resources

Sand, gravel, trees, and soil are all examples of natural resources. If you own a bicycle factory, things like metal, rubber, and energy are some of the important natural resources your factory will need.

Metal is used to make bicycle frames. Rubber is used to make tires. Energy, in the form of

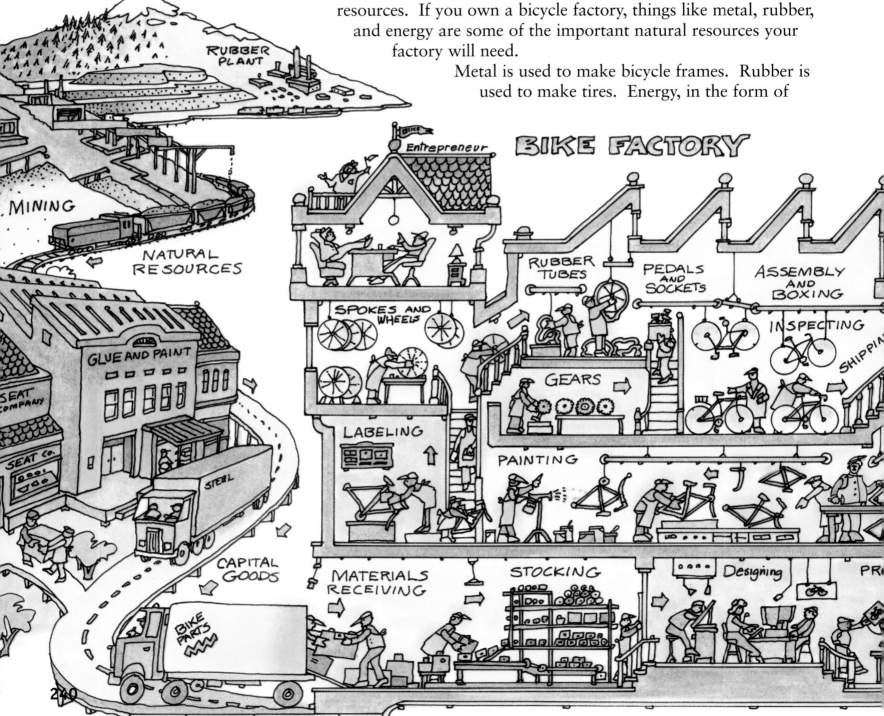

electricity, turns on the lights and machinery. It also provides heat or cool air for factory workers. Can you think of a large structure in Nevada that uses water to create electricity?

Coal, oil, and gasoline are also natural resources that provide energy. Your family lawnmower uses gasoline. Your home may have a gas stove or outdoor barbecue. Business owners try to build their companies or factories close to the natural resources they need.

Capital Resources

Capital resources are those things you need to make your products or goods. For example, a printing press is a capital resource for your city newspaper. It is a necessary part of what the newspaper needs to get important stories out to its customers. Money used to start and run a business is also called capital.

Human Resources

Human resources are made up of people who do the work, or *labor*. Even though many companies use large machines, they need people to run the machines. Businesses also depend on people to work in factories, in schools, as pilots, and as dentists. We need sales people, secretaries, farmers, and all kinds of workers. We will probably always need human resources to make goods and provide services.

Members of a Las Vegas food workers union hold a protest march outside of the hotel and casino where they work.

Labor Unions

During the 19th century, many people worked under difficult conditions for very little money. Some worked in factories or for railroads. Some were loggers or miners. Life was hard for these workers. They had very little say about how they were treated or how much they were paid. Soon people began working together to make things better for workers. They created groups called *labor unions.* Some labor unions tried to solve their problems peacefully. Others used force or violence against the companies they worked for.

In Nevada, the first labor unions started during the Comstock period. Miners argued with company owners about pay, safety in the mines, and other concerns. Because of this, mining unions were formed in Virginia City, Gold Hill, and Silver City.

These early unions opened the way for the labor unions of today. Now there are unions for painters, railroad engineers, journalists, and other types of communication workers. There are also unions for teachers, truck drivers, musicians, actors, firefighters, food workers, plumbers, and more.

"The important role of union organizations . . . is the representation of . . . workers . . . and the development . . . of the common good."

—*Pope Paul VI*

Memory Master

LESSON 2

1. What economic system does our country use today?
2. What must business owners do to make a profit?
3. Describe the difference between a producer and a consumer.
4. List the three factors of production. Give one example of each.

Nevada at Work

Not long ago, almost all the work in Nevada had something to do with mining or *agriculture.* For many years, raising crops and livestock was one of the main industries in our state. Today, people in Nevada do all kinds of jobs, including agriculture.

Our state has workers who design and build homes. Some work for the military or for state or local government. Others work as teachers, firefighters, gardeners, doctors, waitresses, and mechanics. There are also thousands of people who work for one of our state's largest industries—tourism. Let's learn a little more about some of Nevada's important industries.

LESSON 3

WORDS TO UNDERSTAND
agriculture
engineer
kayak
retail

These candymakers at Ethel M. Chocolates in Las Vegas are making a large pan of brittle.

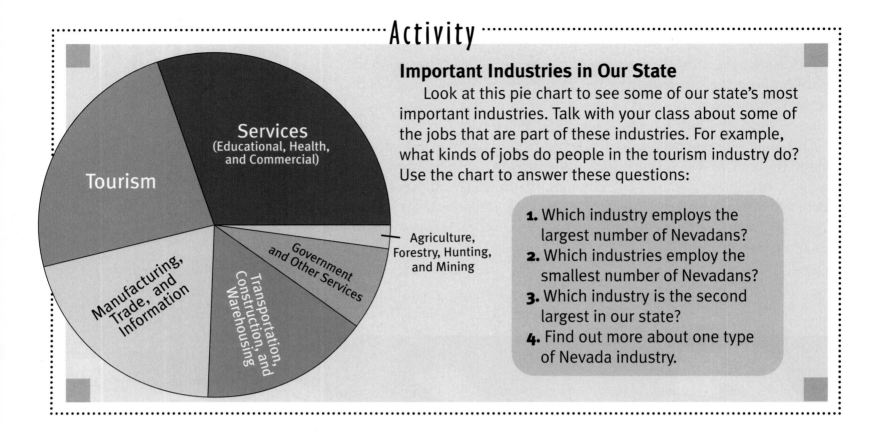

Important Industries in Our State

Look at this pie chart to see some of our state's most important industries. Talk with your class about some of the jobs that are part of these industries. For example, what kinds of jobs do people in the tourism industry do? Use the chart to answer these questions:

1. Which industry employs the largest number of Nevadans?
2. Which industries employ the smallest number of Nevadans?
3. Which industry is the second largest in our state?
4. Find out more about one type of Nevada industry.

Although the Pahrump Valley Winery makes wine, visitors won't see many grape vines there. Vines at the winery were eaten by wild horses. Now the company wine is made from California grapes.

Industries Help Nevada Grow

The city of Henderson has been called the industrial center of our state. More industries are located in that area than in any other part of the state. Industries all over our state have helped it grow for more than 50 years.

Manufacturing has also been an important part of Nevada's growth. Many of these companies do business in Nevada because we have low taxes and a large number of skilled workers. Here are a few of examples of things that are manufactured in our state:

- Ammunition in Boulder City
- Chocolate in Las Vegas
- Scooters in Minden
- Camper tops in Reno
- Beef jerky in Yerington
- Saddles in Elko
- Wine in Pahrump

Tourism

Nevada is one of the most visited places in the world. People come from all over to stay and play in Las Vegas, Lake Tahoe, Mesquite, Laughlin, and Reno. They come to see famous entertainers, major sporting events, and of course, to gamble.

Because tourism is such a big part of our state, many Nevadans work in this industry. Hotels need hundreds of employees to take care of their visitors. Casinos need dealers and cleaning people. Restaurants need servers, cooks, and dishwashers. Thousands of people work in our state's large service industry.

But Nevada has much more for visitors than gambling and shopping. Tourists also come to enjoy our unique scenery and special events. They visit Great Basin National Park, Lehman Caves, Hoover Dam, Lake Mead, the Black Rock Desert, and Red Rock Canyon. People also flood into Elko for the annual cowboy poetry gathering. Outdoor lovers head to Lake Tahoe to fish, boat or hike. Others practice their *kayaking* skills in Reno's Truckee River.

Tourists spend a lot of money in Nevada, which helps our state build a strong economy.

A kayak is a narrow, light-weight boat, similar to a canoe. Kayakers use a special paddle that is flat on both ends.

People from far and near come to Elko each year to hear western music and famous cowboy poets.

These two refiners at the Denton Rawhide mine in Fallon are pouring gold and silver bars.

An engineer is someone who uses science and math to build things.

Modern Mining

Mining in Nevada is very different today than it was when prospectors first came. New inventions have made it much easier to separate the minerals in our soil from the dirt and sand.

After scientists locate minerals in the ground, they send *engineers* to the area to build mills. Large trucks and diggers are used to scoop up the ore and transport it to the mills.

Mining is still a very important part of Nevada's economy. Minerals found in our state, have made a difference in transportation, communication, electronics, engineering, and medicine. Copper, molybdenum, barite, mercury, diatomite, magnesia, perlite, gypsum, and fluorspar are some of the minerals found in our soils.

For almost 30 years, Nevada has been the largest gold-producing state in the nation. We also lead the nation in the production of silver. Because mining companies make so much money from our minerals, the government has asked them to pay higher taxes. Citizens have also demanded that mining companies restore the land they mine. Now, when a mine closes, mining companies level the land and plant native grasses and trees. Many companies also try to improve the communities where their workers live. Some build schools and places for recreation in their towns.

Retail Sales and Warehousing

Another big part of the economy in Nevada is selling goods to tourists and people who live in our state. Visitors from all over the world love shopping in hotel shops and other areas. In Reno, more people work in *retail* and warehousing than in hotels and casinos. Companies can store their goods in Nevada warehouses tax-free. Goods are stored in these warehouses while they wait to be shipped.

Ranching and Farming

Farming and ranching are still a part of Nevada's modern economy. Some of the working ranches in our state are very large, like the Ellison Ranching Company in Tuscarora, the Ninety-Six Ranch in Paradise Valley, and the Nevada First Corporation. But most ranches are small, with less than 500 head of cattle. All of them lease grazing land for their cattle from the federal government.

Many farming businesses in Moapa, Carson, and Smith Valleys also help our economy. They grow things like corn, alfalfa, and garlic seed. They also produce many dairy products.

Warehousing is big business in Nevada, especially in and around the cities of Fallon and Reno.

A rope and a good horse are two of a rancher's most important tools.

Memory Master

LESSON 3

1. Name at least two important industries in our state.
2. Why do companies like to do business in Nevada?
3. What have Nevada citizens demanded mining companies do after they close a mine?
4. Who leases grazing land to Nevada's modern ranchers?

Consider ★ Character

You have studied about character traits and about people who have made good and bad decisions. Which character trait do you think you have studied the most? Look back at all the character traits. Pick the one you think you need to spend more time studying. On your own piece of paper, write the character trait at the top. Then write the definition (you may use this book and a dictionary as a resource). Following the definition, write three examples from Nevada history that show this trait. How has this trait been important to Nevada history? Write down one example of this character trait from your own life. You, too, are becoming a part of Nevada history!

Technology 🔬 Tie-In

In this chapter, we have read about many ways people work to earn money. Almost every job has been changed by modern technology in some way. For example: When miners first began searching for minerals in the ground, they used a pick ax, pan, or shovel. It took them days to cover a small area of ground. Today, new machines allow miners and mining companies to dig and sift quickly through hundreds of tons of ore.

Think about how technology has changed other types of work for people in our state. Select three jobs people do in Nevada. Then on a piece of paper, describe how technology has changed these jobs. Choose from the list below, or create your own list.

- banker
- doctor
- teacher
- farmer
- store clerk
- publisher
- secretary

Geography 🌐 Tie-In

Let's say you want to start a new business in Nevada. What kind of business would you start? Think about where your business would be located. Ask yourself the following questions:

1. Will my business offer goods or services? How will the goods or services get to the customers?
2. What natural features or resources will my business need?
3. How will the people who work at the business get there?
4. Will the business be able to make money in its location?

Share with your class your business idea and location. Tell them why you chose what you did.

Activity

Make Your Own Budget

Pretend you are going on a vacation with your family. You have $2,000 to spend. You will need to make a budget. Where can you afford to go? How will you get there? How much money can you spend on food, hotels, and entertainment? How long can you stay?

You will need to do some research to find out how much things will cost. Fill in a chart to show your budget. You can work with your parents, search the Internet, or find brochures in hotels or other tourist places.

MY FAMILY VACATION TO:

_____

Number of days we'll be gone:

_____

Cost of gas for car:

_____

Food costs:

_____

Hotel costs:

_____

Cost of entertainment:

_____

Other costs:

_____

Total costs:

_____

Glossary

The definitions given here are for the **Words to Understand** *as they are used in this textbook.*

A

abolish: to put an end to
adapt: to adjust; to change to fit new circumstances
adobe: bricks made from mud and straw and baked in the sun
adopt: to take on or assume responsibility
aerobatic maneuvers: special stunts pilots perform in airplanes
agency: a division of the government with certain responsibilities
agriculture: the business of raising plants and animals to sell for food; farming
Allies: countries that came together to fight against other countries during WWI and WWII
amendment: an addition or change to a constitution
ammunition: bullets and other explosive supplies
antique: an object that has special value because of its age
archaeologist: a scientist who studies artifacts and ruins to learn about people who lived long ago
Armistice Day: the early name for the national holiday called Veteran's Day
artifact: something made or used by people from the past
astronomer: a person who studies the planets and stars
atlatl: an early tool for throwing spears
atomic bomb: a bomb with violent explosive power due to a sudden release of energy; a nuclear weapon
auction: a sale where items are bought by the highest bidder

B

ban: to outlaw or put an end to a certain practice
barracks: buildings for lodging a large group of people
barter: to trade one thing for another without the exchange of money
Basque: a person who originally immigrated from the Pyrenees Mountians between France and Spain
Bill of Rights: the first 10 amendments to the U.S. Constitution
bill: a written idea for a law
blasting caps: small caps filled with blasting powder
boomtown: a place that grows quickly and fades away quickly
brand: a special mark that is burned into the hide of a cow with a hot iron
budget: a plan to control how money will be spent

C

cardinal directions: the four directions of a compass rose, north, south, east, and west
century: a 100 year period
checks and balances: a system that limits the power of any one branch of government
cholera: a disease that caused stomach cramps and often death
Civil War: the war fought between the Union and Confederacy from 1861-1865
claim jumper: a person who stole another prospector's claim
climate: the typical weather of an area
Clovis point: a sharpened stone made by prehistoric people and used as a hunting tool
collapse: to fall or break down
colonist: a person who lives in a settlement owned and ruled by another country
communist: one who lives in a social organization where businesses are owned and operated by the government instead of the people
competition: a test in which people go against others for a prize or reward
Comstock Lode: a rich lode of silver ore near Virginia City
concentration camp: a place where prisoners of war are forced to stay
Confederacy: the southern states that fought together in the Civil War
constitution: a set of written laws
consumer: a person who spends money on goods and services
continent: one of the seven large land areas in the world
contribute: to help out or add to
convert: to change from one belief to another
country: a region of land governed by one group or system
county seat: the place where the business of the county government takes place
crib: a box built out of timbers that was used to support a mine shaft
criticize: to find fault; to discuss what one did wrong
culture: traditions and social habits developed by specific peoples
curfew: a set time when people are expected to return home
custom: a way of living, thinking, and acting

D

decade: a period of 10 years
demand: a strong request or need
deposit: a concentration of mineral matter like silver or gold
depot: a railroad station
depression: a time when people can't make enough money to meet their basic needs
dictator: a powerful ruler who makes his or her own rules
discrimination: the unfair treatment of people
disease: sickness
district: an area or region
diverse: many different types

document: a written paper, letter, or form

drought: a long period of dry weather

dynamite: an explosive powder in stick form used for blasting

E

economics: the study of how people make, transport, buy, and sell goods and services

economy: the management of goods, services, and resources

ecosystem: a community of living things that depend on each other in order to function as a unit

elect: to choose something or someone by vote

elevation: how high land is above sea level

emigrant: someone who leaves one country to settle in another

employee: a person paid to do work for another person or company

employer: a person who owns or runs a company

employment: having a job

endangered: in danger of disappearing

engineer: someone who uses math and science to build things

environment: one's surroundings

equator: an imaginary line around the center of the Earth equal distance from the North and South Poles

erode: to destroy or wear down, usually by wind, water or other natural processes

ethnic group: a group of people of the same race or culture

exact location: the location of a place using longitude and latitude

expedition: a journey with a purpose

expense: a cost or money spent

F

fact: something that is true

factors of production: the resources needed to produce goods

fault line: a place where the plates of the earth touch

federal: a government at the national level

fossil: a print of a plant or animal preserved in the Earth or in rock

fragile: easy to break or destroy

free enterprise: an economic system where people, not government, own and run businesses

frontier: land that lies beyond an established settlement

G

geography: the study of the Earth and its relationship with people, animals, and plants

goods: products that are made, bought, and sold

graffiti: writing or painting written illegally on public property

graze: the act of allowing animals to feed on grass or pasture land

grubstaker: someone who paid for the supplies of miners in return for a share of their profits

H

harsh: cruel or unpleasant

hearing: a kind of trial

hemisphere: one half of planet Earth

heritage: something passed down from one's ancestors

historian: a person who studies the past and why things happened

historic groups: groups that have written records about their lives

hunter-gatherer: a person who hunts wild animals and gathers food to survive

I–K

immigrant: a person who lives in a country other than where he or she was born

impeach: to be accused of doing something wrong

income: the money a person earns

independent: someone who takes care of themself

industry: a type of business

influence: to have an effect on

integrate: to bring different ethnic groups or people together

interest: a fee charged for money borrowed

intermediate directions: the directions between the cardinal directions, such as southeast and northwest

invader: someone who comes to a place but isn't welcome

irrigate: the process of using canals or ditches to water crops or land

irrigation: a system of watering dry land through pipes, ditches, or canals

kayak: a narrow, lightweight boat

L

labor unions: groups that help protect the rights of workers

labor: work

landform: a natural feature of the land or water, such as a mountain or valley

latitude: imaginary lines on the Earth that run east and west

lay off: to get rid of workers that are no longer needed

lease: to rent something based on an agreement

legal: within the rules of the law

legend: a story that tells the history of how things came to be

legislature: a governing body that makes the laws

local government: town, city, or county government

longitude: imaginary lines of the Earth that run north and south

M

magnesium: a silver-like metal used in airplanes and bombs

majority: more than half of the people

management: the people who are in charge of other workers

mercury: a metal used to measure temperature

meridian: another word for longitude

microscopic: something so small it can only be seen through a microscope

migrant: a worker who travels in search of work

mineral: something that is mined from the Earth like gold, silver, or salt

minority group: a small part of the population or a group that is different from others in some way

mission: a religious settlement

mochila: a leather mail pouch

monopoly: total control of the market

movement: the act of ideas, goods, or people moving from one place to another

mummy: a body that has been preserved

N–O

natural resource: something found in nature that people use

naturalized: to gain citizenship

nomadic: moving from place to place in search of food

nuclear waste: the garbage left after the process of making nuclear energy

oath: a promise

opinion: a thought or belief

ordinance: a local law

ore: rock that has minerals in it

override: to go against

P

panning: the process that many people used to find gold

patent: a government protection for an invention

pelt: the skin of a furry animal, like a beaver

permanent: something that stays the same

persecution: the act of causing people to suffer because of their beliefs or race

petroglyph: a design carved into rocks by Native Americans

pioneer: a person who is among the first to do something or settle a place

pit house: a home made by the Anasazi

placer mining: an early mining method used to separate minerals from the soil

plate tectonics: a theory that explains the movement of the earth's crust

policy: a plan or way of doing something

portrait: a biography of a person

prairie schooner: a covered wagon

precious: rare

precipitation: the amount of water in the air that falls to the Earth as rain or snow

prehistoric: before written history

prejudice: an opinion made before the facts are known; a judgment made about a person based on race or religion

primary document: an original written record

primary source: something made or written by someone who was there at the time

prime meridian: a special longitude line that runs north and south at 0 degrees

privacy: the right to keep personal things to oneself

producer: a person or a business that makes goods

profit: the money left after expenses are paid

prospector: a miner looking for minerals in the ground

R

radiation: invisible waves of heat or energy

radioactive: having nuclear properties

ration: a little bit of something divided among many people

rebel: to fight against those in power

region: an area of land that has common elements

regulate: to monitor and enforce rules

relative location: a description of a place that involves its relation to other things

relay station: a place where Pony Express riders stopped to change horses

rendezvous: a celebration or large gathering of traders

representative democracy: a type of government in which the people choose representatives to vote and make the laws

representative: someone elected to vote, speak, or act for another person or group

reservation: land where Native Americans were sent to live by the government

reservoir: a place where a large supply of water is stored

resident: a person who is part of a community, town, or city

retail: the sale of goods or services to consumers

ruin: the remains of an ancient home or other building

rural: having to do with the country, not the city

S

secondary source: something written or said by someone who studied an event

segregate: to separate by race; to keep apart

semi-precious: something of value but not rare

service: labor done for others

shadow effect: a unique weather pattern that effects Nevada

shard: a scrap of pottery

sit-in: a type of protest

sluicing: a placer mining method that allowed miners to sift through more dirt in less time

smallpox: a disease in which watery blisters covered the skin

smelt: to melt ore and separate out the metals

smuggle: to buy or send illegal products

species: a classification of living beings

staked a claim: the way a prospector marked the area where he found precious minerals

staple: an important food that makes up a person's diet

steam winch: a machine that pulled something along by winding strong ropes or a cable around a drum

suffrage: the right to vote

supply and demand: an economic rule that says the price of a certain thing is affected by how many are available

surrender: to give up

surveyor: someone who measures the location and distance of an area

suspend: to end for a time

symbol: something that has a special meaning or stands for something else

T

tax: money the people give to the government to pay for services

technology: the use of science to make tools

telegraph: a machine that sends messages by code over wires

tourist: a person who tours or visits places for pleasure

trade-off: a decision to not buy one thing in order to have enough money for another thing

trader: someone who buys and sells things to others

trading post: a place where people bought and exchanged supplies

tradition: a custom handed down from parents to children

transcontinental: going across a continent

translate: to change one language into another

tribe: a group

tule: a tall grassy plant

tungsten: a metallic element used for electrical purposes

turquoise: a blue-green gemstone

U–V–W

unemployed: to be without work

Union: the states and territories in the North that fought together in the Civil War

unique: special

vaquero: a Mexican cowboy with many skills

vein: a pocket of minerals found in rock

veto: to reject a bill from becoming a law

vocational: work-related training

wagon train: a group of wagons that followed one another

weather: day to day temperature and precipitation

Index

Credits

AP/Wide World Photos, 182, 204, 217 (left), 242, 246

Adamczyk, Monika / iStockphoto, 57 (top)

Bancroft Library, University of California, Berkeley, California, 72

Bureau of Reclamation, 203 (top)

Beavers, J. / Shutterpoint, 63 (bottom)

Boulder City Museum and Historical Association, 171 (right)

Brown, Michelle, 109 (top, bottom)

Bruning, Larry, 14 (top)

Brunson, Kris, 12 (top), 13, (center)

Brunson, Nathan A., 92 (top)

Bureau of Reclamation, 203 (top)

Burton, Jon, 214, (bottom), 219, 228-229, 240-241

California Historical Society Library, 113

Carnegie Library of Pittsburg, Pennsylvania Department, 163 (background)

Carnegie Museum of Natural History/ Tom Barr, 53 (top)

Comstock Images / Alamy, 218 (bottom)

Connell, Alan, 109 (center)

Creative Images Photography / Sparks, Nevada, 225 (top)

Ely Renaissance Society / Don and Jared Gray, 139 (top)

Ethel M. Chocolates, Las Vegas, NV/Schadler Kramer Public Relations Group 243

Flag Store, Sparks Nevada, 11 (top)

Foster, Paige / Dreamstime, 28 (center)

Franklin D. Roosevelt Library, 170 (top)

Fujii, Bud, 195

Getty Images, 65

Gibbs Smith Archives, 36 (top), 49 (center, bottom right), 58 (top), 70 (bottom), 77 (top), 107 (left), 116-117 (center), 168 (bottom right), 212 (top)

Gnass, Jeff, 82-83

Goin, Peter, Professor of Art, University of Nevada-Reno, 203 (bottom)

Granger Collection, New York, 90, 98-99, 100, 103, 124-125

Hallstein, Thomas / Alamy, 121

Hansen, Janis, 95 (center), 108 (center), 150 (bottom)

Hopkinson, Glen, 87

Houck, Ramsey / iStockphoto, 32 (top)

Humboldt-Toiyabe National Forest, 29 (center)

Illinois Historic Preservation Agency, 46-47

Jones, Adam / Visuals Unlimited, 12 (bottom)

Klette, Scott / NAMI, 49 (bottom left)

LDS Church Archives, 61, 85 (center)

Lanker, Kippy / Shutterpoint, 28 (bottom)

Las Vegas Veterans Day Parade Committee, 189 (bottom)

Learoyd, Craig / Shutterpoint, 28 (top)

Library of Congress, 64 (top, bottom), 89, 92 (bottom), 110 (bottom), 111, 114, 115, 117 (right), 118, 119, 120 (bottom), 126, 127 (right), 130 (right), 135, 136, 137, 138, 153, 160 (top), 169, 175, 183, 186, 196, 220 (bottom), 227 (top)

Lost City Museum Collection, 53 (bottom), 57 (bottom)

McMillan, Marie, 197, 199 (top)

Miller, Alfred Jacob, 74

Miller, Travis, 37 (bottom)

Mineral Information Institute, 27

Munns, Jeremy, iv (left), v (right), 2-3, 13 (top), 30 (top), 48 (top), 59 (bottom right), 64 (center)

National Archives, 129, 130 (left), 180, 185 (right), 190, 191 (top), 212 (bottom)

National Nuclear Security Administration / Nevada Site Office, 192, 193 (background)

Nations, Jeanne, iv (right)

Natural Resources Conservation Services / Lynn Betts, 174

Nellis Air Force Base, 181 (top)

Nevada Bureau of Mines and Geology, 33

Nevada Department of Conservation and Natural Resources, 42 (bottom), 44

Nevada Historical Society, 17, 62 (left), 75, 76 (bottom), 91 (top), 101, 102, 107, 112, (right), 121 (top), 122 (bottom), 133 (top), 136, 139 (bottom), 140, 141, 142, 144, (bottom), 145, 146, 147 (left), 150 (top), 152, 156-157, 158, 159, 161, 162, 163, 165, 166, 163 (right), 198

Nevada Legislative Council Bureau/ Marilyn Maxfield, 221, 224 (right)

Nevada State Department of Anthropology, 48 (bottom)

Nevada State DMV, 222 (center)

Nevada State Library and Archives / Carlton Watkins, 144 (top)

Nevada State Museum, Carson City, NV, 15 (center), 151, 151 (bottom)

Nevada Tourism Commission, 10, 11 (middle, bottom), 14 (center), 29 (top), 41 (top), 120 (top), 200 (top), 225

New Jersey Historical Society, Newark, 168 (center)

Newmont Mining Corporation, 202

Nichols, Ron / USDA Natural Resources Conservation Service, 29 (bottom)

North Wind Picture Archives, 4, 68-69, 108 (bottom)

Northeastern Nevada Museum, 128, 135

Northwestern University Library, Edward S. Curtis's 'The North American Indian': the Photographic Images, 2001, 58-59 (center)

Oregon Historical Society, 76 (top), 94

PD Photos.org / Jon Sullivan, 26

Photos.com, 8, 9, 13, 25, 59 (top), 66, 86, 91 (bottom), 105 (right), 110 (top), 127, 168 (bottom left), 169 (top right), 193 (right), 207, 214 (top), 215 (right), 218 (top), 227, 230 (bottom)

Rasmussen, Gary, 49 (top), 53 (center), 58 (center), 60 (bottom), 62 (right), 81, 220 (top)

Reno-Tahoe, America's Adventure Place, 37 (top), 116 (bottom), 201

Scottsbluff National Monument, Painting by William Henry Jackson, 79, 84-85 (bottom), 95 (top)

Security Pacific National Bank Photograph Collection / Los Angeles Public Library, 77 (bottom)

Shutterstock, 14 (bottom), 15 (top), 18-19, 35, 38, 39, 40 (center), 42 (top), 52, 55, 73, 178, 205

Smith, Scott T., 40 (top), 208-209

Sorenson, Lance / Shutterpoint, 40 (bottom)

State of Nevada, 224

Stevens, Rick, 222 (left, right)

Streshinksky, Ted / Corbis, 65

Tchernov, Andrei / iStockphoto, 211

Thomas, Harry / iStockphoto, 41 (bottom)

Till, Tom, 50

Tumacácori National Historical Monument, Painting by Cal Peters, 70 (top)

U.S. Atomic Energy Commission / Courtesy of the Nuclear Testing Archive, 194

U.S. Congresswoman Shelley Berkley, 216 (bottom right)

U.S. Congressman Jim Gibbons, 216 (center)

U.S. Congressman Jon C. Porter, 216 (bottom left)

U.S. Forest Service, 32 (bottom)

U.S. Senator Jon Ensign, 216 (top right)

U.S. Senator Harry Reid, 216 (top left)

UNLV Library, Special Collections, 54, 60 (top), 106 (bottom), 131, 147 (right), 148, 149, 170 (bottom), 171 (left), 172, 173, 181 (bottom), 184, 187, 188, 189, 199 (Wilson, Johnson, Sawyer), 200 (bottom)

United States Air Force Thunderbird Library, 182 (left)

University of Nevada-Reno Library, Special Collections, 135 (top), 164, 199 (Kellar)

Utah Historical Society, 71, 77 (top), 78, 104, 106 (top), 133 (bottom), 143, 185 (left)

Wark, Jim / Airphoto, 36 (bottom), 43

White House / Susan Sterner, 215